# HEGELIAN
# MARXISM

---

## SÖDERTÖRN
## PHILOSOPHICAL STUDIES 22
### 2018

# Hegelian Marxism

The Uses of Hegel's Philosophy in Marxist Theory
from Georg Lukács to Slavoj Žižek

*Edited by*
*Anders Bartonek & Anders Burman*

SÖDERTÖRN
PHILOSOPHICAL STUDIES
22

Södertörns högskola
(Södertörn University)
The Library
SE-141 89 Huddinge

www.sh.se/publications

Cover image: *Os vermelhos*, (22 x 28.5 cm, acrylic on paper),
Laercio Redondo, 2017.

Cover: Jonathan Robson
Graphic form: Per Lindblom & Jonathan Robson

Printed by Elanders, Stockholm 2018

Södertörn Philosophical Studies 22
ISSN 1651-6834

Södertörn Academic Studies 75
ISSN 1650-433X

ISBN 978-91-88663-50-4 (print)
ISBN 978-91-88663-51-1 (digital)

# Contents

# Introduction

*Anders Bartonek & Anders Burman*

"It is impossible fully to grasp Marx's Capital, and especially its first chapter, if you have not studied through and understood the whole of Hegel's Logic. Consequently, none of the Marxists for the past half century have understood Marx!!"[1] In this famous aphorism, written in his posthumously published *Philosophical Notebooks*, Vladimir Lenin stresses the importance of Hegelian logic and dialectics on Marx's thinking. When the future Soviet leader made this claim in 1916, one year before the Russian Revolution, his immediate critical concern was with the understanding of Marx that had been allowed to perpetuate within the Second International, a highly conventional and system oriented interpretation to which Lenin was vehemently opposed. Given Lenin's remarks about the significance of Hegel, it seems ironic, then, that the importance of the relationship between Hegelian philosophy and Marxist theory was increasingly underplayed in the official Marxist-Leninism of the Soviet Union, which dogmatically asserted itself after Lenin's death in 1924. Similar to the Second International, the theorists and interpreters of state authorized Soviet Marxism placed exclusive emphasis on the connections between Marx and Engels, rather than reading Marx in light of Hegel.

From the 1920s onwards, the question of Hegelian philosophy's vital influence on Marx as well as to contemporary Marxism was instead investigated with a greater intensity by a number of theorists in, above all, central Europe. One of the basic assumptions of this book is that there are reasons to regard and treat these quite diverse thinkers as Hegelian Marxists. The Hungarian philosopher and aesthetician Georg Lukács and the German

---

[1] Vladimir Lenin, "Abstract of Hegel's Science of Logic", *Collected Works*, vol. 38 (Moscow: Progress, 1963), p. 180.

theoretician Karl Korsch were pioneers in reexamining the relation between Hegel and Marx.

From a variety of perspectives the present anthology addresses the theme of Hegelian Marxism. More specifically, it deals with how some Marxist thinkers, in different historical, political and intellectual contexts during the last century, have employed Hegel's philosophy with the aim of developing and renewing Marxist theory. The principal focus is on a series of well-known theorists from Central and Eastern Europe. Besides Lukács and Korsch—and to some extent also Lenin—the articles included in this volume deal mainly with the thoughts of Herbert Marcuse, Theodor W. Adorno, Walter Benjamin, Evald Ilyenkov and Slavoj Žižek; one text goes beyond the geographical focus of Central and Eastern Europe by highlighting the Italian philosopher Lucio Colletti, who was nonetheless critically engaged in exploring the extent of a (dis)connection between Hegel and Marx. The overall purpose of the book is to investigate if and to what extent these thinkers could be interpreted as Hegelian Marxists, and how they use the Hegelian philosophy with the intention to better understand their own current society as well as situate themselves in relation to orthodox forms of Marxism. Another purpose is to illuminate, from the perspective of intellectual history, how Hegelian Marxism has served as a significant politico-philosophical tradition, with its beginnings in the early twentieth century and reaching up to, and including, today.[2]

To speak of Hegelian Marxism in the singular is indeed a simplification. Still there is enough that unites many (if not all) of these thinkers that thereby justifies an ideal-typical classification of the vast majority of them as Hegelian Marxists. However, it should immediately be noted that the concept of Hegelian Marxism means different things in these theories, and in some cases the concept is not even used by the theoreticians themselves. Nor can it be claimed unequivocally that all of these thinkers are Hegelian Marxists, since some of them, for instance Adorno and Colletti, were critical of much of Hegel's philosophy. All the same, many of the thinkers included in this volume use his highly complex and equivocal philosophy in an affir-

---

[2] The book comprises both texts written within the research project "Hegelian Marxism", which is funded by The Foundation for Baltic and East European Studies, and contributions based on presentations held at the international conference "From Marx to Hegel and Back to the Future", in Stockholm, 25–27 February 2016. Both editors arranged the conference, alongside Victoria Fareld and Hannes Kuch, and we would like to express our gratitude to them. We would also like to thank David Payne for proofreading the entire manuscript.

mative way, often with the ambition of further developing Marxist theory in the direction of some kind of humanism. Hegel, who is usually viewed to be the most abstract of all thinkers, tends in this context to be used with the ambition of formulating a non-dogmatic, Marxist humanism.

Historically speaking, Hegelian Marxism may be described as a radical intellectual tradition that from the interwar years onwards has played a prominent role in political theory and to some extent also in political practice, especially in Central Europe. With their Hegelian interpretation of Marx, often combined with a Marxist interpretation of Hegel, these thinkers are united in the ambition to formulate a critical position between—or rather beyond—the cautious reformism of Western European Social Democracy, on the one hand, and the inflexible dogmatism of Soviet communism, on the other.

Against this background, another common trait of Hegelian Marxists can be perceived, namely that they all in different ways and in different historical contexts respond to what they viewed as the acute or permanent crisis of Marxism. Hegel's philosophy was thus related to and integrated in Marxism as a way of coming to terms with some of the difficulties and blind-spots within the wider theory itself. For many of these thinkers, the underlying question is how is it the case that Marx's (and Engels') work remains insufficient, thus calling for supplementation from Hegel's philosophy, in order to solve certain problems that are preventing Marxism from reaching its critical and emancipatory goals. Importantly, Hegel is here not only highlighted as a historical background figure and a source of inspiration for Marx, Engels and Marxism, rather he is explicitly used as a precipitate for the renewal of Marxist theory. The point is that contemporary Marxism, according to many of these theorists, cannot do without an injection of Hegelian philosophy in order to revivify it.

In thinking the relation of Hegel and Marx, almost all of the Hegelian Marxists place emphasis on the dialectical method. In a wider sense the issues that are generated out of Hegelian Marxism, and the questions for which Hegel's role in Marxism opens up, all point toward an evaluation of the significance of (Hegelian) dialectics for left-wing political theory. Thus the question of dialectics is discussed in several of the articles in this book. This interest in dialectics is arguably in stark contrast to other modern traditions of political theory, which in some way or another can be said to be anti-dialectical. On the one hand, we have the tradition leading from Friedrich Nietzsche to Gilles Deleuze, and on the other, the one that goes from Martin Heidegger and Hannah Arendt to Giorgio Agamben. The comparison with these other traditions is only addressed briefly in some of the texts below. Nonetheless, these other traditions help to constitute a horizon for which the question whether and why Marxism (or political and critical theory in general) needs to be dialectical remains a topic of current interest.

Beyond the general issue of dialectics, it is possible to elucidate some other common Hegelian themes among most of the Hegelian Marxists assembled in this volume, such as, for example, the adoption of a radically historical perspective as well as a preoccupation with the concept of ethical life.[3] More surprising, though, is perhaps what is left unsaid by those Hegelian Marxists surveyed here. Hegel's well-known and often commented analysis of the struggle for recognition, and especially the dialectical play between the master and the slave, plays no prominent role for Lukács, Korsch and Marcuse. This ought to be compared with the Hegelian reception in France, in particular Alexandre Kojève's decisive course of lectures on the *Phenomenology of Spirit* in Paris in the 1930s. Together with Jean Hippolite's *Genesis and Structure of the Phenomenology of Spirit*, published in 1947, Kojève's lectures, with their explicit reference to Marxist themes and their orientation around the problem of desire, became crucial for a whole generation of French thinkers, from Jean-Paul Sartre and Simone de Beauvoir to Georges Bataille, André Breton and Jacques Lacan. Many of them used Hegel's description of the master and the slave as a key to understanding historical development as such, as well as more specific but still complex phenomena, such as—in the case of Beauvoir—the patriarchal relation between man and woman. However, very little of this can be found in the thinking of the Central European Hegelian Marxists.

Maurice Merleau-Ponty was another philosopher who attended Kojève's lectures at the Ecole Pratique des Hautes Études and they left a certain impression on him. With respect to Hegelian Marxism, Merleau-Ponty is important also since he coined the concept of Western Marxism. In his *Adventures of the Dialectic*, published in 1953, one chapter, entitled "'Western' Marxism", mainly focuses on the writings of Lukács.[4] But it was Perry Anderson, almost a quarter of a century later, who popularized the concept of Western Marxism in his highly influential book *Considerations on*

---

[3] See further Anders Burman, "Hegel, Marx, and the Political", in Kaveh Boveiri, Emmanuel Chaput & Arnaud Theurillat-Cloutier (eds.), *Hegel, Marx and the Contemporary World* (Newcastle upon Tyne: Cambridge Scholars Publishing, 2016), pp. 34-50.
[4] Maurice Merleau-Ponty, *Adventures of the Dialectic*, trans. Joseph Bien (London: Heinemann, 1974), pp. 30-58.

*Western Marxism*. In addition to Lukács and Korsch, other thinkers included in his historical treatment of Western Marxism, are the main representatives of the Frankfurt School or critical theory (Max Horkheimer, Adorno, Benjamin, Marcuse), the French theorists of Henri Lefebvre, Jean-Paul Sartre, Lucien Goldman and Louis Althusser, as well as Italian philosophers, such as Antonio Gramsci and Galvano Della Volpe and Lucio Colletti. As one of the characteristic traits of Western Marxism, Anderson stresses "the structural divorce of (...) Marxism from political practice", which he obviously regrets and describes as a kind of inversion of Marx's own development:

> Where the founder of historical materialism moved progressively from philosophy to politics and then economics, as the central terrain of his thought, the successors of the tradition that emerges after 1920 increasingly turned back from economics and politics to philosophy—abandoning direct engagement with what had been the great concerns of the mature Marx, nearly as completely as he had abandoned direct pursuit of the discursive issues of his youth.[5]

The concepts, problems and themes of Hegelian Marxism partly overlap with those that define Western Marxism. To a large extent, they can be drawn together by a series of "family resemblances". The two traditions are marked by an absence of any comprehensive economic analysis, they adopt a more complex and ambivalent analysis surrounding the political possibility of effective emancipatory struggle, alongside an attempt to accentuate the function of theory in the overall ambition of renewing Marxism.

Nevertheless, we would like to suggest that the concept of Western Marxism should mainly be used for the French oriented tradition that goes back to Kojève's lectures on Hegel, while the Hegelian Marxism that emerged with Lukács and Korsch in the 1920s comprises the Central and East European thinkers we are focusing on in this volume. Some of the thinkers discussed here, above all Colletti, may be said to belong equally to the French tradition as much as the Central-European tradition. In most cases, however, we will in the following articles encounter a partially different type of Hegelian Marxism than the one that took root in the French context. To an even greater extent than the post-war French Marxists, the Central European Hegelian Marxists, from Lukács to Žižek, have been occupied

[5] Perry Anderson, *Considerations on Western Marxism* (London: NLB, 1976), pp. 29, 52.

11

with the heritage of Hegel and its positive impact on Marxism. The constellation of Hegel, Marx and Marxism is thus the main problem with which much of this book is concerned.

In the first article, "Back to Hegel! Georg Lukács, Dialectics, and Hegelian Marxism", Anders Burman examines Lukács' Marxist theory and evaluates the extent to which it is informed by Hegel. Since Lukács' Hegelianism antedated his turn to Marx, he can arguably (together with Korsch) be regarded as, properly speaking, the first *Hegelian* Marxist. Lukács' early work, which primarily deals with aesthetic issues, was marked by a romantic anti-capitalist stance and a by a rather vaguely formulated dream of another world. After becoming a Marxist he joined the Communist Party in 1918. Lukács was then to use Hegel for explicitly political ends. In *History and Class Consciousness*, his seminal book published in 1923, Lukács stresses the dialectical method as the crucial element in Marxism, at the same time as he assigns a central role to the proletariat in the current political situation; of decisive importance is that, in order to realize their destiny as a revolutionary subject, the workers must first become conscious of themselves as a unified and political class. In his later works, including *The Young Hegel*, Lukács hardly deviates from the official Soviet Marxist-Leninist line, although he continues to emphasize the Hegelian elements at play in Marxism. He argues that Hegel was a rational thinker who forcefully turned against the irrationalism of the romantics. Lukács emphasizes that today we have to criticize capitalism and fascism in a similar way. It is, in short, necessary to go back to Hegel to be able to challenge capitalism, to revitalize Marxism and to emancipate mankind.

Anders Bartonek's article "Karl Korsch: To Make the Right Marx Visible through Hegel" shows how Korsch seeks to renew Marxism during what he understands as a period of deep crisis for the Marxist revolutionary movement, torn as it was between contemporary forms of vulgar Marxism and the positions of Social democracy. A decisive dimension of Korsch's theoretical effort is to vitalize through Hegel the revolutionary and dialectical foundations of Marxism. Korsch therefore develops a Hegelian analysis of Marxism in order to rediscover the original dialectical scope of its social theory. Here Korsch is seeking to develop a form of Marxism that can give effective expression to the practical needs of the proletariat; he achieves this by bringing forth the revolutionary insights of Hegel. Interestingly, Korsch is able to balance both the need for dialectical theory (Hegel) and the need for revolutionary praxis, and while it may be said that Marx's and Engels' thinking is close to action, Hegel is still needed to make this proximity visible.

A context to which the Central European Hegelian Marxists long had to relate was the contemporary development of the official philosophy and ideology in the Soviet Union. In "Hegelian Dialectics and Soviet Marxism (from Vladimir Lenin to Evald Ilyenkov)", Elena Mareeva and Sergei Mareev provide a broad historical description of the development of Hegelian Marxism in the first official communist country. The article takes as its starting point the early Russian reception of Hegel's philosophy, with thinkers like Alexander Galich and, above all, Alexander Herzen, who interpreted Hegelian dialectics as the "algebra of revolution". It was a theme that Lenin further developed in his work on Hegel's philosophy and its relevance to the contemporary political situation. Much of Mareeva and Mareev's article is however devoted to Evald Ilyenkov, regarded as a philosopher of "the Khrushchew Thaw". Like Lukács, Korsch and many other Central European Hegelian Marxists, Ilyenkov emphasizes the crucial importance of dialectics in Marxism, at the same time as he offers a Hegelian interpretation of Marx. In both of these respects, he ends up on a collision course with the official Soviet dogma of dialectical materialism (Diamat).

As Bartonek shows in his next article "Herbert Marcuse: No Dialectics, No Critique", Marcuse develops a dialectical and negative-critical theory in order to reveal and operate with the contradictions comprising both thinking and reality for the purpose of developing counter images and alternatives to the capitalist system and its destructive (one-dimensional) way of life. In an effort to develop a concrete philosophy based on the immanent needs of humanity in the capitalist era, with the ultimate aim of realizing philosophy in revolutionary action, Marcuse's Marxism continuously takes its sustenance from Hegel's dialectical philosophy, which he takes as his primary source for developing a Marxism adequate to the societal challenges of his own time. It is only through a reinjection of Hegel's dialectical impulse into Marxism that the latter can regain its ability to become the critical force it seeks to be. Marxism must therefore be a Hegelian Marxism.

Many of the thinkers who may be called, to a greater or lesser degree, Hegelian Marxists have also a lively interest in aesthetics. A frequently recurring theme in such related discussions is that of reification and fetishism. This issue is precisely foregrounded in Sven-Olov Wallenstein's article "The Necessary Fetishism of the Work of Art". Based on Marx's analysis of commodity fetishism in *Capital*, Wallenstein shows how this theory became a central component in the aesthetics of both Benjamin and Adorno. Both of them were in search for an art that could transcend the trends of reification in capitalistic society and thus in some way or another be characterized as essentially de-fetishized. In a concluding discussion, Wallenstein, however, points out the impossibility of escaping fetishism in the work of art, at least in our contemporary capitalist society.

Adorno is also at the center of Bartonek's following article, "Theodor W. Adorno: With Hegel Against Capitalism". Here Bartonek makes the case that, despite his ambiguous relation to Hegel, Adorno can nonetheless be understood as a Marxist critic of capitalism (and of Hegel) with help from mainly philosophical categories borrowed from Hegel, but remodeled into a system-critical tool instead of a system-affirmative one: the concepts of identity and non-identity. In this specific sense, Adorno can be viewed as a "Hegelian" Marxist, even if he would never really have understood himself as a Hegelian. Adorno understands and criticizes the Hegelian philosophical system as being an identity-system, which suppresses everything that is non-identical to it. But more importantly in this case, Adorno uses the very same concepts that Hegel deploys in a non-critical way (i.e. "identity" is developed through the integration of the negation of "non-identity"), as a critical tool against capitalism. For Adorno, the system of Capitalism must also be understood and criticized as an identity-system, subsuming and streamlining everything individual and non-identical. Adorno's Marxism is thus essentially informed by Hegel.

In his contribution, "The Revisionist Within: Unity and Unilateralism in Hegelian Marxism and Beyond", David Payne examines the essential stakes at play for Marxists in thinking through the relation between Hegel and Marx, asking ultimately whether any of the stakes that had once served to animate the debates within Marxism, are still relevant for us today. The stakes themselves overlap with what from Lenin onwards are regarded as the three components of Marxism: "science", "politics" and "philosophy". Arguably, Marxism's potency lies in the co-existence of these three dimensions. However, it is precisely the general inability of generations of Marxists to constitute Marxism as a unified whole, by placing equal value and emphasis on its three constituent parts, that haunts Marxism and its history. According to Payne, the risk of "revisionism" has been an immanent effect of a one-sided or unilateralized comprehension of Marxism, which ends up privileging one of its constitutive practices over and above the others. In the article Payne discusses how precisely the question of the relation between Hegel and Marx served as the setting for this dramaturgy to play itself out, where in an attempt to rethink the *philosophical* bases of Marxism, Hegelian Marxists specifically ended up discrediting the role of Marxist Science. In pursuit of the desired but impossible goal of constituting Marxism as the unification of science, politics and philosophy, Payne shows how Marxism must always be in interminable conflict with itself. Payne attributes the effective indexing of this problem to the explicit anti-Hegelian Marxism of Louis Althusser and Lucio Colletti.

To show that Hegelian Marxism remains a living tradition, Burman considers in the final article the work of Slavoj Žižek, in "A Lacanian Hegelianism: Slavoj Žižek's (Mis-)Reading of Hegel". While many thinkers during the past decades have been preoccupied with distancing themselves from Hegelian philosophy, Žižek explicitly refers back and relates to this German nineteenth century philosopher. At the same time, Žižek interprets Hegel in a remarkably idiosyncratic fashion by cross-fertilizing his thinking with Lacanian psychoanalysis. According to Žižek, Hegelian dialectics—with its categories of negativity and the negation of the negation—is still crucial in the analysis of our society and the struggle for a different political and social order.

Taken together, the eight texts in this volume can hopefully contribute to an intensification of discussions about the critical and self-critical philosophy of Marxism today. Since this anthology consists mainly of historical perspectives, the constructive nature of this task shows itself more indirectly (i.e. in the way that these essays may help to rediscover other possible paths in the pursuit of a critical self-examination of Marxism). Thus the book is fundamentally a reminder of some past and present (in the case of Žižek) examples of this self-examination. It is to pose the question: why, according to Hegelian Marxism, is Hegel required in a critical self-examination of Marxism, and in what way do we still need Hegel's philosophy in our own efforts to further develop Marxist theory?

# Back to Hegel!
# Georg Lukács, Dialectics,
# and Hegelian Marxism

*Anders Burman*

As a decisive work in the tradition of Hegelian Marxism, Georg Lukács' *History and Class Consciousness* has been called "a groundbreaking manifesto for a critical, humanist Marxism", which, published in 1923, was "one of the few authentic events in the history of Marxism".[1] With this collection of essays Lukács clarified the Hegelian roots of Marx's thinking and showed, as Peter Bürger has pointed out, how Hegel could be read from a leftist perspective.[2] Indeed, one may say that as a critical intellectual movement Hegelian Marxism arose with *History and Class Consciousness*, together with Karl Korsch's *Marxism and Philosophy*, also published in 1923.

This article focuses on Lukács' version of Hegelian Marxism. The aim is to identify, analyze and to some extent contextualize his specific form of Marxism and the uses he made of Hegel's philosophy for this purpose. So, what kind of Marxism does *History and Class Consciousness* advocate, and what role does Hegel play in Lukács' interpretation of Marx and Marxism? Unlike many other Hegelian Marxists, Lukács was an idealist thinker influenced by Hegel before he identified as a Marxist; he came, so to say, to Marxian materialism from German idealism, not vice versa. As a background to the analysis of *History and Class Consciousness* there are therefore reasons to say something about his early reception of Hegel's philo-

---

[1] Andrew Arato & Paul Breines, *The Young Lukács and the Origins of Western Marxism* (London: Pluto, 1979), p. ix. Slavoj Žižek, "Postface: Georg Lukács as the Philosopher of Leninism", in Georg Lukács, *A Defence of* History and Class Consciousness: *Tailism and the Dialectic*, trans. Esther Leslie (London & New York: Verso, 2002), p. 151.
[2] "Interview with Peter Bürger", in Eva L. Corredor, *Lukács after Communism: Interviews with Contemporary Intellectuals* (Durham & London: Duke, 1997), p. 46.

sophy, and towards the end of the article I will also examine how Lukács' uses of Hegel gradually changed as step by step he distanced himself from the positions he defended in *History and Class Consciousness* in favor of an approach that was more affirmative to the dogmatism of the Soviet Communist Party, even while never entirely abandoning Hegel.

## Aesthetic anti-capitalism

In his early writings, including his important volume *Soul and Form* (1910), Lukács devoted himself almost exclusively to literature, drama and philosophy. He was a theorist of aesthetics with a special fondness for the concept of form. Indeed, there is something almost Platonic regarding his early interest in both the ideas of soul and form. At the same time, one can detect in his writings the strong influence of thinkers such as Immanuel Kant and Georg Simmel. Although at this point Hegel played a less prominent role for Lukács, some Hegelian traits can nonetheless be discerned already in *Soul and Form*, especially in his essays on Novalis, Søren Kierkegaard and Stefan George. As Judith Butler puts it:

> In a sense that is clearly Hegelian, Lukács maintains not only that soul requires form in order to become manifest but also that form requires soul for its animation. Form would be nothing without its substance, and its substance would not be anything without the soul.[3]

In addition, and like many other German artists, writers and thinkers in the early twentieth century, the young Lukács, had a deep aversion to modern Anglo-Saxon culture, which was connected to utilitarianism, liberalism, commercialism and materialism. Germanic society served as a potent counterpoint, associated as it was with higher values such as art, authenticity, spirituality and humanism. At this time, Lukács' disapproval of liberalism in no way implied an allegiance to the socialist or communist cause. Rather his antipathy was rooted in a romantic and politically quite diffuse anti-capitalistic position, and it was this basis on which his criticism of the contemporary situation was formulated.

Nevertheless, Lukács was already familiar with the writings of Marx, including *Capital*, which he read for the first time around 1908. Three years later, in 1911, he wrote: "The system of socialism and its view of the world,

---

[3] Judith Butler, "Introduction", in Georg Lukács, *Soul and Form*, trans. Anna Bostock (New York: Verso, 2010), p. 6.

Marxism, form a synthetic unity—perhaps the most unrelenting and rigorous synthesis since medieval Catholicism."[4] This is in many ways a remarkable quote, particularly given that, already during his pre-Marxist aesthetic period, Lukács always searched for synthetic unity and comprehensive explanations. In that sense he had a kind of structural readiness for the Marxist view on the world, which he would later come to embrace.

Thus it was directly from Hegel, not via Marx, that the young Lukács picked up concepts that would later be central in his works, for instance totality, the typical and the world-historical.[5] These concepts are frequently used already in *The Theory of the Novel* from 1916, his first work to be thoroughly based on a Hegelian perspective. In retrospect, Lukács would claim that, taken as a whole, this study was "the first work in the domain of spiritual interpretation in which Hegelian philosophy was concretely applied to aesthetic problems".[6]

*The Theory of the Novel* deals partly with epic literature in the early, Homeric tradition, and partly with the modern novel. Like Hegel, however, Lukács seeks to come to terms with and overcome various atomizing tendencies present within contemporary society. If Hegel had given a harmonizing role to reason and subsequently to the state, the early Lukács maintains that it is art and aesthetics that have the capacity to overcome the split between the objective and the subjective, or in Kantian words, between *Sein* (being) and *Sollen* (ought). In comparison with *Soul and Form*, *The Theory of the Novel* is a more political text, invested in the hope of a less alienated and a more harmonized world.[7]

In a certain respect it is possible to interpret Lukács' turn to communism, which, it should be added, surprised and even shocked many of his friends, and which to this day continues to puzzle scholars, as the logical extension of his awareness of the increasing atomization and utilitarianization of modern society. Step by step—under the impact of the First World War and the events of the Russian Revolution—Lukács came to realize the limits of art and aesthetics; neither functions as an appropriate response to the most urgent questions in contemporary society. To allude to

---

[4] Lukács quoted in Michael Löwy, *Georg Lukács: From Romanticism to Bolshevism*, trans. Patrick Camiller (London: NLB, 1979), p. 96.
[5] Terry Eagleton, *Marxism and Literary Criticism* (London: Routledge, 1976), p. 14.
[6] Lukács quoted in George Lichtheim, *George Lukács* (New York: The Viking Press, 1970), p. 9.
[7] Georg Lukács, *The Theory of the Novel: A Historico-Philosophical Essay on the Forms of Great Epic Literature*, trans. Anna Bostock (London: Merlin Press, 1971).

Walter Benjamin's famous formulation, one may say that even before the fascists had aestheticized the politics, Lukács chose to politicize aesthetics.[8]

## Hegel as a leading intellectual force

After the October Revolution of 1917, and while the Russian Civil War was taking hold, the Hungarian Communist Party was founded in November 1918. One month later Lukács enrolled as a party member. Hungary was in turmoil and the prospect of founding an entirely new social order seemed to be within reach: the real possibility of creating something new that was radically different from the contemporary liberal capitalism Lukács detested. From now on, communism was for him a promise of a free and humane world, and he dedicated himself wholeheartedly to the party. When the Hungarian Soviet Republic was proclaimed in March 1919, he was appointed Deputy People's Commissar for cultural and educational issues in Bela Kun's government. The Republic was, however, short-lived, and with the Hungarian revolution crushed Lukács was thus forced to go into exile in Vienna.

There he continued to write intensely, now focusing on ideological and political issues. He published a lot of articles in *Die Internationale*, *Kommunismus*, *Rote Fane* and other radical journals. Some of these articles were reworked and then re-published in *History and Class Consciousness*, along with a couple of newly written texts. The book, published originally in 1923, consists of several essays on history, class-consciousness and reification as well as on the questions of historical materialism and the political organization of the party, all interpreted on the basis of a Hegelian infused Marxism. He describes the overall ambition of the book as "mak[ing] us aware of Marxist method, to throw light on it as an unendingly fertile source of solution to otherwise intractable dilemmas."[9] With this emphasis placed on Marx's method Lukács stresses the importance of Hegel. With a solid knowledge of both Hegel and German idealism, Lukács was able to distinguish and analyze the Hegelian elements present in Marx's own thinking. This understanding of the Hegelian Marx—and for that matter even the Marxian Hegel—was novel in the 1920s. But in several key

---

[8] Cf. Walter Benjamin, "The Work of Art in the Age of Mechanical Reproduction", in Benjamin, *Illuminations: Essays and Reflections*, ed. Hannah Arendt, trans. Harry Zohn (New York: Schocken Books, 1968), pp. 217-251.
[9] Georg Lukács, *History and Class Consciousness: Studies in Marxist Dialectics*, trans. Rodney Livingstone (Cambridge, MA: MIT Press, 1971), p. xliii.

respects, it was also a controversial development, something Lukács soon became aware of.

In the preface to *History and Class Consciousness* Lukács discusses Hegel's position and status in Marxism. He recalls certain passages in which Marx points out Hegel's importance for his own thinking, for instance in Marx's letter to Joseph Dietzgen, where he wrote that the "true laws of dialectics are already to be found in Hegel, albeit in a mystified form".[10] Lukács speaks also of Marx's warning about the danger of treating Hegelian dialectics as a "dead dog". According to the author of *History and Class Consciousness*, this is precisely the dominant way in which Hegel was treated in Marxism. The principal purpose of the book was thus to save "the *seminal elements* of Hegel's thought and rescue them *as a vital intellectual force for the present*".[11]

According to Lukács, the crucial element in both Hegelian and Marxian philosophy inheres in the dialectical method. In "What is Orthodox Marxism?", the most programmatic of the essays in *History and Class Consciousness*, he claims:

> Orthodox Marxism, therefore, does not imply the uncritical acceptance of the results of Marx's investigations. It is not the "belief" in this or that thesis, nor the exegesis of a "sacred" book. On the contrary, orthodoxy refers exclusively to *method*.[12]

It is primarily because orthodox Marxism is dependent on the dialectical method, which, according to Lukács, was originally invented by Hegel, that this idealistic thinker occupies such a central place in Lukács' interpretation of Marx and Marxism. Besides Marx's own writings, Hegel's *Logic* and *Phenomenology of Spirit* are in fact the main background sources for Lukács' view of contemporary Marxism. In short, it is necessary to return to Hegel in order to provide an accurate presentation of true Marxism.

Despite—or perhaps on account of—being the first modern thinker to develop the dialectical method, Hegel's understanding of this method was in certain respects limited. The same point applies to Engels, who, according to Lukács, unquestioningly accepted certain shortcomings in Hegel's use of the method. Lukács writes: "The misunderstandings that arise from

---

[10] Marx in a letter to Joseph Dietzgen, quoted in Lukács, *History and Class Consciousness*, p. xlv.
[11] Lukács, *History and Class Consciousness*, p. xlv.
[12] Lukács, *History and Class Consciousness*, p. 1.

Engels' account of dialectics can in the main be put down to the fact that Engels—following Hegel's mistaken lead—extended the dialectical method to apply also to nature."[13] The dialectics of nature, which Engels worked out, and which at the end of nineteenth century was codified into Marxist dogma, was indeed non-Marxian according to Lukács. This means that Lukács, in contrast to most other Marxists in the early twentieth century, was keen to stress that Marx's thought was by no means identical with Engels'.

Hegel's and Marx's method is thus not applicable to nature, but only applies to historical and social processes. By harnessing the dialectical method it is possible to acquire a complex understanding of society as a "totality", a central category in the works of both Hegel and Marx as well as in Lukács. In *History and Class Consciousness*, Lukács writes:

> It is not the primacy of economic motives in historical explanation that constitutes the decisive difference between Marxism and bourgeois thought, but the point of view of totality. The category of totality, the all-pervasive supremacy of the whole over the parts, is the essence of the method which Marx took over from Hegel and brilliantly transformed into the foundations of a wholly new science.[14]

The category of totality is here critically directed against capitalism and the tendency towards specialization characteristic of positivistic science. *"The primacy of the category of totality"*, Lukács maintains, *"is the bearer of the principle of revolution in science."*[15]

## The proletariat and the party

In the decades that followed the publication of *History and Class Consciousness,* and with later representatives of the Hegelian Marxism such as Herbert Marcuse, Karel Kosík and Leszek Kołakowski coming to the fore, this movement became a key challenge to the Marxist-Leninist dogmatism that became hegemonic in the USSR. Against that background, it is notable that Lenin did not pose any main target in *History and Class Consciousness.* On the contrary, the book conveys a quite positive image of the Russian leader. Lukács highlights Lenin's importance not only as a revolutionary activist

---

[13] Lukács, *History and Class Consciousness*, p. 24.
[14] Lukács, *History and Class Consciousness*, p. 27. On the category of totality in Lukács, see Martin Jay, *Marxism and Totality: The Adventures of a Concept from Lukács to Habermas* (Los Angeles & Berkeley: Polity, 1984), pp. 81-127.
[15] Lukács, *History and Class Consciousness*, p. 27.

but also as a theoretician in his own right. For both Lukács and Lenin, not only is emphasis placed on a close connection between theory and practice, but moreover their focus on the dialectical method as the key element in Marxism unites them.

Besides Lenin, Lukács also emphasizes the importance of Rosa Luxemburg. Two of the essays in *History and Class Consciousness* deal explicitly with Luxemburg—"Rosa Luxemburg as a Marxist" and "Critical comments on Rosa Luxemburg's criticism of the Russian Revolution". According to Lukács, Luxemburg, "alone among Marx's disciples, has made a real advance on his life's work in both the content and method of his economic doctrines. She alone has found a way to apply them concretely to the present state of social development."[16] Lukács realizes the great value of Luxemburg's economic analysis and points out that she—unlike many other contemporary socialists and communists—was in fact a "genuine dialectician" with a sophisticated understanding of the concept of totality.[17]

Together with Marx and Hegel, it is with the theoretical help from Lenin and Luxemburg that the author of *History and Class Consciousness* tries to formulate a radical alternative to, on the one hand, Eduard Bernstein's reformist line that many social-democratic parties in Europe followed during the early twentieth century, and on the other hand, the essentially rigid, scientifically-influenced Marxism associated with Karl Kautsky and the Second International. Something that unites Bernstein and Kautsky, according to Lukács, is that neither of them realizes Hegel's crucial influence on Marx or the significance of Hegelian philosophy for contemporary Marxism. On the contrary, they claim that Marxian materialism has nothing to do whatsoever with Hegelian idealism. Lukács says that this anti-Hegelian position—which in practice means an abandonment of the dialectical method—is just one example of the historical fact that many so-called Marxist thinkers have become increasingly bourgeois and social-liberal in their general outlook.

Lukács criticizes, in other words, the deterministic and economistic side of the Second International. Its leading representatives regard history as a predetermined and natural law-bound process. Even though Lukács—just as Marx and Hegel—basically have a teleological (albeit dialectical) view of history, he refuses to agree that something truly transformative in human history can take place automatically—especially the transition from a cap-

---

[16] Lukács, *History and Class Consciousness*, p. xli.
[17] Lukács, *History and Class Consciousness*, p. 182.

italistic to a communistic social system. In *History and Class Consciousness* he formulates the point in this way:

> But the "realm of freedom" is not a gift that mankind, groaning under the weight of necessity, receives from Fate as a reward for its steadfast endurance. It is not only the goal, but also the means and the weapon in the struggle. And here the fundamental and qualitative novelty of the situation is revealed: for the first time mankind consciously takes its history into its own hands—thanks to the class consciousness of a proletariat summoned to power.[18]

Lukács shares Marx's assumption that it is the proletariat who provide the link to the future communist society, the "realm of freedom", an insight that Marx regarded as one of his greatest discoveries. In line with this, Lukács claims that in the current historical situation only the working-class may act as a genuine revolutionary collective subject. In fact, in *History and Class Consciousness* the proletariat occupies an analogous position to the world spirit in Hegel's *Phenomenology of Spirit*: a substance that is also a subject.[19] But in order to fulfill its highest *telos*, the proletariat must first be made conscious—just like the spirit in Hegel's philosophy.

Lukács' strong emphasis on consciousness is a part of the legacy of Hegel and German Idealism. Consciousness means in this context something more than merely having knowledge about something. The main point is that consciousness is not external to the object, but is a part of the object that also changes it. The moment when the workers become conscious of itself as a class, they are transformed. It is only then that the proletariat becomes a revolutionary subject. In this respect class-consciousness is directly related to political praxis.[20] Thus class-consciousness constitutes a precondition for the communist revolution; class-consciousness stands for the subjective element that is necessary—in political analysis as well as in praxis—as a supplement to the objective historical development trends Marx had forensically identified.[21]

---

[18] Lukács, *History and Class Consciousness*, p. 250.
[19] G. W. F Hegel, *Phenomenology of Spirit*, trans. A. V. Miller (Oxford: Oxford University Press, 1977), p. 10.
[20] Slavoj Žižek, *Less Than Nothing: Hegel and the Shadow of Dialectical Materialism* (New York: Verso, 2012), p. 220.
[21] This involves a dynamic interaction between the objective and the subjective, in line with Hegel's and Marx's dialectical method. When Lukács lines up "the crucial determinants of dialectics", he mentions precisely "the interaction of subject and object", but

Together with radical intellectuals, the most advanced part of the prole-tariat constitutes a kind of political avant-garde and thus operates as the central element in the communist party. The question of how the proletariat and the party should be organized is not only a technical matter, Lukács says, but "one of the most important *intellectual* questions of the revo-lution".[22] Leading intellectuals and those elements of the working class who have already become conscious of the situation and the tasks that lay ahead of them, represent the intellectual and political elite at the forefront of the new communist society, which is to say, the party.

When Lukács in this way understood the intellectual and political avant-garde of the party as forerunners of the new communist society, he was clearly influenced by Lenin. But here he gave recognition also to Rosa Luxemburg, even if, according to him, she tended to overestimate the value of spontaneity in the mass actions of the proletariat and concomitantly to underestimate the importance of that kind of conscious organizational work Lenin stressed. The big challenge, Lukács says, is thus to find a midd-le-way, "an interaction between spontaneity and conscious control,"[23] one that constitutes an intermediate standpoint, a negation of the negation, between the position of Luxemburg and the negation of Lenin. In short, even if *History and Class Consciousness* stands closer to Lenin than to Luxemburg, it is the combination of their theories, together with the domi-nant Hegelian influence, that makes the book so fascinating and original in the history of Marxism.

## Criticism and defense

After the publication of *History and Class Consciousness*, Lukács' thinking became in many ways less complex. This, of course, has much to do with the fact that he became more loyal to the Soviet Communist Party as the party itself was gradually becoming more dogmatic. When *History and Class Consciousness* was published, Lenin's theories of capitalism, imperial-ism, the party and the revolution had not yet been codified into dogmas. This canonization of Lenin's writings occurred soon after his death in January 1924.

---

also the "the unity theory and practice, the historical changes in the reality underlying the categories as the root cause of changes in thought, etc." Lukács, *History and Class Consciousness*, p. 24.

[22] Lukács, *History and Class Consciousness*, p. 295.

[23] Lukács, *History and Class Consciousness*, p. 317.

Quickly after Lenin's death, Lukács wrote a short book, *Lenin: A Study on the Unity of His Thought*, in which he gave a very affirmative portrait of his life and thinking. Here too Lukács stresses the importance of the dialectical method in so far as Lenin is said to represent a new phase in the development of dialectical materialism. After decades of decline and distortion by vulgar Marxism, Lenin was responsible for the development and maturation of the method itself. "*Lenin re-established the purity of Marxist theory on this issue. But it was also precisely here that he conceived it more clearly and more concretely.*"[24] That Lukács in this context does not say anything of Lenin's interest in Hegel, may at least partly be explained by the fact that Lenin's *Philosophical Notebooks*—where this interest is clearly expressed—had not been published. Otherwise Lukács would have certainly quoted Lenin's now well-known statement that it is impossible to really grasp *Capital* if one has not read and understood Hegel's Logic.[25]

Despite Lukács' homage to the first Soviet leader, Lukács would soon be subject to harsh criticism from party cadre. The Hegelian interpretation of Marx in *History and Class Consciousness* appeared to be too controversial to pass unnoticed. The criticism against Lukács was delivered by, among others, Abram Deborin, the Russian philosopher, and László Rudas, who was an influential Marxist-Leninist philosopher and a leading figure in the Hungarian Communist Party. Both Deborin and Rudas recoiled from what they identified as Lukács' "revisionism", including his criticism of Engels, his highlighting of Luxemburg's importance, and what they regarded as his strong tendency toward subjectivism in *History and Class Consciousness*.[26]

For a very long time it was thought that Lukács never responded directly to the accusation of "revisionism", deciding instead to distance himself from many of his previous positions. When a new German edition of *History and Class Consciousness* was published in 1968, Lukács took the opportunity in a newly written preface to emphasize that he now regarded much in the book as incorrect and reprehensible.[27] Even before this auto-critique,

---

[24] Lukács, *Lenin: A Study on the Unity of his Thought*, trans. Nicholas Jacobs (London & New York: Verso, 2009), p. 12.

[25] Lenin, "Abstract of Hegel's Science of Logic", *Collected Works*, vol. 38 (Moscow: Progress, 1963), p. 180.

[26] On Rudas's and Deborin's criticism, see John Rees, "Introduction", in Georg Lukács, *A Defence* of History and Class Consciousness: *Tailism and the Dialectic*, trans. Esther Leslie (London & New York: Verso, 2002), pp. 17-25.

[27] Georg Lukács, "Preface to the New Edition", in *History and Class Consciousness*, pp. ix-xxxix. In an interview given at the same time, Lukács says, however, that *History and Class Consciousness* despite all its shortcomings, nevertheless was "more intelligent and

he had renounced his critical treatment of Engels' dialectics of nature.[28] In fact, the later Lukács very seldom criticizes Engels. That he speaks of Engels almost in positive terms is just one example of how, from the late twenties onwards, he did what he could to be close and faithful to the party with its codification of the holy trinity of Marx, Engels and Lenin.

Long after Lukács' death, however, when the secret archives of the former communist countries were opened after the fall of the USSR, a previously unknown response to Deborin's and Ruda's criticism, written by his own hand, was found in Moscow. In this text, *Tailism and the Dialectic*, dated from around 1925 or 1926, Lukács offers a robust defense of *History and Class Consciousness* at the same time as he presents himself as an orthodox Leninist. The overall purpose of the book from 1923, he now describes as follows:

> To demonstrate *methodologically* that the organization and tactics of Bolshevism are the only possible consequence of Marxism; to prove that, of necessity, the problems of Bolshevism follow logically—that is to say logically in a dialectical sense—from the method of materialist dialectics as implemented by its founders.[29]

Instead of taking these statements as a confirmation of what *History and Class Consciousness* really is about—which, for example, John Rees tends to do in his introduction to the English edition of *Tailism and the Dialectic*— Lukács' statements must be understood in their specific context.[30] Given the fact that the dogmatization of Leninism had gone much further in 1925 and 1926 than when *History and Class Consciousness* was published just a few years earlier, there are circumstantial reasons why the author here portrays Lenin as the most obvious authority besides Marx and Engels—or, for that matter, why "Comrade Stalin" is mentioned positively.[31] Even in other ways the new book is more Leninist than *History and Class Consciousness*. While,

better" than most of what was written about Marx "on the bourgeoisie side." Georg Lukács, *Gelebtes Denken: Eine im Autobiographie Dialog*, ed. István Eörsi, trans. Hans-Henning Paetzke (Frankfurt am Main: Suhrkamp, 1981), p. 125.

[28] T. I. Ojzerman, "Lukács' Hegel Interpretation", i Tom Rockmore (ed.), *Lukács Today: Essays in Marxist Philosophy* (Dordrecht: D. Reidel, 1988), p. 197.

[29] Lukács, *A Defence of History and Class Consciousness*, p. 47.

[30] Rees, "Introduction", p. 27 et passim. See also Žižek, "Postface", p. 151-182, and Joseph Fracchia, "The Philosophical Leninism and Eastern 'Western Marxism' of Georg Lukács", *Historical Materialism* 21(1), 2013, pp. 69–93.

[31] Lukács, *A Defence of History and Class Consciousness*, p. 73.

in the original publication, the view of the party was somewhat ambivalent, Lukács now clearly defends Lenin's understanding of the party, instead of Luxemburg's; in *Tailism and the Dialectic* Luxemburg is mentioned only on a few occasions, and on these few occasions they are mainly of a critical character.[32] In comparison with *History and Class Consciousness*, Lukács now tones down Hegel's importance for Marx, although he does make it clear that Hegelian thought is fully compatible with the Marxism-Leninism promulgated by Moscow.

## From the young Marx to the young Hegel

When Lukács wrote *History and Class Consciousness* and *Tailism and the Dialectic*, he had not access to all of Marx's writings. Many of Marx's posthumous texts had still not been published, including *The Economic and Philosophical Manuscripts* and *Grundrisse*, which were rediscovered in the latter part of the twenties.[33] When *The Economic and Philosophical Manuscripts* were published in 1932, Lukács had already been given the opportunity to study them while, in and around 1930, he had worked as a scientific assistant at the Marx-Engels-Lenin Institute in Moscow. Even so, this was still several years after he had penned *History and Class Consciousness*. Paradoxically, the manuscripts from 1844 nevertheless throw an interesting light on Lukács' controversial book, especially its theory of reification.

Central in this theory is the phenomenon of the commodity form and how everything in capitalist society, including relations between people, tend to take "the character of the thing and thus acquires a 'phantom objectivity'."[34] The commodity form is, in short, characteristic of modern, capitalist society, distinguishing it from all previous social systems. Commodities certainly existed earlier in history, but what is new in capitalism is that the commodity form now permeates all facets of society including different manifestations of life. Only in a communistic system could this

---

[32] Lukács, *A Defence of History and Class Consciousness*, pp. 78f.

[33] The writings of Marx to which *History and Class Consciousness* refers is above all "To the Critique of Hegel's Philosophy of Right", *The Holy Family*, *The Poverty of Philosophy* ("his first, mature, complete and conclusive work"), *The Communist Manifesto*, *The Critique of Political Economy*, and the first and the third volume of *Capital*. The references to Hegel are comprehensive and general. The specific works of Hegel that Lukács uses most frequently are *The Difference Between Fichte's and Schelling's System of Philosophy*, *The Phenomenology of Spirit*, *The Science of Logic*, and *The Encyclopedia of the Philosophical Sciences*. See also Rockmore, "Lukács on Modern Philosophy", p. 229.

[34] Lukács, *History and Class Consciousness*, p. 83.

insidious form of reification be overcome. "'The Realm of freedom', the end of 'pre-history of mankind'", Lukács writes with a reference to Marx, "means precisely that the power of the objectified, reified relations between men begins to revert to *man*."[35]

Lukács developed his analysis of reification on the basis of the famous section in the first volume of *Capital* on the fetishism of commodities.[36] With the publication of *The Economic and Philosophical Manuscripts*, the economic analysis in Marx's *opus magnum* was supplemented with a discussion on the alienation of the working class, that is, how the workers in the industrial labor process gradually are alienated not only from the goods they produce, but also from themselves, other people and ultimately from humanity as a species.[37] After their publication in 1932 the manuscripts came to play a key role in the further development of Hegelian Marxism.[38]

Although the Manuscripts of 1844 seemed to support Lukács' humanistic and Hegelian interpretation of Marx, he made no new attempt to defend *History and Class Consciousness*. In fact, he had by that time already accepted the official communist party line. During most of the 1930s Lukács lived and worked in Moscow. The Soviet Union's totalitarian development under Stalin's leadership made it increasingly difficult to openly discuss political issues, and Lukács chose to leave the theory and practice of politics in favor of the theory of literature and aesthetics, although continuing to work from a stringent Marxist perspective.

The primary goal for Lukács from now on was, as Georg Lichtheim has highlighted, to develop "a theory of aesthetics which would do for the world of East European socialism what German Idealism in general, and Hegel in particular, had done for the bourgeois world".[39] Given these ambitions to

---

[35] Lukács, *History and Class Consciousness*, p. 69.

[36] Karl Marx, *Capital: A Critique of Political Economy*, vol. 1, trans. Ben Fowkes (Harmondsworth: Penguin in association with New Left Review, 1976), pp. 163-177.

[37] Karl Marx, *Economic and Philosophical Manuscripts of 1844*, ed. Dirk J. Struik, trans. Martin Milligan (New York: International Publishers, 1972).

[38] Lukács' theory of reification, which demonstrates the connection between reification and the capitalist system, can be compared with Erich Fromm's analysis of alienation. On the basis of *The Economic and Philosophical Manuscripts*, Fromm, who in the thirties belonged to the Frankfurt School, made a kind of anthropological and psychological interpretation of Marx without taking any account of the economic issues. That kind of interpretation is very far away from Lukács, who was always skeptical of psychological explanatory models. Erich Fromm, *Marx's Concept of Man,* with a translation from Marx's *Economic and Philosophical Manuscripts* by T. B. Bottomore (New York: Frederick Ungar Publishing, 1963).

[39] Lichtheim, *George Lukács*, p. 105.

formulate an alternative socialistic and communistic aesthetics, the late Lukács' literary and cultural preferences are strikingly traditional. As he had done during his pre-Marxist period, he still praises Goethe, Balzac, Tolstoy, Thomas Mann and other realistic authors, and the ideals of totality, universality and harmony that still guided his aesthetical analysis made it impossible for him to appreciate the most striking examples of modernist art and literature, including writers such as Franz Kafka, James Joyce and Virginia Woolf.[40]

During his period in Moscow, Lukács also wrote a study on Hegel, entitled *The Young Hegel*, which was completed in 1938 but not published until after the Second World War. If Hegel had been overshadowed by Marx in *History and Class Consciousness*, he stands in the foreground in *The Young Hegel*, and if the reading of Marx in the book from 1923 had been Hegelian, Lukács now interprets the young Hegel's philosophy from a Marxist, historical materialist perspective. (Nevertheless, Lukács claims that *The Young Hegel* also sheds new light on Marx's thinking. In a later added preface he points out that the book tries to clarify how involved Marx is with "the progressive German tradition from Lessing to Heine, from Leibniz to Hegel and Feuerbach, and to prove how profoundly German his works are from the structure of their thought down to his very style.")[41]

*The Young Hegel* consists of four main parts. The first is about what Lukács calls Hegel's early republican phase, from 1793 to 1796, during which he lived in Bern and for which the French Revolution made an especially powerful impression on him. The second part deals with the years in Frankfurt, 1797–1800, during which time Hegel went through a kind of crisis in terms of his view of society. It was at precisely this time that he began to develop his dialectical method. The third part deals with Hegel's period in Jena, between 1801 and 1803, when he worked out his conception of objective idealism. The fourth and final part focuses on the years 1803 to 1807, when *Phenomenology of Spirit* was published and Hegel broke irrevocably with Schelling.

In comparison with *History and Class Consciousness* the study of the young Hegel is less essayistic and, from an academic point of view, we could say more "scholarly". On the whole, the work is solid, even if some of its

---

[40] See e.g. Eugene Lunn, *Marxism and Modernism: An Historical Study of Lukács, Brecht, Benjamin and Adorno* (Berkeley & London: University of California Press, 1982).
[41] George Lukács, *The Young Hegel: Studies in the Relations between Dialectics and Economics*, trans. Rodney Livingstone (Cambridge, MA: MIT Press, 1976), p. xiii.

theses certainly seem less convincing—not least the claim that the young Hegel's theological period is only a reactionary myth.[42] However, the main argument presented in *The Young Hegel* is forceful, namely that Hegel was alone among the German idealistic philosophers to take strong cognizance of the industrial revolution in England and the political revolution in France, and that his dialectical method was elaborated precisely as an attempt to understand and conceptualize this two-sided revolutionary development. Lukács shows how Hegel's philosophy and especially his dialectics were evolved in relation to contemporary socio-economic conditions, including the emergence of modern political economy. Lukács' approach to the book is decisively historical materialist and could, according to the author himself, be regarded as an illustration and application of "the brilliant insight" that Marx formulated in *The Economic and Philosophical Manuscripts*:

> The outstanding achievement of Hegel's *Phenomenology* (…) is thus first that Hegel conceives the self-creation of man as a process, (…) that he grasps the essence of *labor* and comprehends objective man—true, because real man—as the outcome of man's *own labor*. [43]

According to Lukács, *Phenomenology of Spirit* signified a kind of reconciliation with reality (*Versöhnung mit der Wirklichkeit*) after Hegel's rebellious juvenile period. Michael Löwy has drawn certain similarities between Hegel's position in 1807 and Lukács' own situation in the Soviet Union when he wrote *The Young Hegel*: by this time, he too had abandoned his former revolutionary ideals and had become reconciled with the reality of the contemporary political situation.[44]

---

[42] See "Hegel's 'Theological' Period: A Reactionary Legend", in Lukács, *The Young Hegel*, pp. 3-17. While Lichtheim, *Georg Lukács*, p. 115, is skeptical about the academic value of *The Young Hegel*, Ojzerman really esteems it in "Lukács' Hegel Interpretation", pp. 197-220. See also Marek J. Siemek, "Das Hegel-Bild als Problem des philosophischen Selbstverständnisses des Marxismus: Am Rande des 'Jungen Hegel' von Georg Lukács", *Zeitschrift für philosophische Forschung*, 37(3), 1983, pp. 425-441.

[43] Marx, *Economic and Philosophical Manuscripts of 1844*, p. 177.

[44] By the way, the parallel between Lukács and Hegel was highlighted by Theodor W. Adorno already in 1958, in "Erpresste Versöhnung: Zu Georg Lukács' Wider den missverstandenen Realismus", in *Noten zur Litteratur 2* (Frankfurt am Main: Suhrkamp, 1962). It could be added, however, that toward the end of his life, after the totalitarian era of Stalin, Lukács himself explicitly claimed that he never had accepted Hegel's reconciliation with reality. Georg Lukács, "Forord", in Lukács, *Kunst og kapitalisme*, ed. Bente Hansen (Copenhagen: Gyldendals, 1971), p. 7.

The question of Lukács' Stalinism cannot be investigated here, but it is clear he never raised public objections against Stalin during the latter's lifetime. After Stalin's death in 1953, Lukács could indeed express certain criticisms, but even these were in accordance with his constant attempts (from the late twenties) to ingratiate himself with the official Soviet line. During Nikita Khrushchev's famous speech at the twentieth party Congress in 1956, the new Soviet leader denounced the Stalinist terror and Stalin's cult of personality. Lukács did not risk anything when he, for example, in a late interview dismissed Stalin as not any real Marxist and that the large bureaucratic apparatus, which emerged in the Soviet Union under his leadership, was deplorable, or even when he took the opportunity to criticize the cartoon-like depiction of Hegel that circulated during the era of Stalin.[45] Meanwhile, Lukács remained convinced that even the worst form of socialism and communism are preferable to the best kind of capitalism.[46] Seen from that perspective, it is unsurprising he did not object more strongly to Stalin and the other subsequent Soviet leaders.

## To read Hegel for one's own purposes

In both *The Young Hegel* and the later, highly polemical *The Destruction of Reason*, published in 1954, Lukács argues that Hegel was essentially a rationalistic and radical philosopher who turned against the emotional irrationalism of Romanticism.[47] In this way Lukács challenged the image of the young Hegel as a conservative thinker, which had become well established in German-speaking philosophy by the early twentieth century. This alleged "reactionary" interpretation of Hegel was advanced by, among others, Wilhelm Dilthey in his study *Die Jugendgeschichte Hegels* and Franz Rosenzweig in his *Hegel und der Staat*. In these, and other similar studies, Hegel was presented, Lukács says, "as a forefather of the contemporary reactionary bourgeoisie, as a predecessor and accomplice to Bismarck", and

---

[45] John T. Sanders & Katie Terezakis, "Preface", in Lukács, *Soul and Form*, p. ix. Georg Lukács, *Zur Ontologie des gesellschaftlichen Seins. Halbband 1*, ed. Frank Benseler (Darmstadt: Luchterhand, 1984), p. 516.

[46] Harry Redner, *Malign Masters: Gentile, Heidegger, Lukács, Wittgenstein. Philosophy and Politics in the Twentieth Century* (Basingstoke: Macmillan, 1997), p. 3.

[47] Georg Lukács, *The Destruction of Reason*, trans. Peter Palmer (London: Merlin, 1980). Lukács points out the close relationship between *The Young Hegel* and *The Destruction of Reason* in the preface of a later edition (from 1954) of the book on Hegel. Lukács, *The Young Hegel*, p. vi.

Hegelian philosophy—cleansed from all dialectics—became a philosophy of preservation for different reactionary tendencies.[48]

In *The Destruction of Reason* Hegel is positioned as an alternative to a broad range of irrational thinkers—from Schelling, via Schopenhauer and Kierkegaard, to Nietzsche and the *Lebensphilosophen* of the early twentieth century—all of whom, according to Lukács, paved the way for fascism. This means that in the 1930s, when he wrote *The Young Hegel*, as well as during the Cold War when *The Destruction of Reason* was published, Lukács used Hegel as a brother-in-arms in the communist struggle against the irrationalism that had received its clearest expression in Italian fascism and German Nazism, but which also was characteristic of contemporary capitalism. More than any other thinker or scholar, it was Lukács who constructed this strongly politicized image of Hegel as an opponent not only to irrationalism but by extension also to modern fascism and capitalism.[49] Although Lukács consistently uses Hegel for his own communist purposes, he objects to the reactionary form of Hegelianism as an example of mis-readings and abuse of Hegelian philosophy.[50] Nevertheless, even Lukács had to admit that Hegel's philosophy is extremely complex and can be interpreted in a variety of different ways.

Moreover, as Lukács was well aware, Hegel's thinking changed over time. The philosopher who wrote *Phenomenology of Spirit* differs both from the younger and the older Hegel. While the young Hegel was a radical thinker, toward the end of his life, he became arguably more conservative, with indeed his *Elements of the Philosophy of Right* constituting something of a philosophical condensation of his regression into conservatism. It is hardly a coincidence that the latter book is one of the works of Hegel that Lukács uses and writes about the least, even though this particular philosophical work of Hegel's is commonly treated in various synoptic histories of political ideas. In his extensive *oeuvre*—from the early study of the theory of the novel to the late works of the destruction of reason and the ontology of social being—Lukács returned constantly to both *Phenomenology of Spirit*

[48] Lukács, *The Destruction of Reason*, p. 565.
[49] See Jozsef Lukács, "Die Probleme von Religion und Irrationalität im Schaffen von Georg Lukács", in Manfred Buhr & Jozsef Lukács (eds.), *Geschichtlichkeit und Aktualität, Beiträge zum Werk und Wirken von Georg Lukács* (Berlin: Akademie-Verlag, 1987), p. 34.
[50] Lukács treats the Nazi's interpretation of Hegel in "Der deutsche Faschismus und Hegel", in Lukács, *Schicksalswende: Beiträge zu einer neuen deutschen Ideologie* (Berlin: Aufbau, 1948), pp. 37-67.

and the *Logic*.[51] It was mainly based on these two books that he worked out his specific form of Hegelian Marxism.

To summarize, in Lukács' writings from the late 1910s onwards, Hegel and Marx were his main references. He interpreted Marx through Hegel (primarily in *History and Class Consciousness*) and Hegel through the perspectives of Marx and historical materialism (especially in *The Young Hegel*). Although Hegelianism, even more than Marxism, was a kind of "cultural dominant" for his thought, it was through synthesizing these two currents of ideas in *History and Class Consciousness* that Lukács made his most significant contribution to the modern history of political ideas.[52]

In addition, it deserves to be noted that throughout his work Lukács continued to defend not only Hegel's philosophy but also many other concepts and values that he associated with German idealism and the classical humanistic culture—favoring authors such as Lessing, Schiller, Goethe and Thomas Mann. In his later career Lukács defended as well as attempted to bring these constructive elements of the older humanistic culture into the orbit of a modern Marxist worldview. Thus both before and after he had become a communist, Lukács was first and foremost a humanistic scholar with a strong sense for the harmonious and a firm belief in the whole of humanity and humankind.

After the publication of his controversial book in 1923 Lukács' thinking lost much of its complexity as he adapted himself to the quiet simplistic form of Marxism-Leninism that was mandated in Stalinist USSR. At the same time, he continued to emphasize the general importance of Hegelian philosophy and in particular the significance of the dialectical method, not only as a starting point for Marx but also as a tool in the current struggle against the capitalist system, which according to Lukács was a curse for humanity. It was, indeed, to critically challenge capitalism, to re-vitalize Marxism and ultimately to emancipate human beings that Lukács argued it is necessary to go back to Hegel.

---

[51] Hegel's Logic also takes a prominent place in Lukács' last comprehensive treatment of Hegel, which was never completed and published first after his death, *Zur Ontologie des gesellschaftlichen Sein*. Although the sections on Hegel here focus on ontological questions, Lukács also deals with Hegel's dialectics, since this has an obvious ontological side; according to Hegel, the dialectic movements reflect the dynamics of external reality. Georg Lukács, *Zur Ontologie des gesellschaftlichen Seins. Halbband 1*, ed. Frank Benseler (Darmstadt: Luchterhand, 1984).

[52] The concept of cultural dominant is borrowed from Fredric Jameson, *Postmodernism or, the Cultural Logic of Late Capitalism* (London: Verso, 1992), p. 4 et passim.

# Karl Korsch: To Make the Right Marx Visible through Hegel

*Anders Bartonek*

In the following I will examine in what sense the Marxist thought of Karl Korsch (1886–1961) can be understood as a form of Hegelian Marxism, that is, how does Korsch employ Hegel with the purpose of developing a certain type of Marxism? This reconstruction of Korsch's thinking contains two main questions: first, what is the character of his Marxism? And second how can Korsch's interpretation be construed as a Hegelian Marxism? Korsch formulates his Marxist theory in contrast to several other Marxist and Social democratic alternatives, and in doing so, it is the figure of Hegel who plays a significant role in Korsch's undertaking. In 1920, Korsch began his studies of Marx and Marxism.[1] What initiated these studies was an investigation into whether anything had been lost in the disappearance of the Hegelian legacy from both bourgeois and Marxist thought. Here, we can say, Korsch seeks to revive Marxism with some help from Hegel's spirit. This addresses the explicitly philosophical dimension of Korsch's work. In one and the same gesture, though, he tries to keep this theoretical dimension of Marxism alive (seeking to strengthen it) at the same time he seeks to revive the revolutionary force of Marxism. Korsch's second purpose with Marxian theory is thereby essentially extra-theoretical, that is, the end of theory is to prepare and to lead to the fulfillment of the Marxist workers movement in a total social revolution, the result of which would mark the sublation of philosophy.[2] Seung-Hoe Koo formulates this in terms of

---

[1] Michael Buckmiller, "Zeittafel zu Karl Korsch: Leben und Werk", in Buckmiller (ed.), *Zur Aktualität von Karl Korsch* (Frankfurt am Main: Europäische Verlagsanstalt, 1981), p. 165.
[2] See Patrick Goode, *Karl Korsch: A Study in Western Marxism* (London: Macmillan Press, 1979), p. 2; Gian Enrico Rusconi, "Dialektik in pragmatischer Anwendung: An-

Korsch trying to mediate the idea of the proletariat (theory) with the real movement of class (praxis).[3] But at the same time, Korsch continuously points to the significant role that both theory and philosophy play within this historic ambition, and it is precisely for this reason that Hegel is of especial importance. Korsch also underlines how Marx himself defended the Hegelian and dialectical heritage, even if he did this in an inverted and praxis-oriented form. According to Korsch, the role of philosophy within the movement towards revolution cannot be underestimated, even if the proletarian revolution would mean the fulfillment and end of philosophy.

Korsch's theoretical work is being performed in a context of direct political engagement and official work within political parties. During 1919 he was first a member of USPD (Unabhängige Sozialdemokratische Partei Deutschlands) and later enrolled into the KPD (Kommunistische Partei Deutschlands), and during a short period of time he was appointed as minister of justice in the coalition of SPD and KPD in 1923. Already in 1923, Korsch received harsh critique for his book *Marxism and Philosophy*, and by 1926 he was excluded from the party. A further seven years later, Korsch was forced to emigrate.[4] That his theoretical work had a practical purpose becomes further visible in light of a course compendium he wrote on the "quintessence" of Marxism from 1922 (*Quintessenz des Marxismus, Eine gemeinverständliche Darlegung*). There, in a pedagogical manner, Korsch presents the foundations of Marxist and communist economic theory. The compendium consists of a very general account of this theory, and is not specifically connected to Korsch's own research, theoretical work or specific Marxist position.[5]

Korsch's texts can to a large extent be viewed as having been written from the standpoint of Marxism, both as a theory and practice, being in crisis. In the text "The Crisis of Marxism" (1931), he endeavors to formulate this crisis. It is not just a crisis because of the direction that Marxism took after Marx and Engels, but rather it points to a crisis within Marxism itself. The attempts to identify a pure core of Marxism (the theoretical elements of

merkungen zu einer neuen Korsch-Rezeption", in Claudio Pozzoli (ed.), *Über Karl Korsch* (Frankfurt am Main: Fischer, 1973), p. 138.
[3] Seung-Hoe Koo, *Karl Korsch und die Historisierung des Marxismus* (Darmstadt, 1992), p. 11.
[4] Koo, *Karl Korsch und die Historisierung des Marxismus*, pp. 3-14; Goode, Karl Korsch, pp. 1ff.
[5] Karl Korsch, *Quintessenz des Marxismus: Eine gemeinverständliche Darstellung* (Leipzig: VIVA, 1922).

which are constructed by the original architects), only then to view the historical development as a deviation from the original sources of Marxism is for Korsch precisely a symptom of this crisis. Insensitivity toward the theoretical dimension of Marxism is also essential, and Korsch writes that while Marxist theories only can be understood as the joint result of all past class struggles, theory (in his own time) no longer appears to be connected to current class struggle. What therefore is missing is a contemporary Marxist direction that really gives expression to the practical needs of the proletariat.[6] Korsch tries to handle this sense of crisis by formulating what a contemporary Marxism needs to be and in so doing he indirectly tries to become a spokesperson for the proletarian class. A crucial dimension of this theoretical effort is to re-actualize, via Hegel, the revolutionary and dialectical foundations of Marxism. This lesson in crisis management entails not only the development of new forms of Marxism as such, but also necessitates the relativization of earlier and other contemporary positions taken up within the fields of Marxist and social democratic theory. As Koo writes, Korsch deals with the problem surrounding theoretical positions with help from his own historical periodization of Marxism, to which I will return later.[7] It is precisely in being placed in such a historical overview that these positions are relativized and can be transcended.

This essay is divided into two main parts: the first one aims at presenting the central characteristics of Korsch's Marxism in three steps, while the second part aims at a reconstruction of his Hegelian Marxism. Out of Korsch's entire oeuvre, it is his *Marxism and Philosophy* (1923) and *Karl Marx* (1938) that are generally considered to be his two most important works.[8] Therefore these texts will be the principal objects for this study. They are of further interest here, since it is within their pages that the connection between Korsch's Marxism and the philosophy of Hegel reveals itself. Several additional texts, written during the 1920s, are relevant for this topic too, and so will also be considered. The secondary literature on Korsch's interpretation of Marx and Marxism as well as on his understanding of Hegel is generally limited;[9] this is especially the case regarding the

---

[6] Korsch, "The Crisis of Marxism", in Douglas Kellner (ed.), *Karl Korsch: Revolutionary Theory* (Austin: University of Texas Press, 1977), pp. 171ff.

[7] Koo, *Karl Korsch und die Historisierung des Marxismus*, pp. 76ff.

[8] See for example, Goode, Karl Korsch, p. 1; Koo, *Karl Korsch und die Historisierung des Marxismus*, p. 8.

[9] For Marx, see Koo, *Karl Korsch und die Historisierung des Marxismus*; Goode, *Karl Korsch* and Tom Meisenhelder, "The Contemporary Significance of Karl Korsch's

relation of his Marxism to Hegel.[10] There are no studies that discuss in detail Korsch's Marxism as being Hegelian, even if the theme is touched upon more or less superficially in some contributions. This means that, for the sake of space, this particular text will not enter the most controversial questions that have been discussed in relation to Korsch, principally his understanding of Lenin.[11] Interest in Korsch reached its height in connection with the 1968 movement, and this interest was sustained for about ten or fifteen years after these events. This period, we can say, marked a fertile period for Marxist research in general.[12] Thereafter, only occasional works on Korsch's thinking have been published. With respect to the limited discussion on Korsch's Hegelian Marxism—a label that is itself questioned by different commentators—many contributions have only sought to interpret his reception of Hegel in a narrow sense: for them, Korsch is only interested in Hegel as a theoretical instrument for praxis and for purposes of fulfilling the Marxist revolutionary aim (Cerutti, Koo, Rundell). Even if this is true, it is easy to forget Korsch's other main aim with Hegel: to make Marxist theory anew with Hegel.

---

Marxism", *Nature, Society, and Thought*, 14:3 2001. For Hegel, see Koo, *Karl Korsch und die Historisierung des Marxismus*; Goode, *Karl Korsch* and Andrew Giles-Peters, "Dialektik und Empirismus", in: Buckmiller (ed.), *Zur Aktualität von Karl Korsch*.

[10] For Hegelian Marxism, see Koo, *Karl Korsch und die Historisierung des Marxismus*; Giles-Peters, "Dialektik und Empirismus"; Furio Cerutti, "Hegel, Lukács, Korsch: Zum dialektischen Selbstverständnis des kritischen Marxismus", in Oskar Negt (ed.), *Aktualität und Folgen der Philosophie Hegels* (Frankfurt am Main: Suhrkamp, 1971); John Rundell, "Karl Korsch: Historicized Dialectics" (http://journals.sagepub.com/doi/pdf/10.11 77/072551368100300110); Kellner (ed.), *Karl Korsch*, and Rusconi, "Dialektik in pragmatischer Anwendung, Anmerkungen zu einer neuen Korsch-Rezeption".

[11] One should also briefly mention Korsch's relation to Lenin, who was important for his thinking, not least since Lenin was influential in the return to Hegel (Goode, *Karl Korsch*, p. 70). Koo highlights Lenin's significance for Korsch, but also how Korsch later would turn against Lenin. As a member of KPD Korsch was a part of Leninist politics, but in theory he criticized Lenin's undialectical thinking. Some years after he would defend Leninism without criticism, which Koo explains in terms of Korsch's supposed ambition to find an efficient organization for Communism. First in 1927, Korsch turned away from Lenin, and one main argument is again connected to the question of dialectics: since dialectics for Lenin alone belongs within the subject and not within the object, the subject will only be able to be a reflection of the objective processes of reality (Koo, *Karl Korsch und die Historisierung des Marxismus*, pp. 32 ff. and 52ff.). But it was Lenin's early return to Hegel that inspired Korsch to do the same (Goode, *Karl Korsch*, p. 70), but in the end, Korsch understood Lenin as a philosophical, but not a dialectical materialist (Koo, *Karl Korsch und die Historisierung des Marxismus*, p. 58).

[12] Buckmiller, "Aspekte der internationalen Korsch-Rezeption", in Buckmiller (ed.), *Zur Aktualität von Karl Korsch*, pp. 25ff.

## Korsch's Marxism

Korsch opposes several contemporary and older forms of socialism, communism and Marxism, and he seems also to have the self-image of being the righteous manager of the legacy of Marx and Engels. Korsch's Marxism, through its proximity to party politics (in contrast to so-called Western Marxism), as well as through its revolutionary character, is thereby situated in a multi-front-war. It is mainly critical towards, on the one hand, the contemporary reform-oriented social democratic tendency, and, on the other hand, towards Marxist factions, which of course were more radical than social democrats, but still had degenerated into what Korsch calls vulgar Marxism. Although in many ways different, social democracy and vulgar Marxism united around a dismissal of the revolutionary. On the one side, the critique of social democratic reformism exposed the revisionist tendencies of the social democrats; it was a standpoint entirely compatible with contemporary society. What was needed was a theory that could satisfactorily represent the economic effort of the unions and the political effort of the proletariat. On the other side, the critique of vulgar Marxism targeted an approach that was too weighed down by tradition; it held onto the original form of Marxism in a problematic way, such that it became abstract and was cut adrift from new forms of class struggle.[13] To sum up, one can say that Korsch's Marxism is a Marxism that remains close to party politics and a Marxism that refused to consider Marxism having been fulfilled by the Russian revolution. Rather, the revolution remains the task of Marxism. Korsch's unwavering proximity to politics marks out a notable difference to other later Western Marxists (for example Adorno, Horkheimer and Marcuse), who essentially chose to keep their distance from party politics in order to restore a certain theoretical independence from party interests.[14] A main dimension of Korsch's Marxism is also his strong will to hold onto Hegel's dialectical heritage in opposition to anti-dialectical interpretations, where Marxism becomes more a means for the acquisition of power rather than a philosophy of freedom.

Korsch's Marxism will firstly (a) be presented in a general manner, and then, secondly (b), be reconstructed in relation to the concepts of dialectics, revolution and the question of theory and praxis, and finally (c), be examined from out of its understanding of materialist history.

---

[13] Karl Korsch, *Marxism and Philosophy* (New York: Monthly Review Press, 2008), pp. 65ff.
[14] Perry Anderson, *Considerations on Western Marxism* (London: NLB, 1976).

## a) General remarks on Korsch's Marxism

A crucial question for Korsch and for this examination of his thought is the relation between the thinking of both Marx and Engels and those bourgeois thinkers antedating them, especially the philosophy of Hegel. Korsch underlines the importance of Marxist materialism from the perspective of a historical transition away from bourgeois philosophy, in particular Hegelian dialectical philosophy. Both Marx and Engels were "[i]n contrast to bourgeois thinkers (...) fully aware of the close historical connection between their materialist theory and bourgeois idealist philosophy".[15] But for a Marxist materialist theory the main aim, according to Korsch, is the sublation of philosophy, despite its close connection to Hegelian philosophy and to the dialectic. In Korsch's book *Marxism and Philosophy* therefore the question surrounding the relation between Marxism and philosophy has an important status. The task of Marxism not only consists in sublating bourgeois philosophy, as a problematic philosophy, but rather the task is to sublate philosophy as such.[16] Even if socialism derived from bourgeois philosophy, for Korsch this does not necessarily mean that socialism must remain a philosophy. In the same way as Marx and Engels strive not only to transcend some certain state, but the political state as such, socialism aims at transcending philosophy as such. But according to Korsch, philosophy— or materialist theory—plays a decisive role in the struggle for social revolution. Thus an important question is, as Korsch formulates it, the following: what character does the relation between philosophy and Marxism has in that historical stage when philosophy has not yet been sublated.[17] Is Marxism still philosophy? Is it a philosophy working towards the sublation of philosophy? In any case, the relation between philosophy and the social revolution is a crucial issue for Korsch.[18]

Korsch divides the history of Marxism into three distinct phases. The first comprises of the period between 1843 to 1848, that is, from Marx's *Critique of Hegel's Philosophy of Right* to Marx's and Engels' *Communist Manifesto*. The second "begins with the bloody suppression of the Parisian proletariat in the battle of June 1848 and the resultant crushing of all the working class's organizations and dreams of emancipation" and lasts until around 1900. The third phase is, according to Korsch, not yet completed,

[15] Korsch, *Marxism and Philosophy*, p. 47.
[16] Korsch, *Marxism and Philosophy*, p. 49.
[17] Korsch, *Marxism and Philosophy*, p. 52.
[18] Korsch, *Marxism and Philosophy*, pp. 70-71.

but is under development when he writes his book *Marxism and Philo-sophy*.[19] This three-part division contains an understanding of the history of Marxism as, during the first phase, not only a theory of societal develop-ment, understood in the terms of a dynamic totality, but also as a theory about the ongoing social revolution.[20] However, this revolutionary form of Marxist theory changes during the second more reactive phase. For Korsch, the scientific socialism of Marx still consists of "a theory of social revolution comprehended and practised as a living totality",[21] but the different dimen-sions of that theory—the questions of economy, politics and ideology—are now being separated from one another, handled in isolation, for example in Marx's *Capital*. But in Marx, this all-encompassing "practice of the revo-lutionary will"[22] is never too far from sight. The problem is that in the thinking of many of Marx's followers Marxist theory gradually turns into "a set of purely scientific observations, without any immediate connection to the political or other practices of class struggle".[23] Korsch writes:

> a unified general theory of social revolution was changed into criticisms of the bourgeois economic order, of the bourgeois State, of the bourgeois system of education, of bourgeois religion, art, science and culture. These criticisms no longer necessarily develop by their very nature into revolutionary practice; they can equally well develop, into all kinds of attempts at reform, which fundamentally remain within the limits of bourgeois society and the bourgeois State, and in actual practice usually did so.[24]

That the materialistic understanding of history, which Marx and Engels represented, becomes undialectical in the thinking of their epigones is con-nected to this point.[25] This development leads to a division between two positions, both of which have, according to Korsch, lost contact with the task of social revolution. On the one hand: "Revisionism appears as an attempt to express in the form of a coherent theory the reformist character acquired by the economic struggles of the trade unions and the political

---

[19] Korsch, *Marxism and Philosophy*, pp. 56-57.
[20] Korsch, *Marxism and Philosophy*, p. 57.
[21] Korsch, *Marxism and Philosophy*, p. 57.
[22] Korsch, *Marxism and Philosophy*, p. 60.
[23] Korsch, *Marxism and Philosophy*, p. 60.
[24] Korsch, *Marxism and Philosophy*, pp. 63-64.
[25] Korsch, *Marxism and Philosophy*, p. 62.

struggles of the working class parties, under the influence of altered historical conditions." On the other hand:

> The so-called orthodox Marxism of this period (now a mere vulgar-
> marxism) appears largely as an attempt by theoreticians, weighed down
> by tradition, to maintain the theory of social revolution which formed
> the first version of Marxism, in the shape of pure theory. This theory was
> wholly abstract and had no practical consequences—it merely sought to
> reject the new reformist theories, in which the real character of the his-
> torical movement was then expressed as un-Marxist.[26]

The third phase has its starting point within this very situation. But now,
however, a development of, and a reconnection to, a genuinely revolutionary theory occurs.[27] Class struggle now enters a new phase, and new theoretical developments are a response to this. Korsch is not so specific about
the character of this situation, but notes that the "objectively revolutionary
socio-economic position" of the working masses "no longer corresponded to
(...) [the] evolutionary doctrines", as represented by the social democratic
Marxism of the second phase.[28] Not least Lenin re-actualized the question of
the dictatorship of the proletariat.[29] Korsch's own work must be understood
as belonging to this phase, and he writes programmatically that Marxism
must once again become what it was for Marx and Engels, namely "a theory
of social revolution that comprises all areas of society as a totality".[30] Koo's
observation about Korsch—that, because he understood the communist
praxis of his time as itself riven with problems meant that it was necessary
to return to philosophy, in general, and Hegel, in particular, in order to
understand anew which praxis should be followed—appears convincing.[31]

### b) Dialectics and revolution

Central to Korsch's Marxist philosophy is the relation between theory and
praxis. The most essential reason for the need to pursue Marxist philosophy
is for Korsch the need to fundamentally transform society. For the sake of
this, according to Korsch, theory needs to be dialectical, and in *Marxism*

---

[26] Korsch, *Marxism and Philosophy*, p. 65.
[27] Korsch, *Marxism and Philosophy*, pp. 67-68.
[28] Korsch, *Marxism and Philosophy*, p. 67.
[29] Korsch, *Marxism and Philosophy*, p. 68.
[30] Korsch, *Marxism and Philosophy*, p. 70.
[31] Koo, *Karl Korsch und die Historisierung des Marxismus*, p. 68.

*and Philosophy* he describes the relation between theory and praxis as itself essentially dialectical. But "[a]mong bourgeois scholars in the second half of the nineteenth century there was a total disregard of Hegel's philosophy, which coincided with a complete incomprehension of the relation of philosophy to reality, and of theory to practice, which constituted the living principle of all philosophy and science in Hegel's time."[32] Not only had Hegel and this dialectical understanding of theory and praxis been forgotten within the bourgeois history of philosophy, according to Korsch, it becomes increasingly clear how

> Marxists simultaneously tended in exactly the same way increasingly to forget the original meaning of the dialectical principle. Yet it was this that the two young Hegelians Marx and Engels, when they were turning away from Hegel in the 1840s, had quite deliberately rescued from German idealist philosophy and transferred to the materialist conception of history and society.[33]

It is not only the bourgeois canon that has forgotten Hegel and his dialectical understanding of thinking and reality, Marxism itself has placed this heritage out of sight, a legacy that, moreover, was itself formative for both Marx and Engels, despite their public criticisms of Hegel and Hegelianism. Therefore it is plausible to describe, following Michael Buckmiller, Korsch's project as a re-actualization of the Hegelian moments within Marxist theory.[34] But what is the nature of the dialectical principle that Marx and Engels received from Hegel and that plays a significant role in Korsch's own version of Marxism? Even if Hegel continuously is crucial for Korsch, I will here be mainly focusing on his Marxist view on theory and praxis as well as on dialectics. I return to Hegel later.

Korsch discusses how Marx understood the role of philosophy before a revolution as well as Marx's understanding of the relation between philosophy and revolution as such. To begin with, Marx clearly points out that philosophy and ideology are not mere fabrications, but are rather realities in society. Korsch is quoting Marx from an early newspaper-article from 1842, where he writes that "philosophy does not stand outside the world, just as the brain does not stand outside man merely because it is not in his sto-

---

[32] Korsch, *Marxism and Philosophy*, pp. 34-35.
[33] Korsch, *Marxism and Philosophy*, p. 35.
[34] Buckmiller, "Marxismus als Realität. Zur Rekonstruktion der theoretischen und politischen Entwicklung Karl Korschs", in Pozzoli (ed.) *Über Karl Korsch*, p. 15.

mach."[35] Marx's understanding of philosophy contains within it not solely a critique of bourgeois philosophy. What is distinctive about this understanding is the importance it places on philosophy's role for the possibility of revolution. This is the ambivalence of philosophy in Korsch's thinking: on the one hand, as a problem which needs to be sublated, on the other hand as a tool for this sublation. To start with: philosophy is according to its nature already a part of the reality that it seeks to overcome. But this means that at the same time philosophy has a direct contact with this very problem-riddled reality. Not that this insight is sufficient on it own; the relation between philosophy and reality must be further determined. Marx and Engels never rejected, against the backdrop of their critique of bourgeois philosophy, philosophy as mere ideology, but rather took the step from idealistic dialectics to dialectical materialism,[36] which presupposes that "[i]ntellectual life should be conceived in union with social and political life, and social being and becoming (in the widest sense, as economics, politics or law) should be studied in union with social consciousness in its many different manifestations, as a real yet also ideal (or 'ideological') component of the historical process in general".[37] This means that Marxism, in its critique of society and social consciousness, must depart from "the particular forms of consciousness which have found their scientific expression in the political economy of bourgeois society".[38] In any case, Korsch shows that the tradition of Marxist-dialectical theory presupposes that the dialectical understanding of reality is the coincidence of consciousness and reality, and without it "this coincidence of consciousness and reality, a critique of political economy could never have become the major component of a theory of social revolution."[39] Dialectical materialism no longer (in contrast to Hegel) sees scientific thinking as independent from the natural world; rather it views (also in contrast to Hegel) that "forms of consciousness (of bourgeois society) cannot be abolished through thought alone. These forms can only be abolished in thought and consciousness by a simultaneous practico-objective overthrow of the material relations of production themselves, which have hitherto been comprehended through these forms."[40] Here, it is Korsch's ambition to show how philosophy receives a decisive

[35] Korsch, *Marxism and Philosophy*, p. 73.
[36] Korsch, *Marxism and Philosophy*, pp. 76ff.
[37] Korsch, *Marxism and Philosophy*, p. 81.
[38] Korsch, *Marxism and Philosophy*, p. 85.
[39] Korsch, *Marxism and Philosophy*, p. 89.
[40] Korsch, *Marxism and Philosophy*, p. 93.

(but limited) place in the thinking of Marx and Engels, and is not merely understood negatively or as ideology. Crucial here also is how dialectical materialism understands philosophy and reality as dialectically connected, since it is only from this vantage point that philosophy can be regarded as an effective critique of reality. Thinking and social reality must be revolutionized synchronically:

> Theoretical criticism and practical overthrow are here inseparable activities, not in any abstract sense but as a concrete and real alteration of the concrete and real world of bourgeois society. Such is the most precise expression of the new materialist principle of the scientific socialism of Marx and Engels.[41]

In a shorter text on "Der junge Marx als aktivistischer Philosoph" (1924), Korsch discusses the question about the status of philosophy in Marx and Engels and the relation between theory and praxis. In a similar way to *Marxism and Philosophy*, he criticizes the factions of Marxism of his own time for being vulgar Marxists, because they have dropped entirely the contact to its philosophical history (here mentioned as the idealistic tradition of Kant, Fichte and Hegel) and thereby believed to have left every philosophical standpoint behind. But, according to Korsch, this has nothing to do with the dialectical materialism of Marx and Engels and their relation to their philosophical predecessors. Even if, according to Korsch, Marx and Engels were open about the origins of their own thinking, and how they sought to transmit essential dimensions of their heritage from the idealistic philosophy of Hegel, here merely negative aspects of Hegel (when it comes to theory and praxis) are highlighted. Marx tries to transcend the philosophical standpoint, but he does this by not only opposing philosophy, but rather by struggling against the world in its entirety, since this contradiction is not only theoretical, but practical. According to Korsch, Hegel indeed gave philosophy a theory-transcending and practical dimension, but this dimension only contained the insight that reason (as self-conscious spirit) was reconciled with existing reality through its concepts. In Marx, and according to the famous last thesis on Feuerbach, the task of philosophy is not merely to interpret the world, but to the change it. Korsch therefore underlines a contradiction between Hegel's "reconciliation" and Marx's "change", but he remains clear that philosophy does not end being a philo-

---

[41] Korsch, *Marxism and Philosophy*, p. 95.

sophy because it has this revolutionary task. The ambition of philosophy to change the world means that it can no longer remain only theoretical, but rather has an extra-philosophical motivation. In the end, Korsch understands Marx's goal of carrying out its revolutionary struggle within the theoretical sphere, the purpose of which is none other than the sublation of philosophy that runs parallel with society, because philosophy cannot be sublated without being realized.[42] This means that philosophy in this Marxist sense must be theory-transcending and lead to praxis, while Hegel's philosophy reconciles thinking with reality, only for reality to remain untransformed.

In "The Marxist Dialectic" (1923) Korsch highlights Marx's extraordinary theoretical accomplishment for the sake of the praxis of the proletariat's class struggle. Marx gave the existing consciousness of the proletariat an adequate scientific content, seeking though to raise it to a higher level.[43] A main argument for Korsch here is that, within this development, the dialectical method is not something exchangeable for something else, it is instead indispensable to the whole process. Korsch writes in relation to this that "Marx's 'proletarian' dialectic" is "just that form in which the revolutionary class movement of the proletariat finds its appropriate theoretical expression."[44] The main purpose of this text is to highlight Marx's understanding of the dialectical method, as distinct from Hegel's, and to show that this Marxist method is closely connected to the progress of the proletariat, from its undeveloped understanding of the class problem to the scientific formulation of the class question. The proletariat can only become aware of its situation and the need to overcome it through its inherent dialectical method and movement. Where the idealistic dialectics, according to Korsch, reached its endpoint in the bourgeois state and therefore only puts an end to the relation between rich and poor within the idea, the Marxist dialectics is a dialectics that sublates the bourgeois state.[45]

In his text "On Materialist Dialectic" (1924) Korsch discusses the same problem and criticizes his contemporary, Marxist August Thalheimer's formulation of the idealistic dialectics as the demonstration of the connection of the determinations of thought as a system. For Korsch, the content of

[42] Korsch, "Der junge Marx als aktivistischer Philosoph", in *Geistige Politik* (Leipzig 1924), pp. 41-45.
[43] Korsch, "The Marxist Dialectic", in Kellner (ed.), *Karl Korsch: Revolutionary Theory*, pp. 135-136.
[44] Korsch, "The Marxist Dialectic", p. 138.
[45] Korsch, "The Marxist Dialectic", pp. 135-140.

(materialist) dialectics is rather connected to the historical situation: "Apart from its respective concrete historical content a real 'materialistic' dialectic can state nothing at all about the determinations of thought and the relations between them."[46] Materialistic dialectics is not to be understood as one of several sciences, but aims at being "applied concretely in the practice of the proletarian revolution and in a theory which is an immanent real component of this revolutionary practice."[47] This means that philosophy turns into an expression of the proletariat and its struggle, and simultaneously pushes its state of consciousness forward in relation to the prevailing situation. Philosophy must be dialectically directed against the bourgeois order of society.

The dialectical method is also the topic for Korsch's theory in a later text, entitled "Die dialektische Methode im 'Kapital'" (1932). The question treated here is what part does this method play in Marx's *Capital*? According to Korsch, Marx's method is close to the rational core of dialectics in Hegel.[48] Once again Korsch underlines how the dialectical theory in Marx not only is dialectical when it comes to his method or scientific presentation, but the dialectical method is materialist in the sense that it becomes the adequate way to relate to and follow its object. Marx's thinking is dialectical because it develops a science that does not aim at restoring and refining the capitalist order, but to revolutionarily overthrow it.[49] The dialectical method of science is not therefore external to its object, it is rather immanent to it, trying to produce its negation from within. According to Korsch, Marx continuously tries to point out how capitalist society is perishable and how it carries inner contradictions within itself.[50] This question of the method and heritage of *Capital* is also the theme in the preface (*Geleitwort*) that Korsch wrote for Marx's book (1932). Here, Korsch claims that the dialectical method for Marx is not only a theoretical expression, which he uses here and there, it is rather connected to the analysis of an inner principle of the movement of history. For Korsch, dialectics makes Marx's analysis of the entire concrete reality of society possible, its genesis

---

[46] Korsch, "On Materialist Dialectic", in Kellner (ed.), *Karl Korsch*, p. 144.
[47] Korsch, "On Materialist Dialectic", p. 144.
[48] Korsch, "Die dialektische Methode im 'Kapital'", in Korsch, *Die materialistische Geschichtsauffassung* (Frankfurt am Main: Europäische Verlagsanstalt, 1971), p. 174.
[49] Korsch, "Die dialektische Methode im 'Kapital'", p. 177.
[50] Korsch, "Die dialektische Methode im 'Kapital'", p. 177.

and progress as well as its future decay and its inherent seed to a new beginning.[51]

In the book *Karl Marx*, Korsch describes how Marx and Engels realized that the bourgeois and idealistic dialectics in Hegel was no longer enough for proletarian materialism. They broke with it, or rather placed dialectics on a materialist footing, entirely detached from the earlier connection to restoration. Dialectics should no longer, as in Hegel, artfully perform its movement back and forth in order to produce and present its new content by restoring the old, but to let dialectics bury the old in order to reach its scientific and materialist form.[52] The theoretical critique of political economy can only be fulfilled by the proletarian revolution, destroying the bourgeois order of production and changing the connected forms of consciousness.[53] Where Hegel only reaches a point where the alienation of civil society is sublated, Marx, according to Korsch, reminds us that this thinking is insufficient for achieving such a sublation. A practical transition is itself required.[54]

In the end, the form of this dialectics of thinking and reality is not entirely clear in Korsch; rather, he remains caught within formulations that simply state that thinking and reality are "connected". If thinking is a part of reality through a dialectical relation, how specifically does this support the possibility of revolution? Indeed, Korsch's understanding implies that the materialist dialectic must contradict bourgeois philosophy and society in order to produce the negation, which then helps the proletarian sublation of philosophy and society. However, Korsch does not present any detailed answers to how this negativity of philosophy is constituted and how it is supposed to lead to a fundamental transformation in social relations. Nor does Korsch discuss any further how the connection of thinking and reality is connected to the contradiction between, on the one hand, Marxist dialectics and its negation-producing theory, and the bourgeois order, on the other.

---

[51] Korsch, "Introduction to Capital", in Korsch, *Three Essays on Marxism* (New York: Monthly Review Press, 1972), pp. 53ff.
[52] Korsch, *Karl Marx* (New York: Russell & Russell, 1963), pp. 61ff.
[53] Korsch, *Karl Marx*, p. 157.
[54] Korsch, *Karl Marx*, p. 133.

## c) The materialist understanding of history

For Korsch, the question on how to properly understand history was of great importance. He wrote two texts specifically addressing the materialist understanding of history: *Kernpunkte der materialistischen Geschichtsauffassung: Eine quellenmäßige Darstellung* (1922) and "Die materialistische Geschichtsauffassung" (1929). He also broaches this issue in the later *Karl Marx*. The question whether history is materialistic or idealistic is also essentially connected to the question of the relation between Hegel and Marx.

So, then, what is to be understood as a *materialist* understanding of history? In the text from 1922, Korsch writes that Marx's theoretical system contains a science (the new science of Marxist economy) as well as a philosophy (the new philosophical-materialistic understanding of the connection of historical societal events),[55] even if the descriptions of economy and philosophy are themselves not entirely unproblematic, since they remain closely bound up with established understandings. But Marxian theory is, according to Korsch, on the one hand connected to bourgeois thinking, at the same time as it seeks to exit from it,[56] and this ambivalence is a dialectical aspect of history. The political-economical dimension of Marx's understanding of history departs from a critique of bourgeois ideology, but then rather focuses on the real political and economic practices in order to make the real forces that are producing history visible. Through his critique of traditional ideology Karl Marx developed his materialist standpoint, according to which the economic factor, or political economy, appears as the most important and fundamental for the historical and societal life of human kind.[57] This economic and materialist understanding of history and its progression is combined with the more holistic understanding of history as a dialectical mediation of all societal phenomena and a theory about how they are connected. These two dimensions in Marx are interconnected because the economy is the most important factor of mediation. This connection becomes clear when, in *Karl Marx*, Korsch writes that Marx formulates the history of human life as a progress from lower to higher forms of the organization of the materialist states of production. In this development of production lies also the possibility for the transition into a socialist and communist society, introduced and led by the modern indus-

---

[55] Korsch, *Kernpunkte der materialistischen Geschichtsauffassung: Eine quellenmäßige Darstellung* (Hamburg: Verlag Association, 1973), p. 13.
[56] Korsch, *Kernpunkte der materialistischen Geschichtsauffassung*, pp. 12ff.
[57] Korsch, *Kernpunkte der materialistischen Geschichtsauffassung*, p. 12.

trial working class.[58] In *Kernpunkte der materialistischen Geschichtsauffas-sung*, Korsch writes, in relation to this connection of economy and his-torical totality that the anatomy of bourgeois society must be searched for within political economy and that it is the forms of production of material life that determine the social, political and intellectual process of life.[59]

Korsch's understanding of history seems very close to Marx's, not least when he describes how societal being determines human consciousness and not the other way around,[60] or when he describes the process of production as driven by class struggle.[61] But what seems to be a main ambition for Korsch is to reintroduce and re-actualize a dynamic-dialectical version of Marx's thinking in his theory of history, for which Hegel is a crucial source of inspiration. Andrew Gil-Peters points to the fact that, despite under-standing dialectics as a principle of methodology, Korsch mainly develops dialectics as a principle of history.[62] Even if, according to Korsch, Hegelian dialectics is in the end limited and only cements the bourgeois order of society, it is Hegel's principle of dialectics that Marx ultimately uses when he tries to transcend bourgeois society and philosophy. Not that this means that Hegel does not face critique. For Korsch, Marx's understanding of his-tory contains an understanding of society dialectically developed through different forms of advancing antagonism, and for which the modern anta-gonism is the final and strongest.[63] This antagonism must in the end be dissolved through the concrete social revolution in which theory and reality are rendered identical. In this, Hegel provides only an abstract and apparent sublation of the dualism of thinking and being. The antagonism must really and practically be destroyed, it is not enough that it is sublated—conser-ved—as in Hegel. For Korsch, sublation is not to be understood in this con-serving sense, but is rather a sublation of fundamental change and the de-struction of the bourgeoisie. Reality is not changed in Hegel's sublation, but is legitimized in its historically established form. History in Korsch (and Marx) must, in contrast, lead to a total transformation of reality with help from the negating intervention of theory. And, for Korsch, this is exactly what is meant when Marx speaks of Hegel's dialectic as standing on its head (on point of fact of it being abstract and idealistic) and that what is required

---

[58] Korsch, *Karl Marx*, p. 68.
[59] Korsch, *Kernpunkte der materialistischen Geschichtsauffassung*, p. 15.
[60] Korsch, *Kernpunkte der materialistischen Geschichtsauffassung*, p. 15.
[61] Korsch, *Karl Marx*, pp. 167ff.
[62] Giles-Peters, "Dialektik und Empirismus", p. 61.
[63] Korsch, *Kernpunkte der materialistischen Geschichtsauffassung*, p. 15.

is that it be turned around and placed on its feet (become active, able to walk): Hegel's dialectics expressed only its formal and theoretical side, but not the historical-practical dimension, which for Korsch is necessary.[64]

## Korsch's Hegelian Marxism

Despite the fact that Korsch repeatedly presents Hegel's philosophy and dialectics in ways that problematizes both, Hegel nonetheless plays a crucial part in his own contribution to Marxist theory. Indeed, with John Rundell one can say that Korsch is executing a "renewed (Hegelian) analysis [of Marxism] aimed at recovering the original dialectical dimensions of Marxian social theory and philosophy".[65] In the book *Karl Marx*, both the affirmative and problematizing aspects come to the fore in a clear way when Korsch at one point writes of Marx's evaluation of Hegel's dialectic that it received a mystified form by which the predominant state of society was stabilized, but that the rational form of dialectics, on the other hand, as it takes form within Marxism, became a problem for bourgeois society.[66] It might err on the side of exaggeration to call Korsch's thinking a Hegelian Marxism—maybe this over-emphasizes Hegel's role—but Hegel surely is present in Korsch's texts, and arguably he appears most when Korsch is seeking to describe in what the "right" Marx and the "best" form of Marxism consists. To be sure, Hegel is at times only mentioned in order to delimit Marx from Hegel, but overall, Hegel is used and treated as a vital philosophical component for Marxism. Even if, for Korsch, Marx's materialist dialectics transcends Hegel's idealist dialectics it is necessary to highlight how important Hegel is for Marxism. It is precisely through the reconnection with Hegel that Korsch thinks Marxism can reconquer its revolutionary potential.

I will now show: (a) how Hegel's thinking, generally, and his understanding of dialectics, specifically, are limited according to Korsch; (b) in what way Hegel's philosophy still contains a revolutionary potential, and finally (c) I will conclude by considering the question whether Korsch's thinking can ultimately be called a Hegelian Marxism.

---

[64] Korsch, "Die materialistische Geschichtsauffassung", in Korsch *Die materialistische Geschichtsauffassung*, pp. 16-17.
[65] John Rundell, "Karl Korsch: Historicised Dialectics", p. 115.
[66] Korsch, *Karl Marx*, pp. 45ff.

## a) The limits of Hegel

I have already suggested that Hegel's historically significant position is an expression of both his limits and his greatness. On the one hand, Korsch sees how Hegel developed the last great system of classical philosophy and therefore can be seen as the highest point of this tradition, not only as a summary of its entire process, but also through its ability to already show the inner contradictions of classical and modern bourgeois philosophy (and therefore indicates a direction out of it). In Hegel (and Ricardo) bourgeois society reaches its highest level of self-critical insight.[67] On the other hand, Hegel's philosophy is limited because it remains within philosophy and an idealistic version of dialectics. In part, Hegel's idealistic dialectics stay within the realm of thought and the revolution can only be a theoretical one.[68] In part, Hegel remains squarely within and, according to Korsch, unable to exit the bourgeois paradigm and in a materialist manner is incapable of producing the concrete and fundamental transformation needed in society.[69] The connection between these aspects can arguably be formulated in the following way: by remaining within the philosophical realm, Hegel has no interest in the practical task of bringing down bourgeois ideology and contributing to its end.

Here it is important to address Korsch's discussion of bourgeois society and how he understands Hegel's and Marx and Engels' relation to it. For Korsch, to begin with it is problematic that Hegel understands bourgeois society as a timeless concept: even if Hegel writes about it in terms of societal progress, he never transcends the bourgeois understanding of society. His theory of society is bound to bourgeois society and its categories.[70] Even if bourgeois society is understood within the frame of a metaphysical logic of progress, this concept of society is closed and can only see itself in other and earlier forms of society. The new, critical and materialist understanding of society and its concept of progress are in contrast open to all earlier forms of society to itself, viewing them as independent forms rather than as reducible to its present manifestation. As a consequence, it is the materialist understanding of society that is open to the real possibility of transcending bourgeois society. This point is related to Korsch's already mentioned critique of Hegelian dialectics, namely that it has no practical effect, but

---

[67] Korsch, *Karl Marx*, pp. 61-62.
[68] Korsch, *Marxism and Philosophy*, p. 41; Karl Marx, pp. 61ff.
[69] Korsch, *Marxism and Philosophy*, p. 93.
[70] Korsch, *Karl Marx*, pp. 47ff.

remains abstract, remaining within the limits of bourgeois society. In addition, Korsch argues that while for Hegel dialectics belong to the past, it is the tool for revolutionary change for Marxist materialism.[71] According to Korsch, Marx replaces the Hegelian "contradiction", a category too closely tied to bourgeois society, with "class struggle". He substitutes the dialectical "negation" with the proletariat and the dialectical "synthesis" with the proletarian revolution and the transition to a higher historical stage in the history of society.[72] The point here is that Marx regards bourgeois society as a perishable form of societal organization.[73] In Hegel, bourgeois society and the bourgeois state become the political end points. When it comes to Hegel's understanding of the inner logic of the progress of bourgeois society, his fundamental limitation becomes apparent when he can only register the class that Marx will otherwise name the proletariat as the rabble. The rabble is something to be avoided in Hegel, it is deprived entirely of its revolutionary force.[74] For Marx, the proletariat is rather something that needs to be developed as a political agent.

Korsch underlines the fact that Marx took a lot of strength from Hegel's preparatory work, but he took the idea of the state out of the political idea of progress.[75] Bourgeois society shall rather lead to the classless society. One can say that Korsch tries to mobilize Hegel's revolutionary impulse beyond the frames of the bourgeoisie and to inject it into Marxism's political struggle.

### b) Revolution in Hegel's thought

Hegel's dialectics remain a vital impulse for Korsch's version of Marxism. Despite Hegel's limitations, no form of dialectics, not even Hegel's, can entirely be robbed of its revolutionary dimension. Korsch writes:

> For the coincidence of consciousness and reality characterizes every dialectic, including Marx's dialectical materialism. Its consequence is that the material relations of production of the capitalist epoch only are what they are in combination with the forms in which they are reflected in the pre-scientific and bourgeois-scientific consciousness of the period; and they could not subsist in reality without these forms of consciousness. Setting aside any philosophical considerations, it is therefore clear that without this coincidence of consciousness and reality, a critique of

---

[71] Korsch, *Karl Marx*, pp. 24, 52ff.
[72] Korsch, *Karl Marx*, pp. 181-182.
[73] Korsch, *Karl Marx*, p. 22.
[74] Korsch, *Karl Marx*, p. 63.
[75] Korsch, *Karl Marx*, p. 181.

political economy could never have become the major component of a theory of social revolution.[76]

This seems to soften the distance between the idealistic and materialistic dialectic, even if it does not erase it entirely. Also Hegel's dialectics seem, according to Korsch, to contain a revolutionary potential through its inherent point of departure in the coincidence of consciousness and reality. Marx and Engels clearly realize that Hegel's dialectics must be reshaped, but they still, initially and consciously, relate to Hegel.[77] This delimitation from the bourgeois world results in a certain amount of ambivalence on the part of Korsch, since he simultaneously must integrate Hegel in the materialist effort as well as seek to sublate, or rather dissolve, bourgeois thinking and its concomitant societal form.

In connection to the way in which he divides Marxism into three phases, as discussed above, Korsch states how Hegel's dialectics is something to which it is important to hold on: "But the only really 'materialist and therefore scientific method' (Marx) of pursuing this analysis is to apply it to the further development of Marxism up to the present. This means that we must try to understand every change, development and revision of Marxist theory, since its original emergence from the philosophy of German Idealism, as a necessary product of its epoch (Hegel)."[78] This examination he discusses is that of the origin of Marxism and its process of development, as well as the necessity of dialectically understanding all its different forms within its entire historical and societal process.[79] This clearly shows that Hegel and his dialectics must properly be integrated into present and future Marxisms. Dialectics should not only be a method for showing how Marxist theory develops in relation to bourgeois thinking, but dialectical thinking must itself be essential for the possibility of leading thinking and society to its negation.

The philosophical development up to Hegel and beyond is not a mere event within the history of ideas; the process and progress of thought must be thought rather with respect to the societal context and the category of "social totality". This makes it possible for Korsch to connect the philo-

---

[76] Korsch, *Marxism and Philosophy*, pp. 88-89.
[77] Korsch, *Marxism and Philosophy*, p. 90.
[78] Korsch, *Marxism and Philosophy*, pp. 55-56.
[79] Korsch, *Marxism and Philosophy*, pp. 54ff.

sophical development with the existing revolutionary movement.[80] Hegel's dialectics must thereby be freed from its bourgeois framework and be transformed into a tool for materialist and political struggle. According to Korsch, "Hegel wrote that in the philosophic systems of this fundamentally revolutionary epoch, 'revolution was lodged and expressed as if in the very form of their thought.'"[81] For Korsch, this contains a critique of Hegel in terms of how his thinking can only lead to a revolution of thought, as well as a sign that nonetheless reveals the revolutionary dimension that can also be found there. Korsch writes that "[t]he greatest thinker produced by bourgeois society in its revolutionary period regarded a 'revolution in the form of thought' as an objective component of the total social process of a real revolution."[82] Surely, the formulation on revolution having its place in thought implies that the revolutionary is connected to the bourgeois process of liberation. However, this does not stop the revolutionary character of thought from being connected to the historical process. According to Korsch, the bourgeois class lost its revolutionary dimension in its societal praxis and thinking.[83] In Hegel's dialectics the critical and revolutionary principle was present formally, but it was used for the purposes of restoration and reconciliation, and not for change.[84]

In the text "Thesen über Hegel und die Revolution" (1932), Hegel's relation to the question of revolution is presented in more positive terms, or, at the very least, here the aim is to highlight Hegel's positive contribution more clearly, even if this will not mean an absence of critical remarks. Korsch starts by writing that one cannot understand Hegel and his dialectics if one does not connect it to the theme of revolution. Partly, the Hegelian dialectic was developed within the (bourgeois) revolutionary movement, and partly it succeeded in formulating this movement in thoughts. Moreover, a dialectical thinking is revolutionary on account of its formal character: it frees itself from the immediately given, assumes the principles of contradiction and negation, and contains the principles of qualitative change. Having said all this, the revolutionary dimension in Hegel is limited and leads to restoration: his thinking turns dogmatic and

---

[80] Korsch, *Marxism and Philosophy*, pp. 40ff.
[81] Korsch, *Marxism and Philosophy*, p. 41.
[82] Korsch, *Marxism and Philosophy*, p. 41.
[83] Korsch, *Marxism and Philosophy*, p. 43.
[84] Korsch, *Karl Marx*, 55; see also Korsch, *Karl Marx* (Hamburg: Rowohlt, 1981), pp. 30-31.

cements the bourgeois order.[85] But despite this criticism, Korsch's verdict over Hegel is generally affirmative: Hegel's philosophy is not only important historically, it lies in his philosophy to be revolutionary.[86]

With respect to his interpretation of *Karl Marx*, Patrick Goode has described the ambivalence running through Korsch's reception of Hegel, which shifts between a materialist reading of Hegel and a critique surrounding Hegel's restorative tendencies. In the end, this is supposedly to lead Korsch to an understanding of Marx's theory as replacing Hegel's timeless system:[87] "Despite all 'speculative mystifications' Hegel stands out from his idealist contemporaries, the theorists of the organic state and historical school. Hegel had grasped the material relation between men and things, but had concealed this under the apparently speculative connection between concepts".[88] Goode puts his finger on this ambivalence, but I cannot agree with him when he writes that Korsch becomes more critical towards Hegel in his later writings (*Karl Marx*). Rather, I would prefer to say that, throughout his intellectual work, Korsch continuously highlights both positive and negative dimensions in Hegel.

Enrico Rusconi is one of a few who explicitly and thoroughly makes Korsch's understanding of dialectics his main object of analysis. Rusconi focuses on a number of texts written by Korsch around 1930, a period in which he spent most of his time engaged in theoretical reflection and was not as politically involved as before. As far as Rusconi is concerned, this often aporetic connection of theoretical and political activity is in general the most fruitful context for Korsch's work.[89] But this period away from politics is interesting since it clarifies the role Korsch gave to theoretical reflection. In connection with Korsch's defense of the autonomy of theory during this time, Rusconi highlights that Korsch tried to free dialectics not only from Hegel, but also from certain Marxist usages of it.[90] A difficulty detected by Rusconi, which Korsch had reflected upon when he tried to transfer dialectics into a materialist theory, was that dialectics needed to receive a new form and structure, it could not only be a matter of changing the name.[91] Of course, Korsch tries to develop a different and practically

---

[85] Korsch, "Thesen über 'Hegel und die Revolution'", in *Gegner* (3/6 1932), pp. 11-12.
[86] See Koo, *Karl Korsch und die Historisierung des Marxismus*, p. 64.
[87] Goode, *Karl Korsch*, pp. 160-161.
[88] Goode, *Karl Korsch*, p. 162.
[89] Rusconi, "Dialektik in pragmatischer Anwendung", p. 138.
[90] Rusconi, "Dialektik in pragmatischer Anwendung", p. 140.
[91] Rusconi, "Dialektik in pragmatischer Anwendung", p. 146.

potent materialist dialectics, but, as Rusconi writes, there are according to Korsch no clear criteria for how the dialectical method should be used rightly. Hegel "solves" this problem by placing dialectics on the level of the absolute.[92] The text which Rusconi is discussing is Korsch's "Der Empiris-mus in der Hegelschen Philosophie" (1931), in which Korsch examines the connection between empiricism (within the tradition of natural science) and Hegel's philosophy.[93] Rusconi's position seems to be that it is possible to recognize a certain displacement in argumentation between this em-piricism-text and the abovementioned text on Hegel and revolution. How-ever, this is not to be understood as a contradiction. While the text on empiricism defends Hegel on a more formal and scientific level (for ex-ample, when it comes to his expansion of the concept of experience), without denying the political question, the text on revolution more clearly points toward the idea that Hegel's philosophy already contains political dimensions within its formal character, but that these are in themselves not enough. In the end, an epistemological break must occur with Hegel in order to break definitively with the bourgeois world.[94] The risk of an unref-lected transformation of dialectics is that it could turn into a new ideological dogma.[95] It is here that Rusconi's interpretation differs from Goode's, accor-ding to which Korsch supposedly thought that Marx's thinking replaced Hegel's: Hegel's heritage was still present. Rusconi highlights Korsch's difficult theoretical task, which, in the absence of clear criteria for the future usage of dialectics, had to navigate between Hegel's limitations and possi-bilities on the one hand and the potential and existing crisis of Marxism on the other. It is insufficient to only spread dialectics to materialism, impor-tantly one must draw the line between the positive and negative in Hegel, and also to struggle against certain uses (or non-uses) of dialectics within Marxism as well as to distinguish what in Marx and Engels' theoretical legacy is fruitful for the future.

### c) Hegelian Marxism?

There are different positions within the research on Korsch about whether Korsch's theory is to be understood as a Hegelian Marxist or not. On the

---

[92] Rusconi, "Dialektik in pragmatischer Anwendung", p. 147.
[93] Korsch, "Der Empirismus in der Hegelschen Philosophie", in Korsch, *Krise des Marxismus. Schriften 1928–1935* (Amsterdam: Stichting beheer IISG, 1996).
[94] Rusconi, "Dialektik in pragmatischer Anwendung", pp. 149ff.
[95] Rusconi, "Dialektik in pragmatischer Anwendung", p. 140.

one hand, Koo describes him as such. Koo presents Korsch's Hegelian Marxism as essentially directed against Lenin's reduction of dialectics and the relation between societal being and all forms of consciousness to a question of the relation between the subject and object of knowledge.[96] This connection seems quite vague. But it rather contained not only a reintroduction of the Hegelian dimensions into Marxism on a philosophical level, but a reintroduction of Hegel connected to the revival of the revolutionary and practico-critical aspects of Marx's theory. Via Habermas, Koo states that Korsch saw the possibility of saving the philosophical side of Marxism only at the price of its Hegelianization. But for Korsch, this was not only a matter for philosophy, and a strength of Korsch is not only to have opened up for new ways of interpreting Marx. Koo rather states that Korsch was interested in the revolutionary in Hegel, essential for the practical efforts of Marxism. On the contrary, as Koo points out, Korsch meant that it is only possible to understand Hegel on the prior condition that he is related to the revolution. In this regard, Korsch's Hegelian Marxism turns also into a Marxist Hegelianism.[97] On the other hand, Kellner writes:

> Korsch's defense of the importance of philosophy and his claim that understanding the relation between Marxism and philosophy requires grasping the Hegelian roots of Marxism has given rise to the interpretation of *Marxism and Philosophy* as a classic of "Hegelian Marxism", and has led to the picture of Korsch as one of the creators of a current that was in opposition to the dominant Marxist orthodoxy.[98]

Kellner thinks it is inappropriate to call Korsch's theory a Hegelian Marxism, precisely because Korsch's reception of Hegel was hugely selective while also remaining generally critical towards Hegel (as well as towards Marxism).[99]

Kellner's objection seems reasonable and it is important to be cautious when labelling Korsch's thinking in this way. It seems hard to label Korsch a Hegelian in a one-sided fashion, and as a result the concept of Hegelian Marxism becomes uncertain. Instead it seems sufficient to regard him as a Marxist theoretician who strategically used Hegel in order to develop a Marxism needed for his own times. Still, this does not change the fact that,

---

[96] Koo, *Karl Korsch und die Historisierung des Marxismus*, p. 32.
[97] Koo, *Karl Korsch und die Historisierung des Marxismus*, pp. 109-111.
[98] Kellner (ed.), *Karl Korsch*, p. 35.
[99] Kellner (ed.), *Karl Korsch*, pp. 99-100.

from the 1920s onwards, Hegel becomes a steady and indispensable source for Korsch. Without Hegel we would not have Korsch's Marxism. And maybe it was as a result of going first through Hegel that Korsch realized which path is right for Marxism? From this perspective, the label of Hegelian Marxism seems reasonable after all. Even if it is a simplifying and somewhat misleading label, it nonetheless elucidates essential dimensions of Korsch's thinking.

Even Furio Cerutti, who in his text "Hegel, Lukács, Korsch, Zum dialektischen Selbstverständnis des kritischen Marxismus" (1971) discusses the Critical Marxism of Korsch and its relation to Hegel, is skeptical about the concept of "Hegel-Marxism". According to Cerutti, it is better to use the concept of Critical Marxism, instead of Hegel-Marxism or Western Marxism, since it is not the only ambition of Korsch (or Lukács) to reintroduce Hegel into Marxism. Rather such an effort is a part of the bigger project of rediscovering the revolutionary dimensions in Marx.[100] This is a thesis often repeated in the commentaries, but it is not always so clear that Korsch wanted to revive the philosophical dimensions of Marx's work. It is important to establish a balanced perspective on Korsch, ensuring that both these dimensions are equally attended to.

To mediate the essential focus on praxis within Marxism with the theoretical, not only as a necessary evil, but as an absolutely decisive driving force of Marxism, is not an easy task, especially with Korsch's historical situation in mind. But one can say that it was this balancing act that Korsch tried to master: how can Marxism and philosophy be brought together in such a way that both parties become stronger. Philosophical thinking in general (and Korsch's project in particular) arguably aims at strengthening the idea of praxis in Marxism and the concrete political struggle of the proletariat. Marxism and philosophy are continuously balancing on this edge: how to upgrade philosophy and its significance for the political struggle, without establishing a distance to praxis? Korsch refuses to choose between the options of theory and praxis; both are needed, but it should not be a simplifying compromise. Philosophy and politics are made stronger through this encounter. And for this non-compromise Hegel is crucial. Via Hegel, Korsch seeks to present the inherent revolutionary character of thinking and Marxism, as well as to reinforce the centrality of political struggle through this Hegelian and theoretical transformation of Marxism.

[100] Cerutti, "Hegel, Lukács, Korsch", p. 199.

# Hegelian Dialectics and Soviet Marxism
# (from Vladimir Lenin to Evald Ilyenkov)

*Elena Mareeva & Sergei Mareev*

The discussion of the influence of Hegelian dialectics on Soviet Marxism should be placed in a wider historical context, by connecting this to the problem of the proper relation of Hegelian and Marxist doctrines to Russian social life.

This article will seek to understand the formation of the Soviet view on Hegelian dialectics in light of the nineteenth century Russian philosopher Alexander Herzen's term "algebra of revolution". We provide an analysis of the way in which Lenin's understanding of Hegel's and Marxian dialectics changed during his writings that were later to be published as his "Philosophical Notebooks". The article shows how the controversy surrounding Lenin's thoughts regarding dialectical methodology had an impact on discussions in Soviet Philosophy during the 1930s. A further focus for this article is to examine the Hegelian Soviet philosopher Evald Ilyenkov, who argued that dialectical logic is a principal subject for Marxist philosophy. His endeavor was to highlight the process by which formal collectivization transforms into real collectivization in the movement towards communism.

## Russian Hegelianism: Preliminary observations

The first reference to Hegel in Russia can be located in the works of Alexander Galich (1783–1848), one of the representatives of the Russian Enlightenment. The fate of Galich is among those rare instances when a son of a simple lay vicar graduated from a seminary and was then later educated in Germany in the universities of Helmstedt and Göttingen. After mastering in philosophy under the supervision of Gottlob Ernst Schulze (Aenesidene), Galich, as a professor at St. Petersburg University, became a follower of Schelling. In 1818–1819 he published "History of Philosophical Systems" in two parts and concluded it with an exposition of Schelling's system. In "History of Philosophical Systems", Galich mentions Hegel for the first time in the Russian philosophical literature by drawing attention to his works *The Difference Between Fichte's and Schelling's System of Philosophy* and *Science of Logic*. Three years after the German publication of Hegel's Logic, Galich makes reference to this immense work, but he does so only by way of an application of the Schellingian doctrine in logic.[1]

By the end of the 1820s a great number of Russian students were taught in the Berlin University. Dmitry Chizhevsky, a historian of Russian philosophy, wrote, in exile in 1939 that "Hegel's influence has extended without interruption from the early 1830s up to present day. In this regard, one can undoubtedly speak of a steady growth and an increase in his influence".[2] In addition, he stressed that Hegel's dialectics was called upon by life in Russia not only as the dialectics of spirit and social life, but also as the dialectics of nature.

Chizhevsky shows that on the eve of the revolution of 1848 a number of Russian Hegelians were already involved in political life. And even though Hegelianism for many remained a purely theoretical issue, some saw the turn towards practice as an integral part of both Hegel's philosophy and philosophy as a whole. When characterizing the problem of the relation between theory and practice, Alexander Herzen (1812–1870) noted, in his work "The Past and Thoughts", that early in the 1840s the confrontation of the political (revolutionary and practical) and the entirely notional (academic and speculative) issues, had already become evident in pro-Western Russian Hegelianism. Regarding the political, and hence practical trend, to which Herzen also belonged, the central figures were Mikhail Bakunin and V. G. Belinsky, who "were at the top, each of them with a volume of the Hegelian philosophy in hand and the youthful impatience without which there were no cherished and passionate beliefs".[3]

The participation of Bakunin and Herzen in the revolutionary movement in Europe and Russia was still to come. However, already at the turn of the 1840s, Herzen wrote about the division of the Russian Hegelians with the aim of bringing together theory and lived practice. It is characteristic, however, that Herzen identified some necessary prerequisites in order to

---

[1] *Istoriya filosofskih sistem po inostrannym rukovodstvam sostavlennaya* (St. Petersburg, 1818–1819), vol. 2, p. 298.
[2] Dmitry Chizhevsky, *Gegel' v Rossii* (St. Peterburg: Nauka, 2007), p. 20.
[3] Alexander Herzen, *Sochineniya* (Moskva: Mysl, 1986), vol. 2, p. 189.

successfully convert Hegelianism into a practical and political orientation, not only in the character of the Russian people but also in Hegelian thinking itself. In addition, in "The Past and Thoughts" Herzen confronted the "early" Hegel, as expressed in the *Phenomenology of Spirit*, with the "later" Hegel who was principal at the Berlin University. Herzen noted:

> The true Hegel was the humble professor in Jena and the friend of Hölderlin, who saved his *Phenomenology* under his clothes when Napoleon entered the city; at that time Hegel's philosophy did not lead to either the Indian Quietism or justification of the existing civil forms or to the Prussian Christianity; at that time he did not deliver lectures on philosophy of religion (...).[4]

In Herzen's opinion, perhaps due to his age or maybe because of a sense of self-satisfaction with his official position and honor, Hegel "exalted intentionally his philosophy above the ground level". During his professorship in Berlin, he chose "the quiet and non-turbulent sea of aesthetics" trying to avoid the necessity of touching on empirical conclusions and practical applications.

Herzen notes that, within the framework of the adopted theory-practice dualism, practice is substituted for literalism and an actual analysis is substituted with the "idle chatter of dialectics". The solutions of the "damned practical problems" in unreal conditions are shot through with "dialectical complexity", while the dialectical method proper passes into sophistry. Herzen writes:

> If it is not the development of the subject-matter proper (...), the dialectical method becomes a purely external means to drive a farrago of nonsense through a line of categories or an exercise in logical gymnastics, i.e. as it was present among the Greek sophists (...).[5]

Dialectics in the form of vain formalism, on the one hand, and, in the form of arbitrary sophism, on the other, are extreme forms of the same problem. The reason for the transformation of dialectics into both formalism and sophism is the separation of theory from practice or the division of thought from its subject. According to Herzen, however, the power of the dialectical method reveals itself at the very point where this method connects the

---

[4] Herzen, *Sochineniya*, vol. 2, p. 193.
[5] Herzen, *Sochineniya*, vol. 2, p. 193.

movement of thought with the development of the essence of subject "fostering" this essence into thought.

Herzen stresses that a man who "has not outlived" Hegel's *Phenomenology* and has not passed through practical trials, is not of his own times. What is at stake is the movement of a dialectical thought—or, in practical terms the dialectics of a social practice—and the reconstruction of the social contradictions within theoretical thought, as well as their dialectical solution, that they amount to.

## Hegelian dialectics in Lenin's work

It was precisely the idea of dialectics as the "algebra of revolution" that was in focus in Lenin's assessment of Herzen's work and his role in the Russian revolutionary movement. Lenin's text "In Memory of Herzen" was published in the *Social-Democrat* newspaper in May 1912, for Herzen's centenary year. In this regard, the whole context of Lenin's reasoning is notable in "In Memory of Herzen":

> He assimilated Hegel's dialectics. He realized that it was "the algebra of revolution". He went further than Hegel, following Feuerbach to materialism. The first of his *Letters on the Study of Nature*, "Empiricism and Idealism", written in 1844, reveals to us a thinker who even now stands head and shoulders above the multitude of modern empiricist natural scientists and the host of present-day idealist and semi-idealist philosophers. Herzen came right up to dialectical materialism, and halted— before historical materialism.[6]

There are here two notable points in Lenin's reasoning worthy of comment. The first is that, independently of Marx, Herzen has, according to Lenin, developed dialectical materialism; Lenin recognizes this in how Herzen's understands the development of the natural sciences. The second is that, even if there is an anticipation of dialectical materialism present in his work, nonetheless Herzen does not master historical materialism; Lenin analyzes this in detail, in terms of Herzen's interpretation of social processes after the revolution of 1848.

According to Lenin, Herzen's "Letters of Nature Study", with its discussion of the methodological problems of natural science in the nineteenth

---

[6] Vladimir Lenin, "In Memory of Herzen", in *Collected Works*, vol. 18 (Moscow: Progress Publishers, 1975), p. 25; https://www.marxists.org/archive/lenin/works/1912/may/08c.htm

century, introduces an essential dialectical component into this problematic. Even so, we can consider such dialectical ideas of Herzen as the "algebra of revolution" only under certain conditions. Dialectics becomes the "algebra of revolution", Herzen writes quite clearly, at that very point when the revolutionary method corresponds to its subject, and when the theoretical thought strives to comprehend and mediate the social practice with all its revolutionary shifts and paradoxes. A major part of the article "In Memory of Herzen" is devoted to just such a social analysis. Lenin reveals in detail the pros and cons of Herzen's knowledge of the "algebra of revolution".

Thus, while noting the progress that Herzen made with regard to dialectical materialism as the methodology of natural science, on the one hand, and with respect to historical materialism as a study of social contradictions, on the other, Lenin follows the line of two "materialisms" in Marxist philosophy. We might not have paid attention to this dualization in Lenin's interpretation of dialectics in the article of 1912, if this was not also present in his other works from that period, including the criticisms he advances regarding the general theoretical situation as well as his specific analysis of Hegel in his *Philosophical Notebooks*.

In the period from July to November of 1914, when he worked on the material which was later to be included in his *Philosophical Notebooks*, Lenin wrote the article "Karl Marx: A Brief Biographical Sketch with an Exposition of Marxism" for the *Granat Encyclopaedia*. This text is of interest, since it provides an understanding of both how Lenin himself interprets dialectics, and how he indexes the differences between a Hegelian and a Marxist interpretation of the dialectical method. The article is important first of all because of the section on "Dialectics", where Lenin appraises the advantages of Hegel's dialectics in studying nature, in contrast to social life. With reference to Engels, he underlines the problem faced by Marxism, namely how "to rescue conscious dialectics [from the destruction of idealism, including Hegelianism] and apply it in the materialist conception of Nature"? In this section Lenin states that as a result classical philosophy must give place to a separate science of "the general laws of motion, both of the external world and of human thought".[7] However, from where will this new science obtain knowledge about the general laws of being?

---

[7] Vladimir Lenin, "Karl Marx: A Brief Biographical Sketch with an Exposition of Marxism", in *Collected Works*, vol. 21 (Moscow: Progress Publishers, 1975); https://www.marxists.org/archive/lenin/works/1914/granat/ch02.htm

Lenin was inspired by the pathos of constructing an integral scientific vision of the world. However, if dialectical integration of the results of positive sciences is a method for the construction of a scientific vision, then this way will not bring us to a system of dialectical categories. Any philosophical category, including the category of matter, cannot be excluded from neither the study of nature nor the generalization of the discoveries in the natural sciences.

In the section on "Dialectics", Lenin also cites Engels' thought that classical philosophy was reduced to "the science of thought and its laws—formal logic and dialectics."[8] What interested Marx in Hegel's philosophy was precisely this: was it a revolutionary method or a system reconstructing the general derivative laws? The impression may arise that Lenin aimed at combining both vectors in his apprehension, that is, both the methodological and the systematic components, whose vital difference Herzen described very well. Nevertheless, it was Hegel's philosophy that helped Lenin to speak critically about the prospect of a systematics based on the materialist dialectic.

*The Philosophical Notebooks* are ten notebooks with summaries and extracts written by Lenin in 1914–1916. They include summaries of Hegel's *Science of Logic, Lectures on the History of Philosophy*, and *Lectures on the Philosophy of History*. Lenin's fragment "On the Question of Dialectics" is one of his most informative outlines. In this fragment Lenin reached a new level in his understanding of the subject matter and the developing trends of dialectics in Marxism. In this regard, Lenin stressed the shortcomings of the former "metaphysical" materialism, which stopped its development when it reached the ontological problems and failed "to apply *Bildertheorie*, to the process and development of knowledge".[9]

In this connection, the observations of Nikolai Valentinov, whose philosophical stance was criticized by Lenin in his *Materialism and Empiriocriticism*, are of interest. In his work "Meeting Lenin", Valentinov proves that Lenin's *Philosophical Notebooks* bring practically naught to Plekhanov's already established philosophical position. Valentinov writes: "Quite recently, and this is confirmed by his book *Materialism and Empiriocriticism*, Lenin was infuriated merely by the words 'philosophical idealism'. (...) In

---

[8] Lenin, "Karl Marx".
[9] Vladimir Lenin, "On the Question of Dialectics", in *Collected Works*, vol. 38 (Moscow: Progress Publishers, 1976); https://www.marxists.org/archive/lenin/works/1915/misc/x02.htm

his book, he already defended idealism when saying that 'philosophical idealism is just nonsense from the standpoint of rude, common and meta-physical materialism'."[10]

Valentinov emphasizes that Plekhanov, in line with Lenin's *Philosophical Notebooks*, in fact criticizes Kantianism (and agnosticism in general) "from the vulgar materialistic point of view". Hegel's influence on Lenin can be seen in his new assessment: "The clever idealist is nearer to wise material-ism than silly materialism".[11] It is worthwhile reminding the reader here that Valentinov's book was published in 1953 when Soviet "diamat", a metaphysical construction about "general laws of development", became an official philosophical doctrine in the USSR.

In "Meeting Lenin", Valentinov notes the fact that in 1913 the corres-pondences between Marx and Engels were published for the first time. It is in these letters that the problems of dialectics occupy a central place. The attention Lenin paid to this edition is confirmed by the fact that already some weeks after these correspondences, prepared by August Bebel, were published in four volumes in Stuttgart, Lenin took up the writing of a review of the edition that nonetheless remained unfinished.[12]

However, it was these correspondences between Marx and Engels that helped Lenin to be acquainted with the "intellectual laboratory" in which Marx's *Capital* was created. As noted by James White, *The Philosophical Notebooks* in this regard "returned to Marxism's Hegelian roots, redis-covered its dialectical content, and reconstructed the doctrine in the form in which Marx had originally conceived it".[13]

When taking notes on Hegel's work, Lenin looks at dialectics mostly from the standpoint of Marx as the author of *Capital* and not of Engels and Plekhanov. Lenin writes in his *Philosophical Notebooks*: "It is impossible completely to understand Marx's *Capital*, and especially its first chapter, without having thoroughly studied and understood the *whole* of Hegel's

---

[10] Nikolai Valentinov, *Vstrechi s Leninym* (http://fanread.ru/book/3658741/?page=37 01 06 2915).

[11] Valentinov, *Vstrechi s Leninym*.

[12] This incomplete article was first published in the *Pravda* newspaper in 1930.

[13] James D. White, "Lenin and Philosophy: The Historical Context", in *Europe-Asia Studies*, 2015, vol. 67, No. 1, p. 140. In detail, see Elena Mareeva, "Dve traktovki gegelev-skoj dialektiki v rabotakh V. I. Lenina", in *Al'ternativy*, 2015, No. 4, pp. 30-40.

*Logic.* Consequently, half a century later none of the Marxists understood Marx!"[14]

Lenin's philosophical heritage was very much at the center of things during the 20s and 30s, when discussion and theoretical and ideological struggles ensued. These discussions were connected to the idea of the new "Leninist stage" in the development of Marx's philosophy. The Soviet Marxist David Ryazanov, who in 1921 founded the Institute for Marx and Engels Studies and headed it between 1921 and 1931, held his own views about Lenin not being an original philosopher (he simply repeated the ideas of Marx and Engels). The known Soviet philosopher of that time, Abram Deborin (1981–1963), gave an indirect denial of the originality of Lenin's philosophical ideas:

> Lenin in philosophy is, of course, a Plekhanov "disciple", as Lenin stated several times. Both of the thinkers complement each other in a sense. Plekhanov is above all a theoretician, and Lenin is above all a practitioner, politician and leader. But they both achieved much success in developing and deepening our world-view.[15]

The discussions on the views of Deborin and his followers by philosophers and others were held in the Communist Academy, the Institute of the Red Professorship, as well as, more broadly, in higher educational institutions and in the pages of scientific and theoretical periodicals. Their most consistent opponents were two philosophers of the new post-revolution generation, Mark Mitin and Pavel Yudin, both of whom were supported by Stalin. Already in 1931, this confrontation ended in an official recognition of "the Leninist stage" in the development of Marxist philosophy. Ryazanov was exiled, and Deborin was relieved from all his posts. Also in 1931, the Institute for Marx and Engels Studies was renamed to the Institute for Marx-Engels-Lenin Studies, and in 1954–1956 it was named the Institute for Marx-Engels-Lenin-Stalin Studies.

The moment of self-criticism, which was typical for Lenin, was thus rejected for the sake of a confirmation of his absolute innovation. The irony

---

[14] Vladimir Lenin, "Conspectus of Hegel's Science of Logic—Book III (Subjective Logic or the Doctrine of the Notion)", in *Collected Works*, vol. 38 (Moscow: Progress Publishers, 1976), pp. 85-241; https://www.marxists.org/archive/lenin/works/1914/cons-logic/ch03.htm#LCW38_176

[15] Abram Deborin. *Lenin kak myslitel'*, 3 ed. (Moskva & Leningrad: Gospolitizdat, 1929), p. 26.

of all this was that it was Plekhanov's version of Marxist philosophy that finally prevailed over Soviet "diamat".

For many years, *Materialism and Empiriocriticism* (1908) was considered as the central core of "the Leninist stage", although in this work Lenin did not emphasize the advantages of "wise idealism" over "materialism in general"—rather, he mainly used the label of "idealism" to criticize his opponents. But, between 1914 and 1916, this was to change, when he became increasingly under the influence of Hegel's ideas. Lenin's criticism of Deborin and his epigones in favor of "Menshevik idealism"—in particular on the question regarding what Hegelianism meant for the materialist dialectics—was a characteristic moment in the struggle for "the Leninist stage". The essence of such Hegelianization (the convergence of Marx and Hegel's ideas) was considered as resulting in the separation of theory from practice and thus the domination of the former over the latter. Besides, Lenin's reference to the Mensheviks here was not a casual one. After all, Deborin was a staunch follower of Plekhanov, and Plekhanov, being a Menshevik, protested in October 1917 against the armed uprising by reasoning that such practice was not in line with the Marxist understanding of a proletarian revolution. If we separate ourselves from the political labels and accusations typical for that epoch, the question is if Deborin, as well as Plekhanov, by formally recognizing dialectics as a revolutionary method practically, turned it into a theoretical scheme and even a dogma, which was applied from the "outside" onto reality, placing undue emphasis on the development vector of practical life in the name of Marxism. And yet, with respect to the relation between philosophical theory and the development of the natural sciences, such a stance was equally shared by the followers of Deborin in their discussions with "the Mechanists". The discussion of the second half of the 1920s ended in the victory of the Deborin group.

We should note here that *The German Ideology*, written by Marx and Engels, was published in full by the Institute for Marx-Engels-Lenin Studies in the USSR, first in German (1932) and then in Russian (1933). Ryazanov played a decisive role in publishing the most important first chapter of volume one of *The German Ideology*. Through the efforts of Ryazanov it was first published by the Institute for Marx-Engels Studies in Russian in 1924 and then in German in 1926. In chapter one of this book the shape of Marxist methodology appears to be evident and the relation between theory and practice is of central concern. The Old and the Young Hegelian's dependence on Hegel's system is seen by Marx and Engels in the fact that the outer ideal and philosophical schemes of their doctrines continue to

dominate over reality. However, the materialist dialectic differs from idealistic dialectics in a decisive way: thought cannot provide directions for life.
Thus we read in this work:

> The phantoms formed in the brains of men are also, necessarily, sub-
> limates of their material life-process. (…) These abstractions in them-
> selves, divorced from real history, have no value whatsoever. They can
> only serve to facilitate the arrangement of historical material, to indicate
> the sequence of its separate strata. But they by no means afford a recipe
> or schema, as does philosophy, for neatly trimming the epochs of
> history.[16]

The backbone of the Marxist methodology is that it is oriented towards a
movement based on social reality itself, whose theoretical prerequisites are
not given in advance, but are resulting from "the study of the actual life-
process and the activity of the individuals of each epoch".[17] As applied to the
figure of Lenin, this means that in his revolutionary struggle he could not
simply be a practitioner whose role was to realize Marxist theory. Isolated
from a historical process, Marxist theory turns into dogma. Therefore, what
is usually referred to as Lenin's practical intuition is the other side of how
his own theoretical ideas get refined over time. Dialectics as the "algebra of
revolution" is based on an organic unity of theory and practice, according
to which revolutionary practice corrects theory, and the corrected theoretical abstractions prove to be a tool in improving life itself.

In light of the principle of historicism, the content of dialectical categories as "active tools" is enriched in the very process of changing reality. As
Lenin wrote, if "Marxism is not a dogma but a guide for action", then it
cannot be a justification for historical relativism.[18]

The fate of Deborin differed from the fate of many of his colleagues who
perished in confinement camps. Most likely, by renouncing his principles
he escaped the repressions of the 1930s, which continued up to the 1950s;
he even managed to influence the formation of an official version of Soviet
philosophy. This version was officially fixed in the chapter "On Dialectical
and Historical Materialism" in Stalin's *The History of the Communist Party*

---

[16] Karl Marx & Friedrich Engels, *The German Ideology*, in *Collected Works*, vol. 5 (New York: International Publishers, 1976), pp. 36-37.

[17] Marx & Engels, *The German Ideology*, p. 37.

[18] For the difference between historical and logical dialectics in Marx's method, see Sergei Mareev, *Konkretnyj istorizm* (Moskva: Sovremennyj gumanitarnyj unimversitet, 2015).

*of the Soviet Union: Short Course* (1938).[19] In fact, in the version supported by Plekhanov and Deborin the Hegelian dialectics took the shape of an abstract system of logical categories applied from outside to different subjects.

If "diamat" represented a version of "dialectical" natural philosophy, then historical materialism was the Marxist version of the philosophy of history, the central core of which corresponded to the theory of five socio-economic formations abstracted from the works of the Marxist classics. The essence of the official Marxist philosophy as "world schematics" was expressed through a saying from the 1970s and 80s: "If life does not fit well into our schemes, all the worse for life".

The official Soviet philosophy played undoubtedly a conservative role in its total acquiescence with Soviet ideology. Starting from "the Khrushchev Thaw", however, an alternative interpretation of dialectical logic, developed by Evald Ilyenkov, emerged within Soviet Marxism; Ilyenkov understood dialectics strictly as a methodology for scientific and theoretical thinking. It is therefore quite natural that the philosophical semiofficial circles regarded Ilyenkov, with his Hegelian interpretation of both Marx and Lenin, with suspicion and fear.

### Hegelian Marxism of Evald Ilyenkov: Dialectics of a "boiling tea-kettle" and dialectical logic

Evald Ilyenkov (1924–1979) graduated from the Department of Philosophy in the Moscow State University and was a member of the Institute of Philosophy of the USSR Academy of Sciences. He is considered as a philosopher of "the Khrushchev Thaw". The start of his colorful biography is linked with the publication of his theses on the subject of philosophy, theses that were to be condemned officially as Hegelian deviations at the Department of Philosophy in the Moscow State University. As a result, in 1955 the young lecturer Ilyenkov and his friend Valentin Korovikov were discharged from the university. It is of interest to quote a passage from these theses, in which Ilyenkov and Korovikov offer a critical examination of the official version of Soviet philosophy:

> We believe that the interpretation of philosophy as "science of the world as a whole", which exists in our literature, represents *a direct revision of*

---

[19] About the formation of dialectical materialism and historical materialism, see Sergei Mareev, *Iz istorii sovetskoj filosofii: Lukach-Vygotskij-Il'enkov* (Moskva: Kulturnaya Revolyutsiya, 2008), chapter 3.

*classical views* of the subject of philosophy as science, and efforts to develop philosophy as a system of ideas of the world as a whole represent *a reactionary attempt to restore the long deceased natural philosophy and the philosophy of history.*[20]

It is noteworthy that when these theses were first subject to criticism, an attempt was made to accuse the authors of being "menshevik idealists". In fact, it was an accusation of "Deborinism". As we have already seen, Deborin's theoretical stance serves as an important reference point in the dispute surrounding philosophy and dialectics. It should be noted that historians of Soviet philosophy, following critics of Ilyenkov in the 1950s, often interpret his standing as "Deborinism", representing him thereby as a follower of the Deborin school.[21] However, the discrepancy between Ilyenkov and Deborin is essential regarding how one should understand and present the methodological core of dialectics, that is, the system of its principles and categories.

The conversion of Marxist philosophy into a science about "the world as a whole" is necessarily divided into the knowledge of the general laws of the development of nature and knowledge of equally general laws of societal development. It is clear that in such an abstract form these developmental laws can be illustrated by anything. Therefore, Ilyenkov named such dialectics as the "dialectics of a boiling tea-kettle". In such an approach both the "boiling tea-kettle" and "the Great French Revolution" are transformed into illustrative "examples of the relation of quality-quantity categories", he writes in his work from 1974.

> With such an approach both a boiling tea-kettle and the Great French Revolution were only "examples" illustrating the relation of the categories of quality and quantity; but any empirical reality impinging on the eye, however fortuitous it might be in itself, was thereby converted into an external embodiment of absolute reason, into one of the necessary dialectical stages of its self-differentiation.[22]

---

[20] Evald Ilyenkov & Valentin Korovikov, *Strasti po tezisam o predmete filosofii (1954–1955)* (Moskva: Kanon+, 2016), p. 230.

[21] This typical example is Yehoshua Yakhot's assessment of Ilyenkov as a successor of the Deborin line. See Yehoshua Yakhot, *The Suppression of Philosophy in the USSR (1920s–1930s)* (New York: Chalidze Pub., 1981).

[22] Evald Ilyenkov, *Dialectical Logic: Essays on its History and Theory*, trans. H. Campbell Creighton (Delhi: Aakar Books, 2008), p. 228.

However, this "Deborinism" meant also recognition of one further component of Marxist philosophy. In 1929, Deborin had written:

> Marxism, or dialectical materialism, constitutes a holistic world outlook consisting of three main parts, namely, materialistic dialectics as a general scientific methodology (including cognitive theory), natural dialectics and the methodology of natural science (natural-historical materialism), and the dialectics of history (historical materialism).[23]

It should be noted that this interpretation of the dialectical method as a "system of abstract definitions" was very popular in Soviet philosophy during the 1970s and 1980s.

While Deborin's version of dialectics falls into pluralism, Ilyenkov's position constitutes a contrary tendency. When discussing the subject of Marxist philosophy, Ilyenkov insists on the identity of dialectics, logic and the cognitive theory of Marxism. Accordingly, he insists on a literal understanding of Lenin's statement in *Philosophical Notebooks*: "In *Capital*, Marx applied to a single science logic, dialectics and the theory of knowledge of materialism [three words are not needed: it is one and the same thing] which has taken everything valuable in Hegel and developed it further".[24]

For Ilyenkov, dialectical logic is the one and only subject of Marxist philosophy, but laws and categories of dialectics prove to be a cognitive tool only once they are understood as objective forms of thinking. Another of Lenin's observation in *Philosophical Notebooks* is important here: "To be elaborated: Plekhanov wrote on philosophy (dialectics) probably about 1,000 pages (…). Among them, *about* the large Logic, *in connection with* it, *its* thought (i.e., dialectics *proper*, as philosophical science) nil!!"[25] As seen, the tradition of interpreting dialectics as an abstract scientific method and not as the logic of scientific thinking, proceeded from Plekhanov and was stressed by Lenin.

However, already in his early theses on the subject of philosophy Ilyenkov places the emphasis on the *application* of the dialectical method, the merits of which are revealed by no means "alone". If dialectics is a

---

[23] Abram Deborin, *Dialektika i estestvoznanie* (Moskva – Leningrad, 1929), p. 8.
[24] Vladimir Lenin, "Plan of Hegel's Dialectics (Logic)", in *Collected Works*, vol. 38 (Moscow: Progress Publishers, 1976), pp. 315-318.
[25] Vladimir Lenin, "Conspectus of Hegel's Book Lectures On the History of Philosophy: Volume XIV: Volume II Of the History Of Philosophy" in *Collected Works*, vol. 38 (Moscow: Progress Publishers, 1976), pp. 269-300 https://www.marxists.org/archive/lenin/works/1915/cons-lect/ch03.htm#socra.

movement based on the objective logic of the subject-matter, then its study is possible not in an abstract but only in a concrete form. In this context, Marx's *Capital* plays a special role. In fact, Lenin writes in his *Philosophical Notebooks*: "If Marx did not leave behind him a '*Logic*' (with a capital letter), he did leave the *logic* of *Capital*, and this ought to be utilized to the full in this question".[26]

In accordance with Lenin and Ilyenkov, the key realization of the dialectical method was in Marx's *Capital*, where the universal is represented by the particular; therefore the assimilation of the categorial structure of the material dialectic is appropriate whenever it appears as objective forms of thinking. The same holds for dialectics as a method of practical thinking, represented in the revolutionary activities of Marx and Lenin.

However, Ilyenkov's view of dialectics as logic was by no means in line with the generally accepted standpoint. Stalin's own view on Hegel's philosophy was customarily assumed to be an aristocratic reaction to the French revolution and to French materialism. This thesis, advanced by Stalin in conversation with the Soviet Communist Party ideologues, was widely adopted in literature at the turn of the 1940s and during the first half of the 1950s. So when, by the second half of the 1950s, Ilyenkov stated that dialectics was the logic of Marxism, it raised indignation among representatives of certain semiofficial philosophical circles. Nevertheless, the analysis of the method of *Capital* as ascension from the abstract to the concrete became the basis for Ilyenkov's doctoral thesis. His book on this subject, in a severely censored version, was published under the title *Dialectics of the Abstract and the Concrete in Marx's Capital* (1960).

Ilyenkov's psycho-pedagogical theory and practice was related to the so-called "Zagorsk experiment",[27] while his concept of the ideal and his works on aesthetics are to be understood as direct "applications" of dialectics as logic. In a single project encompassing several distinctive aspects, Ilyenkov's philosophy has often been referred to as "the cultural-historical theory" of Soviet "creative Marxism".

In striving to rehabilitate classical dialectics, Ilyenkov upheld the principle of an identity between objective reality and thinking. On this point he

[26] Lenin, "Plan of Hegel's Dialectics (Logic)".
[27] This was an experiment of teaching deafblind children in the Zagorsk boarding school with the goal of intellectual development (1960–1970). After successfully finishing the program, four students managed to graduate from Moscow State University, Alexander Suvorov received a PhD in Psychology.

differed essentially from Deborin, whose abstract version of Hegelian dialectics harmonized with contemplative materialism in the style of Feuerbach. Deborin, following Plekhanov, tried to present the position of Marx and Engels as a direct continuation of the materialistic line proceeding from Spinoza, via the French materialists, to Feuerbach. However, starting from his *Theses on Feuerbach*, Marx does not continue along such a line; he instead criticizes Feuerbach, first of all in connection with the principle of activity, developed by Hegel but absent in Feuerbach. Marx writes: "The chief defect of all previous materialism (that of Feuerbach included) is that things [*Gegenstand*], reality, sensuousness are conceived only in the form of the *object, or of contemplation*, but not as *sensuous human activity, practice*, not subjectively."[28]

Ilyenkov valued Marx's creative and practical understanding of human existence and thinking in the *Theses on Feuerbach*. Further, in his analysis of the problems of dialectical logic in the 1960s and 1970s, Ilyenkov refers to Lenin's works, especially Lenin's theory of reflection, which serves as a possible solution to the problem of the ratio between objective reality and thought. The recognition of Lenin's innovation, resulting in "the Leninist theory of reflection", coincided with the preparation of his centenary anniversary, as well as taking place at a time when there was a struggle to acknowledge "the Leninist stage" in Marxist philosophy. Lenin's theory was regarded as a "new stage" in the development of the cognitive theory of Marxism. It was presented fully in 1969, in the multi-authored work *Leninist Theory of Reflection and Modernity*, a collaborative effort between Bulgarian and Soviet philosophers, and headed by the academic Todor Pavlov. Even in this work, beneath the thin veneer of "the Leninist theory of reflection", there lurked a struggle between two interpretations regarding reflection and contemplation.

An action-oriented understanding of reflection may seem to be an oxymoron, i.e. a combination of the incongruous: activity is reflection because reflection is activity. However, it is the dialectics of the subject-and-practical activity as a purely human method of adaptation to the world that appears as a paradox. Practical transformation of the world is impossible without first reflecting on the laws of nature, but one's reflection about the laws of nature is concordant with the transformation of nature.

---

[28] Karl Marx, *Theses on Feuerbach*, in Marx & Engels, *Collected Works, vol. 5: April 1845– April 1847* (London: Lawrence & Wishart, 1976), p. 3.

In line with the *Theses on Feuerbach*, Marxism unlocks this circle, in terms of practical activity and labor; practice presupposes an adequate knowledge of reality. In line with this, the concept of practice appears to be at the basis of Ilyenkov's dialectical logic. Certainly, "diamat" itself included references to practice as a criterion of the truth of our knowledge. However, Ilyenkov's practice is not an external criterion but an immanent principle of dialectical logic; practice not only tests but it also determines the objectivity of logical forms. A proper understanding of the objectivity of dialectical categories, as well as of the form of their universality, is achieved through the idealizing and generalizing force of subject-and-practical activity.

Thus practice in Ilyenkov's works appears as a mediating moment in the identity of thinking and objective reality. This identity, which is typical for Ilyenkov as well as for Hegel, is not of a straightforward but mediate nature. However, activity is not only an intermediary between thinking and objective reality, it is something where both these moments disjoin dialectically. The clearest trace of Hegelianism in Ilyenkov's writings consists in this, in his understanding of practice.

In works devoted to the history of philosophy, Ilyenkov proceeded from the fact that the subject of productive activity, and even the role of an instrument in the labor process, mediates the man-nature ratio, is an insight already present in German idealism. Here it is worthy to quote Marx's observation on Hegel: "The importance of Hegel's *Phenomenology* and its final result—the dialectic of negativity as the moving and producing principle lies in the fact that Hegel (...) conceives objective man (...) as the result of his *own labour*".[29] These elements of Hegel's historical dialectics are important for Ilyenkov. It was Hegel's ideas of necessity and regularity of historical development, the progress of freedom, the dialectics of the master and the slave that attracted first Marx and later Ilyenkov, in contrast to the idea that "everything develops", which was an interpretation of Hegel's works by many soviet philosophers.

However, the limitation of Hegel's philosophy, as stated by Marx, is associated with the fact that "[t]he only labour Hegel knows and recognizes is *abstract mental* labour".[30] In his work *Dialectical logic: Outlines of history and theory*, Ilyenkov writes:

---

[29] Karl Marx, *Economic and Philosophical Manuscripts* (1844), in *Early Writings* (London: Penguin Books, 1975), pp. 385-386.
[30] Marx, *Economic and Philosophical Manuscripts*.

The fact is that the Hegelian conception of thought represented an uncritical description of the real position of things formed on the soil of a narrowly professional form of the division of social labour, that is to say, on the division of mental work from physical labour, from immediately practical, sensuously objective activity.[31]

In other words, according to Ilyenkov, labor in Hegel's idealism is "self-consciousness of alienated thinking".

It is clear that Marx overcomes the speculative thrust of Hegelian idealism with the idea of the revolutionary dismantlement of alienated social reality. How did Ilyenkov himself appraise this experience, which was obtained in the course of overcoming the world of capital in the twentieth century?

In contradiction to the socialism constructed in the USSR, Ilyenkov saw a confirmation of the fact that socialism, in striving to eradicate the alienation that results from private property, was able to bring this alienation to the last degree. By denying private property *in a simple form,* socialism gives rise to private property *in a general form.* If private property in its simple form acts as the property of one individual, which is not the property of another individual, then a general property acts as property of everybody, and not as the property of anybody in particular. It acts as property of the state but the state itself is, to varying degrees, a social force alienated from society. And Soviet bureaucracy easily seizes the state property, since it is, in reality, private.

If the point of communism is the realization of every individual in the whole of civilization, which up to this point had existed in an alienated form, Ilyenkov believed that this change could not be realized by the mere formal legalistic collectivization of real wealth. In "Marx and the Western world", written for a conference in France in 1965, which he was not allowed to attend, Ilyenkov noted that to socialize property objectively means "to turn it into a real property of each individual, of each member of this society, because, otherwise, 'society' is still considered as something abstract, as something differing from a real total of all participating individuals".[32] It follows from the above that a historical task of socialism is not the "abolition" of private property, but rather its dialectical sublation. However,

---

[31] Ilyenkov, *Dialectical Logic,* pp. 229-230.
[32] Evald Ilyenkov, "Marks i zapadnyj mir", in Ilyenkov, *Filosofija i kul'tura* (Moskva: Respublika, 1991), p. 163.

life proceeds in such a way that revolution becomes a pressing need until the conditions for a real and not formal collectivization are created.[33]

With respect to the tragic collisions that took place within Soviet socialism, as well as the whole experience of constructing socialism in the twentieth century, Ilyenkov took the stand not of moral exposure but concrete historicism, a standpoint that could itself account for the difference between an abstract and real humanism. If "expropriators are expropriated", then it can be only a prerequisite and not a goal. To take away and divide is not an ideal but a forced measure, which in 1917 was associated with famine, breakdown and the civil war in the country. According to Lenin, "war communism" involved the implementation of a number of measures caused by emergencies. He considered the New Economic Policy as a norm of socialism; the socialist construction did not imply the "liquidation" of an owner of private business, but rather *gradual* cooperation with him.

If a socialist revolution is a movement, which overcomes alienation, then the dialectics of this movement is an attempt to solve a contradiction between the market environment and the state dictatorial power. Both references lead to alienation. The first reference leads to the alienation of one producer from another, where both are connected only through the market, and the second reference leads to the alienation of the producer from the real conditions of production, which are formally a property of the state but in fact becomes the property of public officials. In the second case, state property was easily privatized by the party and Soviet officials during "the reforms of the 1990s", and precisely they account for a considerable part of current Russian oligarchical capital. It was much easier to privatize the "nobody's" state property than the private property of individual owners. Therefore the reforms of the 1990s could be carried out without any civil war or bloodshed.

When solving problems on such a large scale (for example, a post-revolutionary situation), it is impossible to rely only on theoretical reasoning. The problem of revolution is solved rather through a concrete historical approach. However, the Soviet theoreticians of "scientific communism" lacked a methodology of concrete historicism. The main contradiction of socialism was finally solved in the USSR in favor of formal collectivization, and socialism went from being a movement into a state—this was seen as "stagnation" by its critics.

---

[33] On the dialectics of formal and real collectivization, see: Sergei Mareev, "E.V. Ilyenkov i socializm", in *Voprosy filosofii*, 2004, no 3 pp. 54-64.

Ilyenkov's writings are far from a "justification" of Soviet reality. This was not the Hegelian "conciliation" with reality as an ideal state. He writes in a letter to Yui Zhdanov in 1968:

> I also got used to think of the current state from the viewpoint of the same categories, i.e. as a phase on the way from formal "collectivization" to a real one to which there is probably a long haul ahead. It is a pity, however, that there is so little of clear theoretical perception and too much of phrases and demagogy in all this movement, which is why the process develops so painfully and with such costs that nearly exceed benefits from formal collectivization and nearly bring them to naught.[34]

In his own time, Ilyenkov was pessimistic about the prospects of transforming dialectics into the "algebra of revolution" that was in practice during the USSR time. In the same letter to Zhdanov he writes:

> It seems that this state of thing will drag on for another two hundred years, if it does not end in misfortune before. (...) I am completely overcome with such feelings. It is difficult to decide to what extent they are justified. However, the integrally intuitive impression is still such that a rotten time starts when everybody, who can do anything interesting, hides in his hole, and every scum creeps out again to the outside...[35]

In 1979 Ilyenkov committed suicide. A decade later, the end of the Soviet epoch, after that the pendulum of history began to swing in the opposite direction. The philosophy of Ilyenkov can be valued as the highest point in the development of Marxist philosophy in the USSR, in contrast to the official "diamat". Ilyenkov's Hegelian interpretation of Marx ran counter to the philosophy of Mikhail Lifshits, another major figure in Soviet "creative Marxism". Meanwhile, other philosophers who today are referred to as bright manifestations of the Soviet "thaw" have no direct relationship to Marxism.

---

[34] Yurij Zhdanov, *Vzgljad v proshloe: Vospominanija ochevidca* (Rostov-na-Donu: Feniks, 2004), p. 390.
[35] Zhdanov, *Vzgljad v proshloe*, pp. 389-390.

# Herbert Marcuse:
# No Dialectics, No Critique

*Anders Bartonek*

The purpose of this text is to reconstruct and to discuss how and why Herbert Marcuse (1898–1979), a Marxist thinker and a member of the Frankfurt School, placed such a focus on Hegel's dialectical philosophy and why this emphasis was decisive for his Marxist thinking. Even if an understanding of Marcuse's reception of Hegel is not reducible to this Marxist "usage", this dimension—that is, Hegel's importance for Marxism—seems to be crucial. The historical connection between Hegel and Marx is well known: Marx's thinking was very much inspired by Hegel's dialectical philosophy of the human, history and society. But this connection will not be at issue for the following examination. Rather, the relevant questions for the present study are: why did Marcuse make such an effort to highlight Hegel's thinking as especially important for his critical and Marxist theory, not only as an implicit background figure for Marx and Marxism in general? And how was this integration of Hegel into Marxist theory achieved? Even if some attempts have been made to explain why Marcuse put so much of his theoretical energy into Hegel, the question cannot be viewed as entirely solved. For instance, Douglas Kellner writes, in his broad-ranging and important study on *Herbert Marcuse and the Crisis of Marxism*, that Marcuse "never really explained why he involved himself in such intensive work on Hegel".[1] Thus, the question remains, why and how Hegel is important for Marcuse's development of his Marxist theory.

During his lifetime, Marcuse wrote two books on Hegel's philosophy: *Hegels Ontologie und die Theorie der Geschichtlichkeit* (1932) and *Reason*

---

[1] Douglas Kellner, *Herbert Marcuse and the Crisis of Marxism* (Basingstoke: Macmillan, 1984), p. 69.

*and Revolution: Hegel and the Rise of Social Theory* (1941), and he also made Hegel an important figure in several other essays and books. Those writings that examine Hegel in the most explicit way belong to the early stages of Marcuse's theoretical career. Marcuse did not write any particular works on Marx, but the fundamental impulse from Marx, like the one coming from Hegel, would be present throughout his entire life's work. Marx's influence on Marcuse begins even before his turn to Hegel; Marx's philosophy can be viewed as the first opening that provided Marcuse the space to think through some "fundamental questions". Marcuse's questions, departing primarily from his early experiences of Marx's thinking, which, like his interest in Hegel, precedes his encounter with Heidegger,[2] although several of the most important issues were articulated in connection with his work on Heidegger's philosophy.[3] There are some big differences between the two Hegel-books. As Andrew Feenberg writes, whereas the first can be viewed as a book on Hegel written for Heideggerians, the second can, on the other hand, be understood as "the work of a Marxist albeit a Marxist intent on recruiting Hegel to the cause".[4]

In order to summarize the horizon of Marcuse's thinking from his earlier texts, in which the influences of Marx, Hegel and Heidegger are woven together, one can say that they carry the ambition of formulating a concrete philosophy of the human and its historical essence, and that this philosophy, which in the spirit of Marxism contains a critique of existing capitalist society, is supposed to lead to radical action and a fundamental change to society through the unity of theory and praxis. This focus can be understood as the core of Marcuse's thinking and it will remain at the core of his entire thinking life, even if the ontological dimension will be weakened by the time he parts ways with Heidegger in 1932 and begins his cooperation with the Institute of Social Research in Frankfurt and their members, such as Horkheimer and Adorno. Like many of the members of the institute, Marcuse fled to the USA during the Nazi regime in Germany and participated in the work of the institute there. Unlike Horkheimer and Adorno, however, Marcuse did not return to Germany after the War, but

---

[2] Kellner, *Herbert Marcuse and the Crisis of Marxism*, pp. 5, 9, 14, 17 and 18.
[3] See Andrew Feenberg, *Heidegger and Marcuse* and Alfred Schmidt, "Existential-Onto-logie und historischer Materialismus bei Herbert Marcuse".
[4] Feenberg, *Heidegger and Marcuse: The Catastrophe and Redemption of History* (New York: Routledge, 2005), p. 48, see also p. 49.

played an equally important role for the student movements of the 1960s in the USA as Horkheimer and Adorno did in Germany.

It is important to distinguish between Marx and Marxism in the thinking of Marcuse. Even if Marcuse tried to deal with problems in Marx's philosophy in relation to societal and historical transformations (at the same time as he held onto Marx during his entire philosophical life),[5] it is foremost in relation to the crisis of Marxism during his own time that he saw the need for new perspectives. It is against this backdrop that a reclaiming of Hegel's philosophy became urgent. Marcuse was a part of what is commonly referred to as Western Marxism—the historical development of Marxism in Western societies that no longer was directly connected to the aftermath of the Russian revolution or to Soviet party politics.[6] Through his Hegel-studies Marcuse was an important figure within the Hegel renaissance during the 1930s and 1940s. Within this renaissance, Korsch and Lukács were other important "Hegelian Marxists", and they also had an impact on Marcuse.[7] The philosophy of Hegel was according to Marcuse well suited to be an instrument for the renewal of Marxism, while at the same time he insisted that Marx's philosophy was in many respects more fruitful than Hegel's. Marcuse localized fundamental problems within the version of Marxism developed in Russia during the period surrounding the Russian revolution, but also within the later decades of Soviet Marxism. According to Marcuse, the crisis of these versions of Marxism amounted to the fact that Russian communism did not answer to Marx's socialist utopia of a classless society, and instead of the "withering away" of the state, a new strong and bureaucratic state established itself. For Marcuse, theory must aim at transcending traditional forms of Marxism and offer new perspectives.[8] Marxism had become a power instrument, when in actual fact it once again needed to be a theory of liberation. Marcuse's attempt at connecting the thinking and writing of Hegel and Marx was a way of redressing this balance.

The question of dialectics will be crucial for this examination. The dialectical method, as the negative motor of critical thinking, was the main dimension of Hegel's thinking that Marcuse claimed for himself. Even if Marcuse was also critical toward Hegel in different ways, he continuously

---

[5] Kellner, *Herbert Marcuse and the Crisis of Marxism*, pp. 5, 6 and 9.
[6] See Kevin Anderson, *Lenin, Hegel, and Western Marxism: A Critical Study* (Chicago: University of Illinois Press, 1995) and Perry Anderson, *Considerations on Western Marxism* (London: NLB, 1976).
[7] Kellner, *Herbert Marcuse and the Crisis of Marxism*, p. 4.
[8] Kellner, *Herbert Marcuse and the Crisis of Marxism*, pp. 6-7.

presented dialectics as an extraordinarily important part of the Hegelian legacy. The question of dialectics was also important for Marcuse's thinking in the way that it made him develop a Hegelian Marxism rather than a Heideggerian or phenomenological Marxism—before 1932 and before Heidegger's commitment to the cause of National Socialism, Marcuse had done both. But the decision in favor of dialectics (and of Hegel) did not only come out of the personal conflict with Heidegger, it emerged out of a certain philosophical questioning itself. When Marcuse made an effort to try to answer his fundamentally Marxist questions on the essence and liberation of the human, he tended to underline the importance of dialectics more and more, even if one can say that the concept of dialectics and the role of phenomenology seemed to get along pretty well in his earliest texts. Especially in the first book on Hegel, which explicitly announces its debt to Heidegger's philosophy, one can identify an attempt to think Hegel's theory of history within a framework of Heideggerian categories. But it still seems reasonable to claim that it was dialectics that led Marcuse away from Heidegger. Marcuse claimed early that phenomenology had to be corrected by the dialectical method,[9] though it is not surprising that the concept of dialectics only plays a minor role in the Heidegger-inspired Hegel-book. In order to preliminary announce the general importance of dialectics in Marcuse's theory, an investigation into Hegel's influence on Marcuse's political Marxist theory is crucial because Hegelian philosophy lays the foundation for that dialectical-negative thinking, without which, according to Marcuse, a critical theory is not possible. Programmatically, we can say that for Marcuse, a critical theory needs dialectics!

My intention is to present a *reconstruction* of how Marcuse's Marxist thinking uses Hegel's dialectical philosophy and to develop a *discussion* about its significance. In this examination I have mainly focused on those texts in which Marcuse explicitly deals with Hegel, and since his own explicit focus on Hegel mainly belongs to his early work—his two Hegel books were released relatively early (1932 and 1941)—this period will be the most important one. Some research already exists on Marcuse's "Hegelian Marxism", even if this in almost every case is reduced to a side question.[10]

---

[9] Herbert Marcuse, "Contributions to a Phenomenology of Historical Materialism", in Richard Wolin & John Abromeit (eds.), *Heideggerian Marxism* (Lincoln: University of Nebraska Press, 2005), p. 2, and Kellner, *Herbert Marcuse and the Crisis of Marxism*, p. 69.
[10] See for example John Francis Kavanaugh, *Whole and Part in Hegel, Marx and Marcuse* (Saint Louis: Washington University, Dissertation 1973); Kellner, *Herbert Marcuse and the Crisis of Marxism*; Seyla Benhabib, "Translator's Introduction", in Marcuse, *Hegel's*

At the same time, there is a larger discussion about Marcuse's Heideggerian Marxism.[11]

## Marcuse's early texts: Marxism between Hegel and Heidegger

In this section I will investigate Marcuse's early texts, that is, those texts written from the end of the 1920s to the beginning of his exile from Germany at the time of Hitler's *Machtergreifung*. Firstly, I will (a) sketch out Marcuse's Marxist questions and impulses (and then clarify how his Marxism is assisted by Hegel). But since Marcuse's thinking during this time moves between the inspirations of Marx, Hegel and Heidegger, he can be said to be experimenting with different paths within this constellation. Therefore I will secondly (b) take into account Heidegger's influence on Marcuse, and the relation between a "Heideggerian Marxism" and a "Heideggerian Hegelianism" will be discussed—these labels seem to fit well with some of Marcuse's thoughts at this time, even if the main question for this section is whether Marcuse's Marxism is, in the last instance, mainly influenced by Hegel or Heidegger. Crucial for this crossroads in Marcuse's philosophical development is, thirdly, (c) the question of dialectics. It is through this question that Marcuse finally chooses the Hegelian and dialectical path and insists on how dialectics and its negative movement is what thinking needs in order to be critical toward existing societal conditions and to instigate radical change.

---

*Ontology and the Theory of Historicity* (Cambridge, Massachusetts: MIT Press, 1987); Anderson, *Lenin, Hegel, and Western Marxism*; Russell Rockwell, "Marcuse's Hegelian Marxism, Marx's *Grundrisse*, Hegel's Dialectic", *Radical Philosophy Review*, 16:1 2013; and Kellner & Clayton Pierce, "Introduction: Marcuse's Adventures in Marxism", in Kellner & Pierce (eds.), *Herbert Marcuse: Marxism, Revolution and Utopia* (New York: Routledge, 2014).

[11] See Feenberg, *Heidegger and Marcuse*; Alfred Schmidt, "Existential-Ontologie und historischer Materialismus bei Herbert Marcuse", in Jürgen Habermas (ed.), *Antworten auf Herbert Marcuse* (Frankfurt am Main: Suhrkamp, 1968); as well as, for example: Jóhann Páll Árnason, *Von Marcuse zu Marx: Prolegomena zu einer dialektischen Anthropologie* (Neuwied: Luchterhand, 1971); Kellner, *Herbert Marcuse and the Crisis of Marxism*; Habermas, *Philosophisch-politische Profile* (Frankfurt am Main: Suhrkamp, 1981); Benhabib, "Translator's Introduction"; Hauke Brunkhorst & Gertrud Koch, *Herbert Marcuse zur Einführung* (Hamburg: Junius, 1990); Wolin, *Heidegger's Children: Hannah Arendt, Karl Löwith, Hans Jonas, and Herbert Marcuse* (Princeton: Princeton University Press, 2015); Wolin, "Introduction: What is Heideggerian Marxism", in Wolin & John Abromeit (eds.), *Heideggerian Marxism*.

## a) Marcuse's Marxist questions

Marcuse's early texts, from 1928 and onwards, are deeply inspired by Marx's philosophy, and my ambition at this point is to sketch out his fundamental Marxist questions. The influence of Marx on Marcuse was strong even in his later writings, which will also be referred to below. In the text "Contributions to a Phenomenology of Historical Materialism" (1928), Marcuse seeks to formulate what kind of fundamental themes are contained in Marx's philosophy. The connection to Heidegger is, as the title suggests, much present in the text, but, for my present purposes, I will ignore this here (even if I will have reason to return to it in the next section). In the abovementioned text, Marcuse underlines the general questions surrounding the "historical" and "action" as central Marxist categories for him. He writes that Marxism not only aims at knowledge in itself (and thereby remaining abstract), but that the knowledge in which Marxism results is always connected to a concrete historical situation and must lead to radical action and ultimately to the liberation of humanity. Marxism stands for the theory of the revolution of the proletariat and consists in the revolutionary critique of capitalist society. Marxism is only a science as far as it contains the insight that revolutionary action is a necessity. Marxism seeks therefore the unity of theory and praxis. The truth of Marxism is not merely a truth of knowing, it is a truth of historical and revolutionary development.[12] Human existence is essentially historical and practical, and these moments are connected: human praxis derives from the historical situation, and its demands and needs. Radical action is an answer to a given situation, but it is also a way of forming and transforming it.[13] For Marcuse, knowledge production is therefore an activity that can never have a neutral value in itself, but rather it always comes out of a historical situation and out of the interests and needs that people have within that situation. Simultaneously Marxist theory points back to the situation that provokes a need for transformation at the same time as it speaks of a liberated society transcending the existing state of affairs, and which calls for revolutionary practice. Theory and praxis are therefore not only identical in the sense that theory seeks to become practical in the revolutionary way, but that thinking initially cannot be separated from human societal life and its practices. This does not guarantee a successful liberation, but theory and praxis must not

---

[12] Marcuse, "Contributions to a Phenomenology of Historical Materialism", p. 1.
[13] Marcuse, "Contributions to a Phenomenology of Historical Materialism", pp. 5ff.

be understood as two separate entities that one should try to connect for the sake of liberating humankind. Something that can be said to be missing in Marcuse's thinking is a positive presentation of the non-identity of theory and praxis, since it seems that—in order to be able to transcend existing society and the false images of societal praxis it harbors—theory must make itself non-identical with society for the sake of a new praxis. The identity of theory and praxis needs a moment of non-identity, although this concept is not used by Marcuse.

Another main theme for Marcuse is the nature of radical action. Even if Marcuse, following Marx and Engels, means that every action in some sense changes the circumstances of human life, every action does not change human existence. It is only radical action that reaches to the core of human essence and that has the ability to change human existence as such. Radical action would in the situation of a capitalist society be the revolution of the proletariat. Through radical action, that which has become unbearable for human existence will be overcome and replaced with what is necessary for humanity, but where this sense of necessity remains immanent to radical action itself. This dimension of necessity, then, comes not from outside; the action is executed because of its inner necessity, a necessity that is essentially historical. Its necessity derives from the human needs within a historical situation, and what is needed is the creation of a genuine, meaningful and true existence, in contrast to the unbearable existence that follows from capitalism.[14] According to Marcuse, the possibility of this action becomes a necessity and a reality when the needs of the situation coincide with the knowledge of the situation and its immanent necessity. The true historical existence of the human will only develop if it also develops knowledge of its situation. Only then is the human in touch with its history and can deal with the challenge which it is now ready to face. The necessity of radical action, therefore, can only become real on the basis of knowledge of the nature of the historical situation. And according to Marcuse, it is the knowledge of the proletarian class, its self-consciousness, which incorporates the historical unity that is able to bear this task of necessity. One can here point out Marcuse's generally uncritical approach towards Marx. For example, Marcuse is not problematizing the possibility for the class to develop a non-false consciousness and its ability to become a revolutionary

---

[14] Marcuse, "Contributions to a Phenomenology of Historical Materialism", pp. 4ff.

subject in the way that, for instance, Adorno would.[15] It appears as if Marcuse assumes an unproblematic continuity from Marx to his own theoretical effort.

Another central aspect of Marcuse's early thinking, which has a close relation to the development of his Marxism, is the question and need of a concrete philosophy. This is formulated in the essay "On Concrete Philosophy" (1929). Although fundamentally Marxist, here we can also trace arguments that are close to Heidegger. In order to stay within the bounds of Marxism, however, one may say that Marcuse generally formulates concrete philosophy as a philosophy that has concrete human existence as its subject. Not that philosophy should only be a practical or concrete science; it is a way of philosophizing in itself: Marcuse underlines that philosophy is a form of human existence—theory and praxis are identical also in this respect. Capitalism is that situation in which human existence finds itself in a crisis, and the task of philosophy is to make its truths visible as counter images to it in a concrete manner.[16]

The discovery of Marx's Paris manuscripts had a crucial impact on Marcuse's thinking and on his formulation of Marxism. This he discusses in the text "New Sources on the Foundations of the Concept of Labor in Economics" (1932). Marcuse highlights especially Marx's theory on the being and essence of the human. Marx's critique of political economy was not only an economic critique, it contained a critique of capitalism as a threat to human essence as such. In capitalist society the human turns into something inhuman, she is alienated and suffers a loss of reality (Marcuse calls this *Entwirklichung*). The human is hindered in its possibility to reach self-consciousness through labor, through which, as a *Gattungswesen,* the human being could liberate herself. But a liberating kind of labor differs essentially from the kind of alienating labor predominant in capitalist society, which is a destructive form of labor, tearing asunder the human, nature and society. In this situation of alienation, human essence and human existence are separated from each other, according to which the lived life does not correspond to its real essence. This is the big challenge that society confronts, namely to end this catastrophe through revolutionary

---

[15] Joan Alway, *Critical Theory and Political Possibilities: Conceptions of Emancipatory Politics in the Works of Horkheimer, Adorno, Marcuse, and Habermas* (Westport: Greenwood Press, 1995), pp. 64ff.
[16] Marcuse, "On Concrete Philosophy", in Wolin & Abromeit (eds.), *Heideggerian Marxism*, pp. 34ff.

action. Moreover, through Marx's reference to Hegel's concept of labor and its merits—that is, his understanding of the human being as realizing itself through its own labor and activity—Marx, according to Marcuse, turns Hegel into a crucial starting point for his own praxis philosophy.[17] Marcuse's aim is precisely to hold onto this praxis philosophy. In their "Introduction: Marcuse's Adventures in Marxism" to the volume *Herbert Marcuse: Marxism, Revolution and Utopia,* Kellner and Clayton Pierce point out that Marcuse's encounter with the Paris manuscripts had the consequence that he came even closer to Marx (distancing himself further from Heidegger), for the potential inherent in Marx's thinking for realizing a concrete philosophy now became abundantly clear to him.[18]

Beside this specific impulse that was set on its way by a reading of the Paris manuscripts, I cannot see any essential change in Marcuse's understanding of Marx during his entire work. I would thus state that one ought to speak of a continuity on this matter. The role of the Paris manuscripts can for Marcuse be seen more as a confirmation of what Marcuse had hoped to find in Marx's thinking. Marcuse will hold onto these fundamental Marxian questions and onto the task of developing a concrete, materialist and historical theory of society and the essence and needs of the human as a critique of capitalist and alienated society. A main focus for Marcuse is always an endeavor to free up those possibilities that speak to the urgent need for radical and revolutionary change. In Marcuse's discussion of Marx in *Reason and Revolution* (1941) these questions are crucial: societal alienation and capitalism; the historical need to overcome these; the question of how the human essence can find its proper place and the idea of a materialist critical theory of the human.[19] In his later book, *An Essay on Liberation* (1969) these themes are still present. The liberation from capitalism is at stake and a politics of liberation should have its starting point in a critical theory which does not remain within its scientific framework, but leads to action—this is what the society demands. What is otherwise rejected as merely "utopian" is what society needs in order to develop. The point of departure is here a materialist theory that grows out of a contem-

---

[17] Marcuse, "New Sources on the Foundations of the Concept of Labor in Economics", in Wolin & Abromeit (eds.), *Heideggerian Marxism*, pp. 95ff., see also, in relation to the concept of labor, p. 94.

[18] Kellner & Pierce, "Introduction: Marcuse's Adventures in Marxism", p. 24.

[19] Marcuse, *Reason and Revolution: Hegel and the Rise of Social Theory* (Boston: Beacon Press, 1960), pp. 273-322.

porary understanding of the nature and needs of the human and deals with the need for a fundamental societal change through radical praxis.[20]

## b) Heideggerian Marxism and Heideggerian Hegelianism

As already mentioned, the young Marcuse finds himself in a constellation of inspiration consisting of Marx, Hegel and Heidegger. The earliest texts (apart from Marcuse's dissertation on the German art novel from 1922)—I referred to a couple of them in the prior section—can be said to incorporate different attempts at orientating himself within this constellation. Taken together, these texts can rightly be considered as containing a "Heideggerian Marxism", even if the Hegelian dimension, also present, is lost in this description. Marcuse's first book on Hegel, *Hegel's Ontologie*—a text with which he initially sought to gain a professorship through Heidegger—could be understood as a Heidegger-inspired Hegelianism, that is, a "Heideggerian Hegelianism". In this book, the Marxist starting point is not apparent, it is rather hidden, even if the fundamental questions surrounding concrete human life and history are themselves present. It is therefore possible to speak of a continuity between this book and the other early essays.

Marcuse's Heideggerian Marxism represents an attempt to formulate a combination of these two philosophies, in which the strengths of both come to reinforce each other, but mutually are used to correct one another's weaknesses. In Heidegger and Marx, Marcuse sees the potential of a concrete philosophy of human essence as a historic phenomenon and for which the historical task of radical action is decisive. How Marcuse formulates his own form of Marxism has already been discussed. The influence that Heidegger exerts upon him becomes apparent, for example, in "Contributions to a Phenomenology of Historical Materialism". The description of the Marxist "situation", the understanding of the human as *Dasein*, as well as the question surrounding historicity, and finally an interpretation of the truth of Marxism as a *Geschehen*, are already important Heidegger-inspired lines of thought. But also the fact that the title of the essay announces Marcuse's ambition to contribute (*Beitrag*) to the phenomenology of historical materialism makes this connection clear.[21] Also the explication of the connection of theory and praxis and Marcuse's formulation that philosophizing is a fundamental way for human *Dasein* to exist has a link to

---

[20] Marcuse, *An Essay on Liberation* (Boston: Beacon Press, 1969).
[21] Marcuse, "Contributions to a Phenomenology of Historical Materialism", pp. 1ff.

Heidegger.[22] In large parts, Marcuse's interest in Heidegger lies precisely in the search for a concrete philosophy, which opens itself toward the possibilities of the historical situation and may lead to radical action and social change.[23] Much of this he finds in Heidegger. But ultimately he also thinks that Heidegger's philosophy is stuck in the presentation of the historicity of its object and therefore never reaches the question of praxis.[24] This is the reason why, according to Marcuse, phenomenology must be criticized and corrected by the dialectical method.[25] But phenomenology can also stand as a counterpoint to Marxism. A theme that speaks for Heidegger is according to Marcuse the positive focus on individual *Dasein*, which in Marx is at risk of disappearing behind the laws of history. However, even here, it is important to see how individuals are not isolated from but in dialectical relation to the whole of society.[26] That which often is formulated by Marcuse as a Heideggerian Marxism is in this text formulated by himself as a "dialectical Phenomenology", and since the text's theme is first and foremost an attempted *rapprochement* between the philosophies of Marx and Heidegger, this concept can be interpreted as a "Marxist-dialectical Heideggerianism". The crucial question surrounding this choice of method (dialectics and/or phenomenology) departs in Marcuse from the thought that the method must be adequate to its object. Both dialectics and phenomenology have according to Marcuse the ambition of growing out of reality and the historical situation itself. The ability of the methods to arrive at the historical dimension of human existence is decisive, and important is therefore how they successfully can be made concrete and ultimately lead to liberating praxis. Even if phenomenology reaches great depths in its analysis, Marcuse thinks that it is only through the dialectical method that action can be prepared and made possible.[27] Below (c), Marcuse's understanding of dialectics will be discussed further.

In Marcuse's first Hegel-book, a "Heideggerian Hegelianism" is developed. This book is therefore of no direct relevance for our inquiry into Marcuse's Hegelian Marxism. But since the book is about Hegel I will refer to it briefly. It remains uncertain whether Marcuse sought to ingratiate

---

[22] Marcuse, "On Concrete Philosophy", p. 34.
[23] Marcuse, "Contributions to a Phenomenology of Historical Materialism", pp. 10ff.
[24] Schmidt, "Existential-Ontologie und historischer Materialismus bei Herbert Marcuse", p. 40.
[25] Marcuse, "Contributions to a Phenomenology of Historical Materialism", p. 2.
[26] Richard Wolin, *Heidegger's Children*, p. 148.
[27] Marcuse, "Contributions to a Phenomenology of Historical Materialism", pp. 17ff.

himself with Heidegger by first embracing a Heideggerian vocabulary more than in the other early texts, and by second placing Marx into the background,[28] for the purposes of making his habilitation in Freiburg for Heidegger easier, a habilitation which in any case would not happen for political reasons. One would have expected that it was Marcuse's ambition to develop a dialectical phenomenology in this book, like in the other early texts. However, this is not the case. The book contains rather a Heideggerian Hegel-analysis that does not highlight dialectics (and that does not accentuate any Marxist perspective). It is difficult to explain the sudden disappearance of dialectics here, in a book on Hegel (the philosopher of dialectics) during a time in which Marcuse wrote other texts emphasizing the importance of dialectics, if not in connection to Marcuse's relation to Heidegger. And this he does afterwards too. All the same, it is relevant to briefly discuss how Marcuse uses Hegel in this book, even if Hegel does not fill the function of strengthening Marxism here.

As the title indicates, the theme of the book is Hegel's ontology and his theory of historicity. The main focus is the concepts of life, history and motion, and one can say that Marcuse, departing from Hegel but operating with Heidegger's concepts, is trying to formulate a theory of the historicity of being.[29] What Marcuse is interested in is whether Hegel's logics and concept of life, as well as his concept of history, really reach all the way down to, and become relevant for, concrete human existence.[30] At this point a connection to many of Marcuse's other writings becomes clearer. But in this book, the question is whether Hegel's ontology really is able to turn life, as a historical category, into the fundamental concept of ontology.[31] For Marcuse, it is therefore crucial whether the historical is understood adequately and whether philosophy in Hegel formulates a concept adequate to history. Here, Marcuse's analysis of Hegel leads him to a critique of Hegel's concept of history. As is the case in the other early texts on the concept of dialectics (to be discussed later), Marcuse criticizes Hegel's theory for becoming unhistorical (despite Hegel's own intentions). It is in the transition of the *Phenomenology of Spirit* into absolute knowledge that Marcuse sees the arresting of the historical. As a result, Hegel's philosophy never really took the form of a genuine historicity: the spirit takes its journey

---

[28] See Benhabib, "Translator's Introduction", p. xii.
[29] Marcuse, *Hegel's Ontology and the Theory of Historicity*, pp. 1ff.
[30] Marcuse, *Hegel's Ontology and the Theory of Historicity*, p. 195.
[31] Marcuse, *Hegel's Ontology and the Theory of Historicity*, pp. 195 ff. and 229.

through history only because he knows history cannot hurt him. History can only take the path of spirit.[32]

### c) The question of dialectics and leaving Heidegger

In the already mentioned shorter early texts, Marcuse tried to combine the philosophies of Heidegger and Marx. But, he would soon turn his critique toward phenomenology, claiming that the lack of dialectics was itself a limitation. During those same early years Marcuse wrote two other essays, which he called "On the Problem of the Dialectic (Part 1)" (1930) and "On the Problem of the Dialectic (Part 2)" (1931). These essays can be viewed as his first attempts to develop the concept of dialectics as being discovered as a certain deficiency in Heidegger. The dialectic would thus be made into a fundamental concept in his own theory. But Heidegger's influence is present even here. The concept of dialectics will be discussed later with respect to Marcuse's later writings—it plays a significant role in his entire work, not least in his book on Freud and his critique of Soviet Marxism—but here I will discuss the beginnings of his elaborations on this concept.

In the first of these essays,[33] Marcuse makes an initial point that both reality and the relation of philosophy to reality are dialectical. Thus, dialectical thinking cannot be understood as a mere external method, which tries to grasp a one-sided and homogenous reality. This also means that reality is inherently contradictory and that thinking can only relate to it in dialectical terms. Marcuse finds these dialectical insights into the relation between philosophy and reality in both Plato and Hegel. But in Hegel, in contrast to Plato, dialectics are thought historically, which for Marcuse is crucial. Dialectics becomes the principle of becoming. Reality is becoming by being dialectical. In Hegel, the point of dialectics is to rip being out of its stagnated and isolated existence and transform dialectics into the life nerve of its development. It is important to understand the singular in its negativity, by which its own singularity is negated and becomes a part of a higher form of being. In Hegel, reality is simultaneously dialectical and historical (and for Marcuse, only that being that is historical is also dialectical). But for Hegel, being as historico-dialectical is also subject. Therefore Hegel understands thinking, as the self-reflection of being, as dialectical

---

[32] Marcuse, *Hegel's Ontology and the Theory of Historicity*, pp. 305ff.
[33] Marcuse, "On the Problem of the Dialectic (Part 1)", in Wolin & Abromeit (eds.), *Heideggerian Marxism*, pp. 53-67, see also Marcuse, "The History of Dialectics", in Marcuse, *Marxism, Revolution and Utopia* (London: Routledge, 2014), pp. 142ff.

and as the method for conceptualizing reality. After his discussion of this, Marcuse speaks briefly of Marx and his understanding of dialectics, which presupposes Hegel's understanding, but also stands for a critique of Hegelian dialectics. While reliant on Hegel's dialectics, Marx develops a more concrete form of dialectical thinking, which in contrast to Hegel can lead to a genuine and historically situated realization of the human. One can conclude here that in this text Marcuse mostly refers to the concept of dialectics of other thinkers; he has not as yet worked out his own philosophical position.

In the second essay on dialectics, formulations surrounding the movement of dialectics become clearer and more detailed. Marcuse describes dialectics with a quote from Hegel as the *Sichselbstgleichheit im Anderssein*. According to this understanding the human becomes identical with itself by becoming different from itself. Marcuse also writes that dialectics in Hegel is a process of a continuous *Aufheben* of otherness. Sublation means here that both the human and society progress by relating to their contradictions and negate themselves through those contradictions in order to sublate them. They dedicate themselves to their otherness in order to sublate it and reach fulfillment through this process. According to Marcuse, Hegel shows how this process is formative in every concrete form of being. This means for Marcuse that dialectics essentially also is a movement through which the current state of existence is transcended.[34] And the possibility of this transcending will be decisive as to why Marcuse turns the concept of dialectics into the core principle of critical thinking. Dialectics makes the transcending of the societal situation possible, which is a possibility that already is rooted in the inner dialectical "nature" of reality. Through a dialectical interpretation of reality, theory makes the inner contradictions of reality come forth, and thereby it becomes possible to create counter images to the contemporary state of society. In "Contributions" Marcuse writes that dialectics puts every established and stagnated form into motion.[35] Despite this positive description of Hegel's concept of dialectics, Marcuse criticizes Hegel with help from Marx. Hegel, after all, undermined a real transition of society despite his philosophy being dialectical. The reason for this, according to Marcuse, is that the historical dimension ultimately disappears in Hegel's system. Because Hegel seeks to lift his dialectics, founded in the historical determined life process, to become an absolute totality, the his-

---

[34] Marcuse, "On the Problem of the Dialectic (Part 2)", in Wolin & Abromeit (eds.), *Heideggerian Marxism*, pp. 68-85.
[35] Marcuse, "Contributions to a Phenomenology of Historical Materialism", p. 17.

torical dimension is arrested. In contrast, Marx's dialectics makes a real movement of transcendence possible, which is prepared through the analysis of the situation that is historically given.[36]

Even if Marcuse tries early on to formulate a dialectical phenomenology, the concept of dialectic can be seen as a symbol for why Marcuse and Heidegger part ways. Even if a dialectical phenomenology tries to acknowledge the benefits of Heidegger's analysis of existence and its concrete historical situation, it was the ability of the dialectical method to concretize theory and give it its fruitful practical perspective that made it attractive for Marcuse's thinking. Marcuse rather tried to build on both Hegel and Marx in order to develop his own political theory on the possibilities for radical change. The concepts of dialectics and negativity play big parts in this. Marcuse's Marxism therefore chooses the path of Hegel and dialectics, rather than via Heidegger. Regarding the central focus for our study—that is, how and why Hegel was important for the development of Marcuse's Marxism—one can say that Marcuse highlights the importance of Hegel's thinking and of dialectics from out of an essentially Marxist perspective.

## Hegel and Marcuse's Critical Theory

I have now arrived at that phase of Marcuse's writing which coincides with the establishment of his cooperation with the Institute of Social Research and its members Horkheimer, Adorno, Löwenthal and others. At this point the Heideggerian influence undergoes further weakening, and instead Marcuse's thinking is increasingly informed by the development of the critical theory of the Frankfurt School. Marcuse will also become a leading figure within this school of Critical Theory and be very important for the student movements of the 1960s, first of all in the USA and in Germany.

This section departs (a) with a discussion on how Marcuse, in dialogue with Hegel, examines the beginnings of social theory as well as the relation between philosophy and critical theory. Marcuse's book *Reason and Revolution*, in which the dialectical and subversive potential of Hegel's Logic is presented, is essential for this (b). The third part (c) consists of one of the most important discussions for this text: Marcuse's concept of dialectics in relation to Hegel, Marx, and Marxism. Finally (d), one of Marcuse's late and most famous works about the one-dimensional man will be addressed, in which he identifies a crisis for negative and critical thinking, a discussion

---

[36] Marcuse, "On the Problem of the Dialectic (Part 2)", pp. 77ff.

relevant here since this must also be understood as constituting the crisis of dialectics.

## a) Hegel and the Critical Theory of Society

The main focus in this part will be Marcuse's second Hegel-book, *Reason and Revolution*. In this book, Marcuse identifies the limitations of Hegel with help from Marx, but still it is clear that Marcuse cannot undertake this critical task without the dialectical impulse from Hegel. It is difficult to find precise formulations in which Marcuse directly highlights Marxism's need for Hegel—in this book one rather finds formulations limiting Hegel's potential—but I interpret Marcuse's position as saying that Hegel's dialectical theory is needed explicitly in order to place at the center the dialectical and an idea of negativity, both of which are present in Marx's thinking, though in a slightly different way. Although Marx went further than Hegel and thereby prepared the ground for Critical Theory, it is crucial to hold onto Hegel, from out of which the life nerve of critique comes. As will be seen below in the discussion on dialectics in Hegel and Marx, Marcuse often and unsurprisingly thinks that there is a path leading from Hegel to Marx, but the Marxist Marcuse nevertheless writes two books on Hegel in order to hold onto dialectics. It is clear that it is not enough to stay within Marx's thinking. Rather, Marcuse constructs an aggregate of the Hegel-Marx-constellation, which for him becomes necessary for the possibility of critical theory and for the movement toward the liberation of the human.[37] To summarize, one can say that Marcuse's highlighting of Hegel has the ambition to: (1) show how Hegel has a critical and revolutionary function for Marx's thinking and the following Marxist tradition; (2) show that Hegel not was a conservative thinker, but essentially a critical thinker, and (3) with help from Hegel, save dialectical and negative thought for the sake of a critical theory of society, which is yet to be developed.

An important dimension of *Reason and Revolution* is that it defends Hegel against, at that time, the common accusation of Hegel as a totalitarian philosopher and who could be connected to fascism.[38] I will not focus on

---

[37] In his article on Marcuse's *Reason and Revolution*, Kevin Anderson quotes Raya Dunayevskaya's understanding of Marcuse's theory—that is similar to my understanding—as having "re-established the revolutionary dialectic of Hegel-Marx". Kevin Anderson, "On Hegel and the Rise of Social Theory: A Critical Appreciation of Herbert Marcuse's Reason and Revolution, Fifty Years Later", *Sociological Theory* 11:3 1993, p. 258.

[38] See for example Marcuse's later written afterword in *Schriften* 4 (Springe: zu Klampen, 2004), pp. 369ff., see also the translator's afterword, p. 375.

this theme here, although it is remarkable how affirmative Marcuse is in his interpretation of Hegel, especially when compared to the thinking of his colleague Adorno. The abovementioned book is to a large extent of an introductory character. The whole first half treats the main dimensions of Hegel's work: the phenomenology of spirit, logic, political philosophy and the philosophy of history. But for Marcuse it remains an ambition to use Hegel as a foundation for the construction of a critical social theory. According to Marcuse, Hegel founded social theory precisely because his theory and dialectics were derived from an analysis of reality. His thinking was partly a reflection on the historical development of reality, but it was also partly the case that reason needed to be realized in the social and political institutions of social reality in order to truthfully become real reason. Hegel's dialectics are not closed off to the reality of the social, but in Hegel reason starts to respond to and realize itself in different forms of society. Marcuse depicts Hegel's system as the culmination and end of the modern era, an era that had interpreted the world from out of reason and self-consciousness and that had thus subordinated nature and history under the criteria of thinking. At the same time, Hegel acknowledged that societal and political life were man-made constructs and that these structures themselves served as the foundations upon which reason realized itself. But here Hegel, according to Marcuse, brings philosophy to its negation and thus to its end. This confrontation with society results, despite Hegel's intention, in the closed immanence of reason. Hegel's theory instead turns into a link that bridges the old form (Kant) and a new form of critical theory (Marx). Hegel also serves as a link connecting philosophy and social theory. The principal difference between Hegel and Marx consists in the fact that Hegel's concepts—although they can be viewed as being informed by economics and politics—belong to philosophy and remain locked within its framework. In contrast, Marx tried to develop a theory that represented a negation of philosophy. Additionally, Hegel's concepts strengthen and confirm the existing order, while Marx's categories all the time are seeking to become the negation of that political order. The problem with Hegel is that he allows reason to fully realize itself within the static status quo of the state. But for Marcuse, the method of dialectics survives Hegel's state and even transcends it. Even if Hegel meant that politics finds its fulfillment and end in the state, his critico-dialectical method endures and becomes the instrument for (i) Marx's materialist thinking and (ii) Marcuse's version of a critical theory.[39] Against this background, Marcuse has the ambition of examining how philosophy can and must be transcended in order to make room for a new adequate critical social theory. This he tries to do with Hegel's dialectics as a foundation.

Marcuse discussed this path from philosophy to a critical dialectical theory as early as in the 1930s. One essay, "Philosophy and Critical Theory" (from 1937),[40] stands out here. In this essay, Marcuse tries to describe in what a critical theory must consist and how it is to differ, but also depart from philosophy (mainly Hegel's). Here, philosophy comes across as belonging to the old world, and Marcuse writes that philosophy, as an enterprise trapped within the extant division of labor, has lived of the fact that it has not realized itself (in Marx's sense). But while Hegel meant that the freedom of man was realized in the state, Marcuse claims that Hegel only identified freedom with necessity, and that both the human and society were trapped in an apparent necessity and therefore man was not free. Reality is reconciled with reason, but reality is not fundamentally altered. Economic structures are sublated in Hegel, and are therefore fundamentally conserved, and this is not enough for Marcuse. Philosophy must rather find its end through real societal change. Critical theory differs from philosophy in so far as it participates in political struggle, which aims at liberating humanity from capitalist alienation.

Karl-Heinz Sahmel, for instance, criticizes Marcuse's negative thinking; he sees within it the risk that Marcuse's theory of society as a negative whole makes a critical position impossible.[41] My interpretation of Marcuse is rather that he understands the whole as both problematic and negative, but that its inner antagonisms make room for critical reflection and critical distance it demands.[42] Society is not entirely homogenous.

---

[39] Marcuse, *Reason and Revolution*, pp. 251-257.

[40] Marcuse, "Philosophy and Critical Theory", in Marcuse, *Negations: Essays in Critical Theory* (Boston: Beacon Press, 1996).

[41] Karl-Heinz Sahmel, *Vernunft und Sinnlichkeit: Eine kritische Einführung in das philosophische und politische Denken Herbert Marcuses* (Königstein: Forum Academicum, 1979), pp. 223ff.

[42] This touches on a question that makes possible a certain comparison between Marcuse and Adorno. Even if Sahmel is referring to Adorno in order to ground his questioning of Marcuse, Adorno himself was often criticized in the same way, for example by Habermas. In my book *Philosophie im Konjunktiv: Nichtidentität als Ort der Möglichkeit des Utopischen in der negativen Dialektik Theodor W. Adornos*, I try to show how Adorno's concept of the non-identical is the concept that opens up the possibility for the critical position. Marcuse, though, seems to lack a concept like this.

## b) The subversive content of Hegel's Logic

Marcuse's treatment of Hegel's *Logic* in his second monograph on Hegel consists, despite its thematic content, in perhaps Marcuse's strongest arguments in favor of a subversive potential for Hegelian dialectics, which is far from self-evident since his *Logic* is devoid of political content.[43]

An important entrance into this issue is that Hegel's *Logic*, in contrast to many of its predecessors, can be said to be a "materialistic logic", and hereby he is also paving the way for Marx's materialism. It is not merely an idealistic logic, but stands for a critique of a traditionally accepted demarcation between categories and forms of thought on the one hand, and their addressed content on the other hand. Rather, the categories express the dynamics of reality. Hegel does not accept the existence of a ready-made world outside of thinking, with which thinking then deals. This would mean that thinking would have to accept the world as it is, and resign from the ambition of reconciling reality with truth, that is, to make reality into what it should be. According to Marcuse, Hegel rejects all attempts to sanctify certain forms of being or society. Reality in its immediate shape must rather be negated and destroyed. With its negative character, dialectics belongs in essence to the domain of logic. The task of thinking is to negate reality in order to sublate its current forms and to let their inherent potential for reason be realized. Crucial is that reality needs to be negated and therefore become what it is not. Only by not being permitted to remain what it initially was, can reality become what is has potential for. According to Hegel, it is the whole and the common that must be developed; the negation, on the other hand, is fulfilled through the singular or individual, a negation that is sublated by the common in order to secure its progress. Here, dialectics is positive despite its negative method.

It is also essential to highlight how the concept of essence stands for the negative and the antithetic dimension in the Hegelian concept-triad of being–essence–concept. When something turns into its own contradiction it is expressing its own essence, and this means at the same time that the inner contradictions of being appear in its essence (and then will be sublated). Essence is the form of being through which being is set in motion and transcends itself. Through this motion being also turns into something else. The process of being's transformation, which shall lead to itself, has

---

[43] Marcuse, *Reason and Revolution*, pp. 121-168 and Alasdair MacIntyre, *Marcuse* (London: Collins, 1970), p. 32.

begun. This process and the relation between the concepts of essence and being correspond to Hegel's theory of reality as negative: reality develops by mobilizing its inner contradictions. In this mobilization one can find the critical potential of Hegel's thinking. Marcuse also shows, against the backdrop of Hegel's concept of dialectics, how Marx's concept of capitalism is another example of a concept that brings out the critical significance and concept of essence. Within the play of societal contradictions, the (false) essence of society comes forth, it shows its right face. This possibility to make visible inherent contradictions is the subversive potential of Hegel's *Logic*. But Marcuse also inherits the ambition to let reason permeate reality from Hegel.

In the end, Marx's dialectics is more fruitful for Marcuse. Why does Marcuse prefer Marx, and what role is Hegel playing in this discussion?

### c) Marcuse's understanding of dialectics between Hegel, Marx, and Marxism

In this section I will examine how Marcuse formulates the concept of dialectics of Hegel and Marx. I shall also address Marcuse's later discussions of this concept. First, however, I start with Marcuse's exposition of dialectics in *Reason and Revolution*, where he admittedly joins Marx and identifies the limitations of Hegel's understanding of dialectics. Nonetheless, despite this critical undertaking, Hegel remains in a powerful position. Hegel and Marcuse share the understanding that the dialectic operates as the immanent negation of reality, itself the principle of movement and creativity. The societal praxis of the human includes negativity, as the possibility of transition. One may say that Marcuse's concept of negativity includes both a constructive and a destructive aspect: on the one hand, for example, the negativity of private property as the obstacle for a genuinely humane community, but on the other hand the negation of this obstacle would be positive in the sense that it is the overcoming of what is destructively negative. He writes that the negativity of capitalist society lies in the alienation of labor, but that the negation of this negativity would lead to the end of alienated labor.[44] Christian Fuchs argues how Marcuse uses the concept of negativity in a double sense, namely as a description of the problematic society and as the method for tearing it down. A negation of the negation

---

[44] Marcuse, *Reason and Revolution*, p. 282.

would thus mean revolution.[45] According to Marcuse both Hegel and Marx understand dialectical reality as the whole of reality—truth lies in the whole—which they at the same time understand as a negative totality. But Hegel and Marx view this totality differently. Whereas for Hegel the whole is the ontological whole and a closed system of reason, which has become identical with the progress of history, for Marx dialectics is entirely disconnected from this ontological understanding. In Marx negativity instead turns into a historical premise that must not be hypostatized into a metaphysical fact. Totality in Marx is the class society, to which its historically developed form and its inherent negativity belong. Here, Marx turns the dialectical method into a historically determined method, which loses the general and universal meaning it has in Hegel. No longer, then, can the idea of a negative totality be used in relation to all things. Dialectics now grasp things as elements of a certain historical totality from which they cannot be separated. This kind of dialectics then include both the existing negativity of capitalist society and its negation. Although dialectics is the driving force of history in Hegel, dialectics as such, according to Marcuse, become timeless in a problematic way, both with respect to its generality and universal applicability.[46] What for Hegel is history, is only pre-history for Marx.[47] But in *Reason and Revolution*, Marcuse mentions Hegel's understanding of history in a positive manner. Hegel's optimism consists of an understanding of reality in a destructive way, namely that what exists finds itself in a dissolving movement initiated by reason and as such will not persist. Reason will transform reality until reason corresponds with reason. Dialectics stands for the view that all reality is impregnated with negativity and contradictions, and therefore is the counterpart of all positivism.[48] According to Marcuse, Marx concretized Hegel's dialectics and his theory of alienation, as well as the idea of transcending alienation within capitalist society and its specific situation.[49]

In *Reason and Revolution* and in his book on Soviet Marxism (1958) Marcuse discusses the crisis of Marxism as a lack of dialectics. This is

---

[45] Christian Fuchs, *Herbert Marcuse interkulturell gelesen* (Nordhausen: Bautz, 2005), pp. 22ff. and 31; see also Richard Bernstein, "Negativity: Themes and Variations", in Robert P. Pippin, Feenberg & Charles P. Webel (eds.), *Marcuse: Critical Theory & the Promise of Utopia* (Basingstoke: Macmillan Education, 1988), p. 14.
[46] Marcuse, *Reason and Revolution*, pp. 312ff.
[47] Marcuse, *Soviet Marxism: A Critical Analysis* (Harmondsworth: Penguin, 1971), p. 8.
[48] Marcuse, *Reason and Revolution*, pp. 26-27 and 36-37.
[49] Kellner & Pierce, "Introduction: Marcuse's Adventures in Marxism", pp. 26-27.

crucial for my focus in the present text, because it means that Marcuse uses both dialectics and Hegel to conceptualize the crisis of Marxism. In *Reason and Revolution* Marcuse means that the reduction of dialectics and of Hegel's significance within Marxism, which took place both before and after Lenin, mostly coincided with the attenuation of the revolutionary dimension of Marxism. Lenin himself questioned the naturalistic version of Marxism and defended the need for dialectical thought. According to Marcuse, Lenin meant that it was dangerous only to connect the possibility of revolution with the necessity of economic laws and only to follow economic goals. The goal of politics must be to rule economics, and dialectics is a counterpart to the necessity of history and the overthrow of the prevailing order.[50] The dialectic also plays a significant role in Marcuse's criticism of Soviet Marxism. The main aim is to examine and immanently criticize some of the significant tendencies within Soviet Marxism. Marcuse writes that there might be no question better suited to show the direction of the development of Soviet Marxism than how it deals with dialectics.[51] What has happened with Marxism in the USSR is worse than a revision: what was once a critical way of thinking has developed into an extensive worldview and a method with fixed frames and rules. Instead of being the tool for revolutionary consciousness and praxis (as was the case for Marx), Marxism is now placed within the established power system. But dialectics is rebellious against this kind of doctrinal framing, and, according to Marcuse, this significantly is shown in the difficulties that Soviet Marxism encountered in developing a textbook on dialectics. Dialectics cannot be fixed into a homogenous system, but contains rather a resistance against the systematic. In Soviet Marxism, dialectics tended to stagnate into a general system in which the historical process merely was understood as a pattern of nature. The Soviet regime made dialectics harmless to itself, it was put to rest in order to protect an established form of Marxism.[52] An important task for Marcuse is thus to reconnect Marxism with dialectics.

During the late period of his thinking, Marcuse wrote several texts with dialectics as their main focus. For example, in 1960, Marcuse formulated his position regarding dialectics and negativity in a pithy way in a new preface to *Reason and Revolution*: "A Note on Dialectic". What is again at stake is

---

[50] Marcuse, *Reason and Revolution*, pp. 398-401.
[51] See also Marcuse, "Dialectic and Logic Since the War", in Kellner & Pierce (eds.), *Herbert Marcuse. Marxism, Revolution and Utopia* (New York: Routledge 2014).
[52] Marcuse, *Soviet Marxism*, pp. 114ff.

the possibility for negative and critical thinking as well as the possibility and need for reawakening it in order to negate the existing state of society. According to Marcuse, the world is inherently contradictory and therefore is continuously contradicting itself. With help from negative thinking it is possible to abstract from reality, a critique that is performed from within these contradictions. The crucial aspect is not only to revive Hegel, but it is in Hegel that dialectical thinking is first developed into a reality-negating method, a thinking essentially alienated from the established universe of discourse and action. The fact that it is alienated in this sense marks out a potentiality: not to be totally included in that which is supposed to be criticized, but to keep a distance to reality and screen it. According to Marcuse, dialectics depart from an experience of the world as unfree; the human being is also alienated in this sense: one does not live one's life as oneself. The interpretation of the world should according to Marcuse not only be made on the basis of what it is, but essentially on the basis of what it is not, that is, in relation to what is excluded and prohibited from developing.[53]

If it now can be determined that Marcuse's theory is in a fundamental way Marxist, it is also without a doubt that Marxism has continuously a need to return to and use Hegel's dialectical thinking. Marcuse strengthens his Marxism through Hegel.

### d) One-dimensional man and the crisis of negative thinking

Marcuse's late book *One-dimensional Man* (1964) is neither explicitly a book on Hegel nor directly about the question of dialectics. Rather it is an analysis of capitalist society, which is more pessimistic than many of his earlier works. Nonetheless, even here, he still seeks out those possibilities for revolutionary praxis. The relevance of this book for our study here is that, indirectly, Marcuse makes dialectics into a key question surrounding the possibility of resistance within advanced industrial societies. Because both the human and society are characterized by one-dimensionality, dialectics and the two-dimensional possibility of negative and critical thinking is lacking.

The advanced industrial society contains two contradictory tendencies: on the one hand society, it has the ability and the tools to prevent qualitative changes. Industrial society, as an irrational society despite the semblance of reason, blocks social transformation and paralyzes critique. On the other

---

[53] Marcuse, "A Note on Dialectic", in Marcuse, *Reason and Revolution*, pp. vii-xvi.

hand, there are forces within society that could break through these embankments.[54] But the potentialities of critique are undermined in that they are limited to certain platforms, with oppositions integrated and rendered harmless. Society has built a semblance of reason so strong that all contradictions appear as irrational and every resistance seems thereby impossible.[55] Marcuse still places his hope in a negative thinking that is supposed to make visible how irrational existing society is, and to show up the ways in which the negation of negativity is possible. But one-dimensional society does everything to triumph over its contradictions. A two-dimensional thinking, on the other hand, is dialectical, and it would not try to win over the real contradictions, but rather depart from them in a productive way. Such a way of thinking presupposes an experience of the world's antagonism, which is (at least) two-dimensional. If philosophy is guided by this experience it can, according to Marcuse, distinguish between semblance and reality, untruth and truth or unfreedom and freedom, and thus initiate a movement that can resist the totalitarian form of society.[56] But it is the two-dimensional way of thinking or the two-dimensional character of dialectical logics that makes it possible for thinking to grasp the antagonistic reality,[57] and to develop counter images to reality.[58]

To some degree Marcuse in this book also discusses Hegel's philosophy in order to strengthen his own materialist theory. With help from Hegel, Marcuse tries to emphasize the importance for dialectical thinking to let itself be guided by the nature of its object. According to Marcuse, Hegel criticized the critical philosophy of his time for being afraid of its object, and he demanded instead that philosophy fully grasp how its logic is concretized in its objects. Dialectical logics cannot be merely abstract and formal since it is determined by concrete reality. Marcuse thinks that if the historical content of reality enters into a relation with the dialectical concept it can reach concretization. Logical truth thus also becomes historical truth.[59] Thinking absorbs the antagonistic content and real tensions of a historical situation in order to process its dialectic and to oppose its apparent one-dimensional structure.

---

[54] Marcuse, *One Dimensional Man: The Ideology of Industrial Society* (London: Sphere, 1968), pp. 9-15.
[55] Marcuse, *One Dimensional Man*, pp. 19ff.
[56] Marcuse, *One Dimensional Man*, pp. 105ff.
[57] Marcuse, *One Dimensional Man*, pp. 111-112
[58] Marcuse, *One Dimensional Man*, pp. 112ff.
[59] Marcuse, *One Dimensional Man*, pp. 116ff.

In the end, the positive and one-dimensional thinking risks overcoming the negativity of two-dimensional thinking, since the positive affirms whatever is actual and does not construct any counter images of it.[60] This suffocation of the oppositional forces leads to the possibility for reality to be ruled under its own positive form and can develop its repressive violence in an undisturbed way.[61] But it is important to highlight the fact that Marcuse in this book also explicitly discusses Hegel's philosophy in order to establish his own idea of a critical thinking that seeks to resist one-dimensionality. Even if his theory is essentially informed by Marx, Marcuse's Marxism makes itself dependent on Hegel's dialectics, as a form of dialectics that has the ability to realize and concretize the rational.

At the same time it seems possible to question Marcuse's general affirmation of and maybe naïve position in relation to Hegel. Marcuse does not reflect on society's ability to integrate contradictions and critique, in order to undermine them as being strictly a Hegelian problem. In contrast, Adorno tries to explain society's ability to make its own negation into a part of its functioning as a principle that indeed comes from Hegel. In Adorno, the question of negative thinking is therefore shot through with ambivalence. Adorno sees in it both the way that the system maintains its grips as well as providing the possibility for real subversive critique. Also other commentators have put Marcuse's affirmation of Hegel into question. How much of Hegel's theory is Marcuse really embracing? Kellner notes, for example, that Marcuse's second book on Hegel is barely at all critical of Hegel; Marx was more critical than Marcuse.[62] In addition, Alasdair MacIntyre problematizes the fact that Marcuse assumes several doubtful dimensions from Hegel, for example the thought that Hegel is realizing history (and then letting Marx take over).[63] Martin Jay writes that Marcuse tends to formulate an identity philosophy, whereas it is precisely this dimension of identity in Hegel which Adorno will criticize later, as the principle oppressing the non-identical.[64] Nevertheless, all this points to the general importance of Hegel for Marcuse's Marxism.

---

[60] Marcuse, *One Dimensional Man*, pp. 120ff.
[61] Marcuse, *Schriften 4*, p. 370.
[62] Kellner, *Herbert Marcuse and the Crisis of Marxism*, pp. 144ff.
[63] MacIntyre, *Marcuse*, pp. 31ff.
[64] Martin Jay, *The Dialectical Imagination: A History of the Frankfurt School and the Institute of Social Research 1923–1950* (Berkeley: University of California Press, 1996), pp. 60ff.

It is not until his text "Zum Begriff der Negation in der Dialektik" (1966) that Marcuse discusses Hegel's dialectics in a critical way similar to Adorno. He here puts forward its conformist tendencies, which are actualized when the negation is only a semblance in Hegel. The negation is no real negation, rather it serves to stabilize Hegel's system. In the end this always means that it is the existing state of affairs that is reproducing itself, such that the negativity does not become a source for change. In Marcuse's view, Marx risks also falling into this trap as long as theory does not distance itself from the idea that the future has its source within, and therefore gets stuck inside, the actual state of affairs.[65] The only hope for negativity is to find ways to disturb the prevailing order from outside. It is therefore in relation to this critique of Hegel that resistance can take both anarchic and chaotic forms.[66] But in another text from the same period, about the history of dialectics, Marcuse is, with help from a Marxian argument, arguing in favor of an understanding of the revolutionary dimension of dialectics as its idealistic core, and not just a specific aspect. Even if the uncritical moment in Hegel's dialectic consists in the organization of the contradictions in the harmony of the whole, the critical and radical moment for Marcuse is alive in the singular moments of Hegel's system, which according to Marx means that dialectics are fundamentally revolutionary.[67] Marcuse seems unable to choose between these paths, but dwells in this twilight of Hegel-critique and Hegel-affirmation. Nevertheless, in Marcuse, Hegel reconquers his critical edge.

[65] Marcuse, "The Concept of Negation in the Dialectic", in Marcuse, *Marxism, Revolution and Utopia*, pp. 128ff.
[66] Marcuse, "The Concept of Negation in the Dialectic", p. 131.
[67] Marcuse, "The History of Dialectics", in Marcuse, *Marxism, Revolution and Utopia*, pp. 247 ff., for a similar Hegel-critique, see Marcuse, "A Note on Dialectic", pp. xiiff.

# The Necessary Fetishism of the Work of Art

*Sven-Olov Wallenstein*

> Kultur ist Müll, und Kunst, einer ihrer
> Sektoren doch Ernst als Erscheinung der
> Wahrheit. Das liegt im Doppelcharakter
> des Fetischismus.
> Adorno, *Ästhetische Theorie*

I will approach our theme from an aesthetic angle, or perhaps from an angle that signals something like a limit of the aesthetic, where it passes over either into sociology or economy, or inversely into religion and theology. This angle will be provided by the concept of fetishism, which in a particular way weaves together the aesthetic, the social, and the religious, and has had a long trajectory in the social and human sciences from Marx, through Freud, and up to various versions in contemporary thought.

I will look at this concept in four steps: *first*, the initial formulations in Marx, which have at least an indirect bearing on art; *second*, the debate on the possibility of a de-fetishizing of art that took place between two great Marxist thinkers, of which at least one was also Hegelian, Benjamin and Adorno; *third*, I will trace the consequences of this discussion as they were developed and thought through in Adorno's final work, *Aesthetic Theory*; and *fourth*, by way of a conclusion, I will add a few reflections on the transformations of fetishism in contemporary aesthetics, which will elucidate my title, the necessity of fetishism in the work of art.

## Marx and the fetishism of commodities

The concept has its origins in the mid-eighteenth century, in the early stages of ethnology, and specifically the writings of Charles de Brosses, whose 1760

treatise *Du culte des dieux fétiches* seems to have put the term into circulation.[1] While the concept was known to Hegel, it only surfaces inciden-
tally in his writings and plays no role in the analysis of the present; for
Hegel, it belongs to a superseded stage of development.[2] It is rather in Marx
that it appears as the means for an analysis of the present. Marx too was an
avid reader of anthropology and ethnology,[3] but here I want to stress something else, namely the background of the theory of commodity fetishism in
a particular aesthetic experience, or more precisely the encounter with the
kind of display culture that emerged around the time of the 1851 London
World Exhibition.

In a trajectory that leads from the initial London exhibition, through the
subsequent but lesser known exhibitions in New York ("Exhibition of the
Industry of all Nations," 1853) and Dublin ("Great Industrial Exhibition,"
1853), and up to the "Exposition Universelle" in Paris 1855, a visual culture
emerges in which the juxtaposition of commodities and artworks generated
what we could call an *immersive experience of modernity*. Immersion here
means that artifacts and artworks henceforth would exist in the same space,
not just in order to overthrow or re-evaluate values—to elevate industrial
objects to art, or bring artworks down from their pedestals—but also, and
more importantly, to let us sense the dimension out of which objects
emerge, and to invest them with a magical quality that has the power of
drawing us into their radiance and power. Marx's reaction to the 1851
exhibition in London is paradigmatic when he in *Capital* I: 4 analyzes the
logic of the commodity and shows how it generates, seemingly out of itself,
a particular kind of magic:

[1] On the context of de Brosses' work, see Madeleine David, "Les idées du 18e siècle sur
l'idolatrie, et les audaces de David Hume et du Président de Brosses," *Numen*, vol. 24,
No. 2 (1977): pp. 81-94. For overarching contextualizations of the term, see Emily Apter
and William Pietz (eds.), *Fetishism as Cultural Discourse* (Ithaca: Cornell University
Press, 1993), and Paul-Laurent Assoun, *Le Fétischisme* (Paris: PUF, 2002).
[2] See the fragment on *Volksreligion* in *Werke*, eds. Michel & Moldenhauer (Frankfurt am
Main: Suhrkamp, 1986), 1: pp. 28 and 40, where fetishism is described as an external and
objective mechanism in which spirit evaporates; in the lectures on the philosophy of
history the emphasis instead lies on subjectivity, and the fetish is understood as deprived
of religious autonomy, because it is only a reflection of the believer's will in an inert
object: see *Werke* 12, pp. 123, similarly in the lectures on the philosophy or religion,
*Werke* 16: pp. 294f. In neither case is there however any claim that the concept of fetishism would apply to the present.
[3] See the excerpts in MEGA IV.1, pp. 320-367. For a discussion of the background to
Marx's theory of fetishism, see Antoine Artous, *Marx et le fétichisme: Le marxisme com-
me théorie critique* (Paris: Éditions Syllepse, 2006).

A commodity appears at first sight an extremely obvious, trivial thing. But its analysis brings out that it is a very strange thing, abounding in metaphysical subtleties and theological niceties. So far as it is a use-value, there is nothing mysterious about it, whether we consider it from the point of view that by its properties it satisfies human needs; or that it first takes on these properties as the product of human labour. It is absolutely clear that, by his activity, man changes the forms of the materials of nature in such a way as to make them useful to him. The form of wood, for instance, is altered if a table is made out of it. Nevertheless the table continues to be wood, an ordinary, sensuous thing. But as soon as it emerges as a commodity, it changes into a thing which transcends sensuousness. It not only stands with its feet on the ground, but, in relation to all other commodities, it stands on its head, and evolves out of its wooden brain grotesque ideas, far more wonderful than if it were to begin dancing of its own free will.[4]

Three aspects of Marx's analysis will be highlighted here: *first*, the magic and phantasmagoric power that holds the subject captive—or better: that produces a particular subject of captivity, a subject that exists precisely as a knot in the force field of the phantasma; *second*, how movement, agency, and autonomy are transferred onto the objects because of the inversion of the use-exchange relation, which in turn, and more surprisingly, will form a new bedrock for the idea of aesthetic autonomy; *third*, the new sense of matter and materiality that emerges in between the inherited terms of matter and spirit, folding a spectralized matter and a materialized specter into each other.

First, on the most straightforward level, what is analyzed here is a doubling of use value and exchange value, in which things have become crystallizations of a common social substance, i.e. the force of labor expended in producing them. This doubling, which produces a spectral twin of the real object, is what makes up the fetishistic character of the commodity, and corresponds to the superimposition of symbolical value on everyday objects in religious fetishism. That Marx's concept draws on a tradition in anthropology and comparative religion—as we noted, he probably picks up the term "fetish" from de Brosses—is no doubt what provides his description with its resonances of magical irrationality, but it also records an experience whose result was intended by the organizers of the exhibition. As has been

[4] Karl Marx, *Capital*, vol. 1, trans. Ben Fowkes (London: Penguin, 1976), p. 164.

proposed by Giorgio Agamben,[5] Marx's reflections on the fetish character of the commodity form echo the intentions of the organizers when they opted for Paxton's Crystal Palace project: this would be a building where the "atmosphere" has itself become perceptible, so that the spectator would experience the distant parts of the pavilion as "enveloped in a bluish halo"[6] in which all items on display are enveloped in the same experiential field. The architecture with its play of light and shade, fusing inside and outside in a nature-artifice continuum in this way becomes an extension of the aura of the commodity, or more precisely, an apparatus for the *production* and intensification of the aura as an experience that extends to all objects in its domain.

This idea seems to have been picked up by the organizers of the Paris sequel in 1867. The official guidebook states that the public needs something that will make them "halt, astonished, before the marvels of industry," and what the public desires, they suggest, is to "contemplate an enchanted scene (*un coup d'oeil féerique*), and not similar products, uniformly grouped."[7] Thus, in the Paris version the task seems to have been more about finding a way of countering a development in which the aura would already be in a process of decay, by an intentional re-enchantment of an industrial commodity characterized by seriality, similarity, and uniformity. But regardless of whether the aura is to be intensified or recreated, the strategy of immersion remains the same: to overwhelm the spectator, to produce a sense of awe and wonder that envelops all things.

As for the second point, beyond the fascination exerted by the visual spectacle, Marx's description can also be applied to the idea of the autonomous artwork, in a way that at first might seem paradoxical. On the one hand, the transformation of all things into commodities implies that the sanctity of art is lost; it is cast down from its pedestal. On the other hand, its entry into a sphere of circulation makes it possible for the Kantian framework, which once established autonomy as a distance from the world of utilities, to be derived from a commodity logic in which use value is gradually absorbed into exchange value. Henceforth, it is *because it exists as a commodity*, severed from its former use as moral or religious instruction, that the artwork can be understood to create its own value in a sphere of

---

[5] Giorgio Agamben, *Stanzas: Word and Phantasm in Western Culture*, trans. Ronald L. Martinez (Minneapolis: University of Minnesota Press, 1993).
[6] Mary Merrifield, "The Armory of Colours as Exemplified in the Exhibition," cited in Agamben, *Stanzas*, p. 39.
[7] Cited in Agamben, *Stanzas*, p. 38.

pure, abstract exchange. The artwork is the ultimate fetish, the supreme commodity, and the pure differential relations of economic exchange value are as it were realized exorbitantly in the artwork, whose price is just as open to infinite contextual fluctuations as its aesthetic value.

Put in more sociological terms, this is the moment when the artist's entry into the market creates a new mobility, transforms the audience into an indeterminate public, and gradually comes to render the hierarchies, vocabularies, and codes of the academic tradition obsolete, which for the artists was just as much felt as a liberation as a threat. Here it must be emphasized that commodity fetishism is not a psychological structure, not some perceptual or intellectual mistake that should be corrected, but an objective social structure that determines consciousness and its products. Thus, if art becomes autonomous in the same way as the commodity becomes a fetish, this process cannot be undone by a shift in perception, or a return to a natural object form, since the unfolding of the commodity form irreversibly draws all things into its orbit. On the level of consciousness, this is the condition that allows for art and artists, in a paradoxical counter-movement to the social logic that conditions them, to claim the position of *truth* (an art that saves, preserves, or redeems a dimension of authenticity) against falsity (a commodity that alienates, levels and perverts all human values). This doubling, moving ceaselessly between market value and aesthetic value, and yet upholding an invisible though strict border between them, opens the game of a modernism that locates itself at the critical limit of capitalism while still being dependent on it—tied to its other with an "umbilical cord of gold",[8] as Clement Greenberg noted—with all the shifting alliances, projections, and mutual aggressions that such a game entails.

Third and finally, we must note the particular status given to materiality in Marx's account. Nature still furnishes the materials, the wood whose form is changed when it is turned into a table; but when the table enters into the sphere of exchange and circulation, it is transformed into a thing that "transcends sensuousness," in Fowkes' translation, or, closer to the German: "a sensuously super-sensuous thing" (*ein sinnlich übersinnliches Ding*). It is important here to retain the paradox; the thing is not only *both* sensible and supersensible, but supersensible in a *sensuous, sensible way*, so that the material dimension, while not simply disappearing, becomes as it

---

[8] Clement Greenberg, "Avant-Garde and Kitsch" (1939), repr. in Greenberg, *The Collected Essays and Criticism. Vol. 1, Perceptions and Judgments, 1939–1944*, ed. John O'Brian (Chicago: University of Chicago Press, 1986), p. 11.

were de- or immaterialized, and then reinscribed in a movement of doubling or "spectralization," which in turn produces a system of mediating and differentiating frames that separate and mediate the two sides—the "visor effect," as Derrida has called it.[9]

So, the three aspects of the artwork that would seem to emerge from this are the following: it holds us *captive* by exerting a particular fascination that is inextricably bound up with, yet not identical to, that of commodities; it is endowed with an *autonomy* precisely because, by entering into the world of commodities, it not only becomes severed from earlier ties, but also appears to transcend the commodity logic that conditions it; and, it has a peculiar *materiality*, sensible and supersensible at the same time, two sides that call upon each while being mediated through a particular structure of framing.

## Aura and autonomy

A particularly complex take on this occurs in the debate between Adorno and Benjamin, on the occasion of the latter's essay on the work of art in the age of its mechanical reproducibility.[10] The main exhibit, apart from Benjamin's essay, will be Adorno's famous letter to Benjamin from March 18 1936, from which I will only extract the particular problem of the possibility of overcoming fetishism.

Benjamin's Reproduction essay precisely identifies the three aspects of fetishism that I have delineated above—magic, autonomy, and the materiality—and he does so in the multi-faceted concept of the *aura* that he

---

[9] See Derrida, *Spectres de Marx* (Paris: Galilée, 1993). The visor effect refers to how material frames and devices become props or instruments for the ghostly return of the dead. Derrida develops this on the basis of a reading of *Hamlet*, where the father's ghost always requires a technical supplement, more precisely the material structure of the armor, in order to appear as present at the very limit of appearing and presence. At the same time, this spectralizes materiality, so that the technical supplement, in relaying the two, at once belongs to and does not belong to the empirical world.

[10] The essay exists in three different versions, printed in *Gesammelte Schriften*, eds. Rolf Tiedemann & Hermann Schweppenhäuser (Frankurt am Main: Suhrkamp, 1980). I/2 (first and third version) and VII/1 (third version); for a discussion of the differences between these versions and the publication history, cf. the editorial remarks in *GS* VII/2: pp. 661-90. English translation by Harry Zohn, in *Illuminations*, ed. Hannah Arendt (New York: Schocken Books, 1969). Henceforth cited: German/English. The exchanges between Adorno and Benjamin on early drafts for the Arcades project would also be important for our theme, but I leave them aside here.

suggests belongs to the traditional work of art,[11] and which he now proposes must be dismantled for a new, political art to emerge.

*First*, Benjamin stresses the magical qualities of the aura: it is derived from the model of the monk in his cell, and infused with a presence that sets the subject apart in a non-social space of contemplation. Just as the artist taps into a magical source, there is a mystical attitude required on the part of the beholder for the work to release its secrets, and Benjamin contrasts the attitude of the magician, who performs an *actio in distans* so as to trans-figure the object, to that of the surgeon, who enters into the object, takes it apart in order to understand its structure.

This comes across in cinema, where the distancing built into the pro-ductive apparatus encourages the spectator to "test" the actor, and where identification occurs only through the technological mediation. The actor is estranged (*verfremdet*) from himself, since his performance is broken up into a series of discrete moments. If the traditional painter employs a magic charm in order to release the inner essence of the object, the filmmaker penetrates the object in order to decompose it in a series of analytical operations. The new analysis of movement and social space made possible in cinema in fact renders it analogous to psychoanalysis—and Benjamin famously speaks of an "optical unconscious"—where the seemingly mar-ginal slips in our discourse are brought to attention.

*Second*, the artwork has aspired to a condition of singularity and ori-ginality, to an autonomy that would set it apart from other forms of pro-duction; but as we saw, this it could do by drawing on commodity fetishism in order to safeguard its own stance vis-à-vis the sphere of other things; as an absolute fetish, existing only in the space of exchange—it has no use, which is why it can attain an infinite economic value—it escapes the sub-stitutability of the commodity. For Benjamin, this is now being transformed because of technical reproducibility, which enters into the substance of the work: the new technological forces of production render the idea of originality obsolete, and the work steps out of its transcendent space-time in order to become a thing among other things, which means undoing its fetishistic magic, making it available for mass consumption, and providing it with a capacity for political agency.

---

[11] The concept of "aura" in Benjamin is obviously complex and highly stratified, and the remarks here only relate to the use of the term in the Artwork essay; for an overview of different senses of the term, see Josef Fürnkäs, "Aura," in Michael Opitz & Erdmut Wizisla (eds.), *Benjamins Begriffe* (Frankfurt am Main: Suhrkamp, 2000), pp. 95-147.

*Third*, while in the Artwork essay aura is defined as the authority and singularity of the original, Benjamin also adds an analogy to the aura of "natural objects," which points to a another and equally decisive dimension: an *interior, singular, and unique distance* impossible to abolish by any physical proximity, "the unique phenomenon of a distance, however close it may be" (*"einmalige* Erscheinung einer Ferne, so nah sie sein mag," I/2, 441). In one sense this points to the transcendence of the work over and above its material incarnation, the fact that it belongs to a realm of aesthetic objects by being removed from ordinary space-time. But it also relates back to the *Einmaligkeit* of ritual and sacrificial events, and so to the magic origin of art.

The ritual dimension, Benjamin suggests, was perfected in Symbolism, as in the case of Mallarmé's at once sacral and formalist poetics, where secular officiates are to read aloud from the great Book, *Le Livre* (which was Mallarmé's great, unfinished, and no doubt interminable project), so as to regenerate the world on the basis of an art that is nonetheless entirely pure, that goes beyond the world by being altogether Word. But this aura, Benjamin suggests, cannot survive the structure of technological reproducibility, which in modernity has been inscribed into the very core of the object—immediately in cinema and photography, and in a mediate way in the other arts, such as painting, sculpture, literature, each of which in their respective ways find themselves drawn into the force field of the first two, so that they will increasingly tend to appear as reproduced already from the outset. Things now come closer, they shed their distance, and they appear more similar.

This severs the object from its traditional context in a process that is equally destructive and liberating. Benjamin speaks rather brutally of a "liquidation" (*Liquidation*) of the tradition,[12] although for him this in fact promises the emancipation from the burden of an oppressive history. If the aesthetic work of art in its insistent uniqueness originated in a secularization of the religious cult object, and in the guise of a substitute fetish was developed to perfection in Symbolism, this residual ritual dimension now disappears in the era of reproduction, where there is no more transcendence or mystery, only what Benjamin, perhaps somewhat surprisingly,

---

[12] This brutal vocabulary is no coincidence, and it can be found throughout Benjamin's writings, which in fact contain a rich array of such "destructive" terms that are not only limited to the sphere of aesthetics: *Liquidierung, Zertrümmerung, Zerstörung, Verwischung, Zerstörung, Vernichtung,* etc. For an overview, see Dag T. Andersson, "Destruktion/Konstruktion," *Benjamins Begriffe,* p. 183.

calls the "exhibition value" (*Ausstellungswert*). This seems at once to refer to the work as commodity (as in the world exhibitions, although magic indeed returned here in the guise of fetishism and phantasmagoria) and to the work's capacity to communicate and enter into the fabric of social life.[13] Divested of its cult value, the work of art steps out of the aesthetic sphere, and this loss of autonomy renders it useful for new purposes, which for Benjamin means agitation and the active shaping of communal life.

Thus, by dispelling commodity fetishism the destruction of the aura returns art to practice rather than sets it up for contemplation, it gives us a positive approach to serial production and typical objects, and finally, shows us the work as a material construct made up of parts, rather than a mysteriously unified whole. The proximity of this to Bauhaus, Constructivism, the discourse of the artist-engineer etc., has often been noted, and Benjamin himself develops this in other adjacent texts that deal with architecture and literature, for instance "Experience and Poverty" and "The Author as Producer," although I will say no more about this here.

To these claims, then, Adorno's letter proposes a series of powerful counterarguments,[14] which will subsequently also form the bedrock for his final claims in *Aesthetic Theory*, where they were developed into a fully-fledged theory of the necessity of fetishism.

First, against the immediate revocation of the artwork's use value Adorno proposes that the reification inherent in the traditional artwork in its separation from the immediacy of life should not be seen just as a loss or deprivation, but, more fundamentally, as a necessary condition for its capacity to resist society and attain a certain transcendence in relation to the actual world, which is the very precondition for its power to act as a *critique*. It is just as "bourgeois," Adorno claims, to deny the reification of the subject in cinema (the aura of the theater actor that disappears in the technical dimension of montage), as it is naïve and all too hasty—"it would border on anarchism" (129)—to deny the reification of the autonomous work in favor of an immediate use, i.e., in favor of an art that would lay claim to direct inventions in the praxis of life.

---

[13] Benjamin explains the term by reference to the development of cult objects in religion, which become more accessible as they are put on display, and not directly in terms of institutions like museums; as we will see, his argument can however also be linked to the practices of the avant-garde of the time.
[14] See the letter from March 18, 1936, in Benjamin and Adorno, *The Complete Correspondence 1928–1940*, ed. Henri Lonitz, trans. Nicholas Walker (Cambridge: Polity Press, 1999). The following citations with page number are from the same source.

There is indeed for Adorno too an essential disenchantment of the aesthetic moment that occurs through the advance of technique, but the difference is that this has to be understood precisely as an *artistic* technique, in terms of the immanent laws of construction for the work itself. Mallarmé's poetic materialism, which shows us that poetry is made of words, blanks, and the spacing of the page, as well as Schönberg's dodecaphonic method of composing that imposes a seemingly foreign set of "objective" parameters on the composer's subjectivity, dissolve the traditional idea of creation as a mystical act much more efficiently than the practices of the feuilleton writer or the industrial division of labor in the movies, whose disenchanting effects Adorno perceives as vastly exaggerated.

"I cannot express my feelings about the entire piece more clearly than by telling you how much I would like to see a study of Mallarmé precisely as a counter-point to this essay" (128), Adorno writes, a counter-point which implies that it is only when *l'art pour l'art* is seen as essentially related to popular art, as its *precise and determined other*, that we can understand the dialectical totality as a contradictory whole. The aura is broken down just as much in the autonomous work as in the art of mass consumption, but in the first case it is because of an inner, formal development while in the second it is because of external demands, and thus, reification and fetishism are neither simply a loss nor a gain, but both of these at once. In this sense, fetishism cannot be undone in the name of a return to the real, to life, or to immediacy, even though all ways of assuming its challenge are not equal: one can simply give in to it and accept the conditions that it imposes on production, or, which I think is Adorno's Hegelian moment, while understanding it as the necessary condition of modernity, one can at the same time attempt to disentangle a moment of truth that through this necessity also points beyond it, which is the dimension of reconciliation that cannot however be simply presented as a content.

The two extremes, autonomous and popular art, touch each other, but only if they are credited with the same dialectical value, whereas Benjamin appears to simply reject one of them as if it were, in Adorno's expression, "counter-revolutionary" (128). And, he continues, it would be either a bourgeois or a proletarian romanticism, but in both cases a romanticism, to opt exclusively for one of the two versions. In a famous and often cited phrase Adorno summarizes his critique of Benjamin's project to directly transform art to life, when he writes of the respective works of the avant-garde and mass culture that they both "bear the stigmata of capitalism, both contain elements of change (…) Both are torn halves of an integral freedom, to which, however, they do not add up" ("Beide tragen die Wundmale des Kapitalismus, beide enthalten Elemente der Veränderung (…) beide sind die auseinandergerissenen Hälften der ganzen Freiheit, die doch aus ihnen nicht sich zusammenaddieren lässt") (130). The true is not the whole (a figure on which Adorno will constantly elaborate, up to his dense formula in *Negative Dialectics* in which the whole is the *untrue*) but the *whole differs from itself*, it is split into two halves that can just as little be reconciled as one of them can be simply discarded. And as we will see, the hinge between the two halves will have an essential relation to the fetishism of the work as something that must be worked through, both in theory and practice.

### The concept of fetishism in *Aesthetic Theory*

The debate with Benjamin that unfolded around the Reproduction essay would continue to inform Adorno's postwar writings, and can be taken as one of the essential threads that run throughout his work: it engages the crucial features of art's autonomy, its relation to the social means and relations of production as well as its own immanent technical procedures, how art is encountered as a phenomenological given,[15] and ultimately its claim to a "truth content" (*Wahrheitsgehalt*) that would be both conditioned by society and set apart from it. While Adorno's analysis of this passes through many stages, I will here limit myself to considering the analysis of fetishism proposed in *Aesthetic Theory*, where the concept is dealt with in a way that draws out all of its conflicted and even contradictory implications.

The concept is, to be sure, never given a sustained treatment, and we must extract elements of a theory from its many occurrences in shifting contexts that seem to preclude a systematic analysis; and yet, a synoptic overview of his claims show them to be distributed along three lines. *First*, fetishism is perceived as a *negative* process that obscures true relations and processes, whereas art would have the power to counteract its mystifying force; fetishism belongs to the logic of commodities, and if it enters into art, it is as a destructive force. *Second*, fetishism appears as a fundamentally *ambivalent* phenomenon, in being both what art has to fight against and its

---

[15] Shortly after the exchanges with Benjamin, Adorno develops this aspect in the essay "Über den Fetischcharakter der Musik und die Regression des Hörens" (1938), where it is explicitly linked to sensory apprehension, and shows that the fetish cannot be located solely within the domain of material objects, but must be understood in terms of a general objectification independent of substrate.

inescapable condition; there is no art that is not caught up in commodifi-cation, and the task must be to fight it from within. And *third*, as a way of interlacing the first two claims, fetishism is not just a negative although unavoidable external condition of art in the administered world, but also, and more fundamentally, it is the *condition of possibility for its truth content*: it is the rigidifying power of aesthetic objectification that gives art its necessary distance to society, and the good and bad are not external to each other, but as it were two sides of the same loop, so that truth belongs to falsity just as much as falsity to truth.

In this, fetishism is inscribed in the movement of negative dialectics that pits concepts against themselves, not just in order to distinguish a positive sense from a negative one, but more fundamentally to see how they are inextricably intertwined and require a strategic refunctioning.[16] In order to approach this final intertwining, it is however useful to begin by sorting out various claims listed above in a schematic fashion, even though this un-doubtedly does some violence to the "paratactic" organization of the text, which does not describe a cumulative movement from one argument to another. As Adorno writes in a letter to Rolf Tiedemann: "a book's almost ineluctable movement from antecedent to conclusion proved so incompat-ible with the content that for this reason any organization in the traditional sense (...) proved impracticable. The book must, so to speak, be written in equally weighted, paratactical parts that are arranged around a midpoint that they express through their constellation."[17]

1. As a *negative* concept, which threatens to overtake art, while the latter still retains the capacity to propose a series of countermoves, fetishism enters into art as the idea of the artwork as a thing that can be possessed, in analogy to the idea of an exploitable property within the psychic economy of the self that can be assessed in terms of a balance sheet: "heard the Ninth Symphony tonight, enjoyed myself so and so much" (27/16). The demand for possession that aspires to treat the spiritual like the material makes a

---

[16] Elsewhere I have tried to trace the trajectory of "realism" in Adorno; see my "Adorno's Realism," *Baltic Worlds*, Vol. IX (4) (2016), pp. 28-34. The matrix for his use of the term was in fact established roughly at the same time as the debate with Benjamin, in the quarrel in the late thirties over expressionism that set Lukács against Bloch (a debate in which Adorno himself never took part), and it is developed in Adorno's postwar writings, ushering in the final complex stance in *Aesthetic Theory*.

[17] Cited in Tiedemann, "Editorisches Nachwort," *Ästhetische Theorie* (Frankfurt am Main: Suhrkamp, 1973), p. 541; "Editor's Afterword," *Aesthetic Theory*, trans. Robert Hullot-Kentor (London: Continuum, 1997), p. 462. Page references given directly in the text are henceforth to these two editions: German/English.

fetish of works and their hope of duration in the face of the vicissitudes of time, and pushes them into a false eternity that is nothing but a "sickness unto death" (49/36); rather than the mourning that for Adorno must accompany the acknowledgment of art's finitude and inescapable link to time, it wants to immortalize that which is necessarily bound up with the movement of history.

Seemingly opposed to this fetishist desire for permanence, and yet a consequence of it, the enjoyment procured, as a rest of the mimetic impulse that lies at the origin of art, can in turn be "bartered off as a commodity" (32/22). This indicates the extent to which traces of this archaic fetish at the origin of art still linger on in the present, although in such way that they become reduced to consumable stimuli: "The consumer arbitrarily projects his impulses—mimetic remnants—on whatever is presented to him." (33/23) Inversely, there is a false and equally fetishistic return to nature that is nothing but a "pantheistic subterfuge" (115/96), which appears as the mask of an endlessly repetitive fate: natural beauty, to the extent that it wants to reach back beyond the mediation through modernity, would contain such a threatening refusal of subjectivity, almost as an overcompensation for the unbridled subjectivization that reduces the work to a bundle of stimuli.

Against these three forms of fetishism—the intrusion of the commodity as a model for possession, the work's dissolution into stimuli, and the fateful return to nature as a regressive countermove—Adorno proposes that the "darkness" of art might be a way to "cancel the spell that this world casts by the overwhelming force of appearance, the fetish character of the commodity," first and foremost since artworks "by their very existence (...) postulate the experience of what does not exist and thereby come into conflict with the latter's actual non-existence" (93/76).

The power of the fetish can however also enter into the very structure of the work, so for instance in the idea of an essential "intuitability" (*Anschaulichkeit*), such that it itself becomes a fetish if it is severed from the conceptual moment: the demand for immediacy violates the fact that art is neither concept nor intuition, but precisely a way of protesting against their separation (148/126). On another level, the very idea of the production of art as dependent on a conception of genius, which from Kant onward began to be understood as a "separated, abstract subjectivity" (255/224),[18] harbors its particular fetishism, this time oriented toward the depth of the artist; finally, at the other end of the artistic spectrum, the technical forces of production should not to be fetishized in art (323/284), just as little as, more generally, the rationalization of means (439/377), which echoes the earlier critique of Benjamin.

2. As an *ambivalent* concept, fetishism denotes something that does not just threaten to overtake the work from the outside—in order to eventually reappear in its internal structures, as in reified forms of intuitability, genius, and technique—but it belongs to its very mode of existence. If the new becomes a fetish by being drawn into the logic of the commodity, this cannot be dispelled by simply rejecting the latter, but must be criticized from within the work; it expresses "the paradox of all art that is no longer self-evident", that "something made exists for its own sake" (41/29), and in this sense, it is one with the claim to autonomy. New ways of conceiving works, such as musical notations that rebel against fixation and aspire to create a new latitude and openness in composition and performance practices, are in one sense regressive, Adorno suggests, and their attempts at resuscitating "neumic-graphic imitations of musical gestures" are "simply reification of an older level (154/130), and yet they have a validity in registering how the work suffers from being a thing, from the fetishization of what in itself is a process: autonomy is a "rigidification" (*Erstarrung*) that breeds insurgencies, and yet there is no way back. In a slightly different context, where the issue is the capacity of art to deliver meaning, he notes the theological roots of this conception, but underscores that it must not be conflated with revelation, since this would "amount to the unreflective repetition of its unavoidable fetish character on the level of theory." (162/139)[19]

The fetishism inherent in autonomy however requires that art always be looked at from the outside as well as from the inside, so as to remind us of its dual character: it is at once autonomy and *fait social*, both of which contain their respective forms of fetishism. In an almost Cagean moment Adorno suggests that we think of music piped into a restaurant, where the

[18] Trans. mod. Hullot-Kentor gives "dirempted, abstract subjectivity", but Adorno's point in this context is not that this subjectivity would be characterized by an inner split, but that it is set apart from its social conditions; it is *abgetrennt*, not *entzweit*.
[19] Trans. mod. The adjective "unavoidable" (*unausweichlich*) has unfortunately disappeared from the translation, which somewhat skews the argument. Adorno's claim is rather that fetishism *must be*, cannot *not be*, repeated on the level of theory, since it is unavoidable, but that this repetition must be carried out in a reflexive way.

"hum of conversation and the rattle of dishes and whatever" (375/328) become part of the work; similarly, the positivist aesthetics that he had denounced earlier for its dissolution of the work into consumable stimuli, for being a fetishism of sensory surfaces, can just as much be marshaled against the "fetishization of artworks that is itself part and parcel of the cultural industry and aesthetic decline," and it points to the "dialectical element that no artwork is ever pure" (399/347). Fetishism is inevitable, inevitably positive as well as negative, which is why its destructive aspects on one level can be marshaled against those on another; it is a split pheno-menon, as it were ceaselessly mutating into its other and back again.

3. As the *condition of possibility for truth*, fetishism first of all sets the work apart from empirical reality, so that simply by virtue of such distance, not because of its actual content, it stands for something else; through its alienation it is also something positive, and what is set up as an "alien and rudimentary fetish that endures in opposition to the subject is the pleni-potentiary of the nonalienated" (173/149). This distance, the alienation into an illusory pure spiritual sphere, is itself the result of the work's spiritual-ization (*Vergeistigung*),[20] which makes it stand apart from the world through its inner facture, its being made into a self-enclosed unity.

In the section that develops the most detailed explication of fetishism (334-338/295-298), by the German editor subtitled "Art's double character: *fait social* and autonomy; on the fetish character,"[21] Adorno stresses that the modern phenomenon of art's emphatic opposition to society is what gives it a social content, not its use of technologies or the empirical stuff that enters into it: art is something "crystallizing in itself as something unique to itself" (335/296), and its seeming asociality is in fact the determinate negation of a

---

[20] An analysis of the series of terms clustering around *Geist* and *Vergeistigung* could be undertaken, which would be analogous to the one here proposed for the term fetish with its cognates. Spirit is on the one hand that into which artworks can be alienated, the domain of the otherworldly, purely ideal etc., on the other hand that which emerges from the inner articulation of the work and exists by virtue of its material configuration. As Adorno often suggest, the process of "spiritualization" in modern art is what from the point of view of traditional art leads toward its becoming non-art, *Entkunstung*, since it increasingly demands that coherence be derived from an internal logic and not from external models. In this sense, a "materialism of the signifier" (to use a term foreign to Adorno's lexicon, to which he would possibly object, although for other reasons) in literature, or a pure materialism of color in monochrome painting, would be wholly con-sistent with a fully spiritualized art.

[21] The headings are not Adorno's own, but have been inserted in the table of contents by the editors, and they greatly facilitate the reader's orientation; in the 1997 Continuum edition cited here they have unfortunately been omitted.

determinate society. This however leads into a series of paradoxes: arts' only function is to be functionless, its enchantment is disenchantment, its essential quality is to contradict itself, all of which with respect to commodity fetishism ushers in the claim that "[u]nless it [art] reifies itself, it becomes a commodity" (335/296). It is true that works seal themselves off from what they truly are, i.e. determinate negations of society, and this turns them into ideology to the extent that they posit something spiritual outside of society, but, at the same time, this spiritual dimension—*Geist* now understood not as a sphere outside of the material, but as the *facture* of works, the interplay of their constituent parts that takes them beyond the world of *facts*—is what gives them their critical purchase on reality.

This is why being guilty of fetishism is not in itself disqualifying; nothing is outside of guilt, and the truth content of artworks is predicated upon the fetish character that sets them apart from the empirical world and its instrumentality, to the effect that only what is *useless* is capable of prefiguring another *use* beyond the equation use-exchange value that is the precondition for commodity fetishism. This is a dimension of the fetish that goes beyond commodities, and artworks can neither exclude nor deny it; they must insist, fetishistically, on their coherence, their *Stimmigkeit*, on being that absolute that they cannot be, whereas simply divesting themselves of fetishism would enmesh them in a false consciousness and a shortsighted praxis that in fact prolongs blindness. Thus, while artworks are never simple things, they nevertheless participate in reification by being modeled on external things, which is why aesthetic objectivation always entail fetishism just as much as it provokes rebellion, as comes across for instance in the idea of "classicality" (441/378), which is a petrification that works must ceaselessly and perhaps even hopelessly fight since it emerges from their own thinghood and from their aspiration to transcend time. In this they are both part of the cultural apparatus and its commodification machinery—they are, in Adorno's stark words, "refuse" (*Müll*, 459/392)—as well as the "appearance of truth" (*Erscheinung der Wahrheit*), they are how truth appears to us as, although broken through the lens of untruth: such is the inescapable double nature of fetishism. If, on the one hand, they always tend to relapse back into a fetishism in which they were rooted already in their archaic origin, and which today has been transformed into the most insidious of processes, on the other hand, "without the fetishism that now verges on becoming art's untruth," there would be no *truth*, since "[o]nly through fetishism, the blinding of the artwork vis-à-vis the reality of which it is a part, does the work transcend the spell of the reality principle as something spiritual" (596/432).

## Transformations of fetishism

By way of a conclusion, then, a few words on what seems like emergent features of fetishism today, located as it is on the threshold between the fetishism of autonomy and that of the commodity, or rather in the loop that binds them together in a structure that "verges on becoming art's untruth."

On a general level, we may detect a process that shifts the parameters of commodity fetishism by transferring the logic of the spectacle back onto production itself: the commodity is no longer primarily a material object that crystallizes labor and hides its origins, but it is itself an immaterial entity called information, almost as if the process of ideology would transform its own production into a spectacle to be enjoyed. If Marx in *Capital* I: 4 proposed that the material production process was concealed in order to endow the commodity with a spectral and mysterious life of its own, making it into "a very strange thing, abounding in metaphysical subtleties and theological niceties," it is now the process itself that is displayed, often couched in a vocabulary of participation and interactivity. While this process is not particular to art, it is here that it reaches a self-reflexive visibility, precisely by folding this visibility back on itself, which in turn produces a subject of captivity even more insidiously caught up in itself than before.

Looking back at the historical avant-garde, which without being explicitly named formed the backdrop for the debate between Benjamin and Adorno in the thirties, we can see how Benjamin's suggestions were linked to a set of new exhibition strategies, which, even though they may have been unknown to him, provide a particular resonance to his conception of "exhibition value." From the experiments of the Russian Constructivist avant-garde to its German counterparts, from El Lissistzky to Alexander Dorner, there emerged a vast spectrum of techniques for displaying artworks that in one respect drew on the kind of immersive experience that had been inherited from the nineteenth-century world fairs, while also wanting to foster a critical and reflective attitude—"testing," as Benjamin said—in their audiences.[22] This was an attempt to bring art back to life and everyday experience, to dispel its magical aura and endow it with a political

---

[22] For a discussion, see Charlotte Klonk, *Spaces of Experience: Art Gallery Interiors from 1800 to 2000* (New Haven: Yale University Press, 2009).

agency. The same argument recurs in the 1960s, notably in Conceptual art, where the very identity and materiality of the work itself was at stake (sometimes phrased in terms of a "dematerialization")[23] and audience involvement extended not just to judging, but sometimes even to actualizing the works themselves. With varying levels of clarity and success, the target was the work as a commodity, as a thing that could be bought and sold, and whose value was predicated on being enclosed in the enchanted sphere of the aesthetic.

Processes, contexts, framing conditions, or more generally ideas, were precisely that which emerged as commodities at the moment when Adorno was about to finish his *Aesthetic Theory* in the late 1960s. In a certain way, these are sensuously supersensuous things, *sinnlich übersinnliche Dinge*, but also, inversely, supersensuously sensuous things, *übersinnlich sinnliche Dinge*: they are ideal objects that can be materialized in a manifold of ways, of which a whole tradition of conceptual and post-conceptual art provides us with a vast array of specific modalities. Adorno's reluctance toward these new works, which he observed primarily in the open forms in music, to a lesser extent in the visual arts, is well known, and in many respects his criticisms echo those against Benjamin in the thirties: their claim to become part of the real world by removing the framing conditions that provide their transcendence converts them into a set of stimuli and deprives them of the capacity of pointing beyond themselves, and they undo the capacity of the subject by abandoning themselves to the blind powers of processes or of the material—all of which, as Adorno at one point remarks scathingly (his target is Cage and the power of pure natural sound), "degenerates at once into culture."[24]

Adorno's resistance to the new forms of artistic production in the sixties was in hindsight misguided, in the end a losing battle, and in this respect it might seem as if Benjamin would have had the last word. But maybe it is more fruitful to see their dialectical exchange as continuing into the present, and to use the concept of fetishism as an analytical tool, rather than as something that at one point would be undone, overcome, or something that simply sinks into irrelevance. For in the process suggested above, the trans-

---

[23] See the rich collection of sources for this development in Lucy Lippard, *Six Years: The Dematerialization of the Art Object from 1966 to 1972* (Berkeley: University of California Press, 1973).

[24] Adorno, "Vers une musique informelle" (1961), in *Quasi una fantasia, Gesammelte Schriften* (Frankfurt am Main: Surhkamp, 1978), 16, pp. 534f.

feral of immersive power from the finished object onto production itself, where the production of images is laid out before us as a spectacle to be enjoyed, and in which we are called upon to verify our own participation and agency, constitutes a transparence that is itself immediately commodified and offered up for consumption. But even though certain essential features of this machinery will remain hidden, it would be too simple to say that everything remains the same, and that the workings of ideology production would remain in the same state of concealment as before: the fetishizing of the means of production does not abolish fetishism, but pushes it to a new level, that of a fetishism unfolding through the visible and transparent, in which the desire that holds the subject captive is its own desire to itself become part of this very visibility; to monitor and to be monitored, in the end to assure itself of its own existence by applying the panoptic machinery to itself. It is as if the analysis of ideology once proposed by Marx—the mechanism of a *camera obscura* that gives us the image of the world turned upside down, so that ideas, endowed with an agency of their own, would be the source of reality instead of reality the source of ideas—would have been transformed into a theater of sorts, in which the desire to have the real thing is what drives the illusion.

This is one of the reasons why the aloofness and interior distance of the work that Adorno wanted to uphold, against what he perceived as Benjamin's premature rejection of the aura, no longer seems directly applicable: it is the de-auratization of the work that has become a commodity, or in other words, it is that which formerly was understood to resist the commodity form that now functions as the avant-garde of commodification. The question is whether this is a mere inversion, which like most inversions leave the basic premises delineated by Marx intact, or whether it signals, as I think, a more profound mutation in the very form of objects, which in turn calls for a renewed analysis of fetishism. Here too, artworks are somehow clairvoyant entities, just as in the time of Marx, because they, unwittingly or not, prefigure what is to come.

# Theodor W. Adorno: With Hegel Against Capitalism

*Anders Bartonek*

How and why does Theodor W. Adorno use the philosophy of Hegel in order to strengthen his Marxist theory and its perspective? This is the question that this essay will try to answer. Against the background of an outline of Adorno's thinking, as far as it is Marxist, the purpose is to reconstruct in what way he is using essential aspects and concepts of Hegel's thinking in order to develop his own philosophical contribution to Marxism. The main thesis, which will be constructed around Adorno's ambivalence towards Hegel, is that Adorno uses his own critique against Hegel's system of identity in his critique of the principle of capitalism, and that, when doing this, Adorno harnesses his adapted version of Hegel's notion of non-identity as a critical tool against both Hegel's identity system and the system of capitalism. This means that, with help from Hegel, Adorno secures a possibility of criticizing Hegel and capitalism (as well as Marx's own tendency toward closure), doing so from a Marxist and system-critical perspective.

In quite different ways, the philosophies of Hegel and Marx play a crucial role for the Western Marxism of the Frankfurt School, of which Adorno is one of the most prominent members.[1] Marx's thinking was a cornerstone already when the institute was founded by Felix Weil,[2] that is, at an earlier stage than when the now most famous members joined. For Max Horkheimer, who became the head of the institute in 1930, Marx played a significant role in the formation of a critical theory that avoided becoming a scientific theory adequate to and the preserve of modern capitalist society.

---

[1] See Kevin Anderson, *Lenin, Hegel, and Western Marxism: A Critical Study* (Chicago: University of Illinois Press, 1995) and Perry Anderson, *Considerations on Western Marxism* (London: NLB, 1976).
[2] Rolf Wiggershaus, *The Frankfurt School* (Cambridge: Polity Press, 1994), pp. 9ff.

The aims of critical theory were rather to contribute to societal change. Horkheimer wrote about this in his programmatic text on "Traditional and Critical Theory" from 1937, giving the thinking of the Frankfurt School its name: Critical Theory. Horkheimer's text contains explicit Marxist leanings, it is steeped in Marxist concepts and perspectives (i.e. class, capital, labor, etc.), and is versed in the promise that theory can lead to the demystification of society.[3]

Hegel's influence is not equally significant for the institute as a whole, but rather a very crucial source of inspiration for some of the members, such as Horkheimer, Adorno and Herbert Marcuse. Marcuse wrote two books on Hegel, and the second, *Reason and Revolution: Hegel and the Rise of Social Theory* (1941), is especially worthy of mention, for it is in this text that Marcuse argues how Hegel can be regarded as the foundation for a critical and dialectical theory of society.[4] At the same time, Marcuse was always more affirmative toward Hegel than Adorno. While Marcuse embraced Hegel's total system of thought, Adorno in general was suspicious toward Hegel's, and Marx's, proclivities for system-building—as far as both can be said to have totalizing tendencies—even if he still uses both thinkers in his own critical philosophy.

Those writings of Adorno relevant for this text are those that deal specifically with Marx and/or Hegel, and in particular those that can be said to set out on a Hegelian Marxist direction. In most cases, one of these dimensions is mainly emphasized. Adorno's more systematic work on Marx and Hegel—that is, in the sense that it can be viewed as itself a form of Hegelian Marxism—is mainly concentrated to the later phases of his thinking, in contrast to, for example, Marcuse, who, from an early stage of his thinking, sought to articulate Marx with Hegel.[5] When it comes to Marx, Adorno's understanding was greatly informed by both Georg Lukács and Ernst Bloch.[6] However, it was not until he returned to Germany after his time in the USA during the second world war that Marx plays a more expli-

---

[3] Max Horkheimer, *Critical Theory, Selected Essays* (New York: Continuum, 2002).

[4] See for example the chapter on Hegel's logics: Herbert Marcuse, *Reason and Revolution: Hegel and the Rise of Social Theory* (Boston: Beacon Press, 1960), pp. 121-168.

[5] Douglas Kellner, *Herbert Marcuse and the Crisis of Marxism* (Basingstoke: Macmillan, 1984), pp. 5, 9, 14, 17 and 18.

[6] Stefan Müller-Doohm, *Adorno: Eine Biographie* (Frankfurt am Main: Suhrkamp, 2003), pp. 59-61; Susan Buck-Morss, *The Origin of Negative Dialectics: Theodor W. Adorno, Walter Benjamin, and the Frankfurt Institute* (Hassocks: Harvester Press, 1977), pp. 25ff. and Brian O'Connor, *Adorno's Negative Dialectic: Philosophy and the Possibility of Critical Rationality* (Cambridge: MIT Press, 2004), pp. 8ff.

citly significant role in his publications, for example in *Negative Dialectics* (1966) and some of the sociological writings, although present earlier.[7] In addition, Adorno's Marxism can be understood as a form of Western Marxism, with no direct connections to party politics. The same goes with Adorno's Hegel interpretation. It is only later, when Adorno deals with the question of identity,[8] that Hegel becomes more systematically important for his thinking. The preponderance of the identity-question in Adorno's later work is crucial here for the formulation of Adorno's Hegelian Marxism.

Several essays and books of Adorno will not be discussed here since they are not directly relevant for our present aims, even if they are very important writings for Adorno's thinking, as a whole: "Die Aktualität der Philosophie" (1931), "The Idea of Natural History" (1932), *Kierkegaard* (1933), *Minima Moralia* (1951) *Against Epistemology: A Metacritique* (1956) and *The Jargon of Authenticity* (1964). And while his *Aesthetic Theory,* and his other aesthetic and musicological texts often adopt a Marxist perspective,[9] there will be no room for a discussion of these either. Instead, the most relevant texts for the theme addressed here are *Hegel: Three Studies* (1963), *Negative Dialectics* and several of the sociological essays published in the volumes *Kulturkritik und Gesellschaft I–II* and *Soziologische Schriften I–II.* Furthermore, Adorno's lectures on negative dialectics, philosophical terminology, moral philosophy and sociology are relevant and will be consolidated, but only as a compliment. *Dialectic of Enlightenment* (1947), which Adorno co-wrote with Horkheimer, focuses neither on Marx nor on Hegel, but uses several Marxist categories, such as reification, the role of capital and the negative logics of civil society and money. But one important theme in this book that will be of significance is the theoretical connection that Adorno and Horkheimer make between the critique of capitalism and the critique of the instrumental reason of science, and I will have reason to discuss this later.

Published debates surrounding Adorno's relation to Hegel and Marx are comparatively high in number.[10] And yet there has not been much written

---

[7] Dirk Braunstein, *Adornos Kritik der politischen Ökonomie* (Bielefeld: Transcript, 2011), pp. 43ff.
[8] Anke Thyen, *Negative Dialektik und Erfahrung, Zur Rationalität des Nichtidentischen bei Adorno* (Frankfurt am Main: Suhrkamp, 1989), pp. 102ff.
[9] See Oskar Negt, "Adorno als Marxist", in Joachim Perels (ed.), *Leiden beredt werden lassen: Beiträge über das Denken Theodor W. Adornos* (Hannover: Offizin, 2006), p. 14.
[10] When it comes to Adorno's relation to Hegel, these contributions can be mentioned: John Holloway, Fernando Matamoros & Sergio Tischler (eds.), *Negativity and Revo-*

about Adorno's combined reception of them in terms of his possible contribution to Hegelian Marxism.[11] What could be the reason for this? It cannot be regarded as entirely unproblematic to deal with Adorno in terms of Hegelian Marxism, since his critique of Hegel appears so fundamental. This is an issue this article will broach directly.

The text will begin with a reconstruction of the Marxian concepts used by Adorno, showing how his thinking is Marxist. Thereafter, Adorno's relation to Hegel will be reconstructed, and both his critique and reception of Hegel will be presented. Finally, I will formulate in what way Adorno develops the Hegelian concept of non-identity such that it becomes an indispensable tool in his critique of capitalism.

## Adorno's Marxism

In what way is Adorno's thinking Marxist? Adorno can be understood to have assumed central parts of Marx's theory of society and the critique of

lution: *Adorno and Political Activism* (London: Pluto; 2009), Natalia Baeza, *Contradiction, Critique, and Dialectic in Adorno* (Notre Dame, Indiana, 2012) and Dimitri Vouros, "Hegel, 'Totality', and 'Abstract Universality' in the Philosophy of Theodor Adorno", *Parrhesia*, No. 21 2014. Among earlier studies, these are worth mentioning: Thyen, *Negative Dialektik und Erfahrung. Zur Rationalität des Nichtidentischen bei Adorno*, Drucilla Cornell, *The Philosophy of the Limit* (New York: Routledge, 1992), and Mauro Bozzetti, *Hegel und Adorno* (Freiburg & München: Alber, 1996). When it comes to the relation to Marx, these can be mentioned among the newer contributions: Sybe Schaap, *Die Verwirklichung der Philosophie* (Würzburg: Königshausen & Neumann, 2000), Simon Jarvis, "Adorno, Marx, Materialism", in Tom Huhn (ed.), *The Cambridge Companion to Adorno* (Cambridge: Cambridge University Press, 2004), Christoph Ziermann, "Dialektik und Metaphysik bei Marx und Adorno", in Wolfram Ette (ed.), *Adorno im Widerstreit: Zur Präsenz seiner Denkens* (Freiburg & München: Alber, 2004), Negt, "Adorno als Marxist", Hendrik Wallat, *Das Bewusstsein der Krise: Marx, Nietzsche und die Emanzipation des Nichtidentischen in der politischen Theorie* (Bielefeld: Transcript, 2009), Holloway, Matamoros & Tischler, *Negativity and Revolution: Adorno and Political Activism*, Braunstein, *Adornos Kritik der politischen Ökonomie*, Baeza, *Contradiction, Critique, and Dialectic in Adorno*, Christopher Cutrone, *Adorno's Marxism* (Chicago, Illinois, 2013) and Werner Bonefeld, "Emancipatory Praxis and Conceptuality in Adorno", in Holloway, Matamoros & Tischler (eds.), *Negativity and Revolution: Adorno and Political Activism*.
[11] Here Nigel C. Gibson, "Rethinking the Old Saw: Dialectical Negativity, Utopia, and Negative Dialectic in Adorno's Hegelian Marxism", in Gibson & Andrew Rubin (eds.), *Adorno: A Critical Reader* (Oxford: Blackwell, 2002) and Robert Lanning, *In the Hotel Abyss: An Hegelian-Marxist Critique of Adorno* (Leiden: Brill, 2014) can be mentioned. But these texts do not develop this theme in an elaborated sense. The latter does not read Adorno as a Hegelian Marxist, but rather develops a Hegelian-Marxist critique of Adorno. But Gibson adequately defines Hegelian Marxism as a Marxism that "both emphasizes the Hegel-Marx relationship and uses Hegelian categories to creatively reactualize Marxism within their own context" (p. 286).

society, and to have made those into motivating driving forces in his own theory. Even if Adorno did not publish any particular work on Marx, Marx and his critical impulse are present in Adorno's work in a continuous way. As already mentioned, Adorno discovered Marx early through the contrasting interpretations of Lukács and Bloch. My intention is not to present an entire image of Adorno's Marxism, but rather to focus on those Marxist elements that are important for his Hegelian Marxism. The main purpose here is to connect Adorno's questioning and critique of identity with the Adornian critique of capitalism. Dirk Braunstein, for one, supports the importance of this connection in Adorno.[12] Nonetheless he does not discuss this in terms of Hegelian Marxism or in relation to Adorno's reception of Hegel. Nevertheless, Adorno's critique of capitalism is held together by a dismissal of capitalism as a phenomenon that erases differences and creates conformity. The unique character of the singular is grinded down, reduced to an object possible to smoothly handle on the market. But Adorno's critique of capitalism presupposes and thus requires his critique of identity. Adorno's critique of capitalism problematizes capitalism as identity.

Adorno's Marxist way of engaging with Hegel must be related also to other understandings of Marxism during his own time and the critiques he leveled at them. As Braunstein shows, the Frankfurt school had already criticized Marxism's approach to Social democracy and it had also distanced itself from the image of Marxism as a general science of the laws of nature and history, which seemingly turned into a forever valid theory of the absent revolution.[13] In relation to this, Adorno shows how the materialism in Marx never can be reduced to an anti-philosophical doctrine of nature. Adorno criticizes the way in which Marx's materialism "in the East" was transformed into a vulgar materialism, degrading the very idea of a materialist point of view. Moreover, Adorno finds in Marx a critique against any philosophical attempt to derive abstract principles, out of which it is possible to deduce reality. A crucial moment in Marx's thinking is the relation between theory and praxis, and Marxist theory can therefore never only be a theory about reality as it is, it must transform it.[14]

The following parts of this section will: (a) present three Marxist concepts which are especially important for Adorno; (b) continue by way of

---

[12] Braunstein, *Adornos Kritik der politischen Ökonomie*, p. 274.
[13] Braunstein, *Adornos Kritik der politischen Ökonomie*, p. 130.
[14] Theodor W. Adorno, *Philosophische Terminologie*, Bd. 2 (Frankfurt am Main: Suhrkamp, 1974), pp. 255ff.

the utopian and the ban on images, and finally (c) account for Adorno's materialism. The latter themes are important because it is out of these that Adorno can be said to develop a novel Marxist perspective.

### a) Marxian concepts

Marx's influence on Adorno is extensive, using many concepts that are traceable back to Marx. Some of them are used in a crucial and programmatic way, while others do not have quite the same essential function for his negative dialectics, although often they are used frequently. Some of these concepts that do not have such systematic significance are ideology,[15] class,[16] labor,[17] reification,[18] and fetishism.[19] *Dialectic of Enlightenment* contains several Marxian perspectives and they are essential for the argument of the book, even if it is difficult to decide if they derive from Adorno or from Horkheimer, who co-wrote the text. In any case, the dimensions of classification, calculation and domination over nature are presented therein as instrumental reason and connected with the capitalist principles of civil society. *Dialectic of Enlightenment* therefore suggests an alliance between the calculations of science with the power-logic of capitalism: what makes these spheres similar is their way of leveling out what is otherwise different and unique.[20] Both calculative capitalism and rationalizing science are criticized by Adorno (and Horkheimer) as examples of forms of identity. Already here a seed can be found for a critique of capitalism made possible through a critique of identity. But at this point, this mode of critique has not reached its point of maturity.[21] I will start by presenting Adorno's usages of three concepts that are especially important for Adorno: *capitalism* (and the

---

[15] See Adorno, *Soziologische Schriften I* (GS 8) (Frankfurt am Main: Suhrkamp, 2003), pp. 457-477 and *Negative Dialectics* (London: Routledge, 1990), pp. 197ff.
[16] See Adorno, "Reflections on Class Theory" (https://platypus1917.org/wp-content/Up loads/readings/adorno_classtheory1942.pdf).
[17] See for example, Adorno, *Hegel: Three Studies* (Cambridge: MIT Press, 1993), pp. 17ff. and *Critical Models: Interventions and Catchwords* (New York: Columbia University Press, 1998), pp. 167ff.
[18] See for example, Adorno, *Negative Dialectics*, pp. 189ff., and Gillian Rose, *The Melancholy Science* (London: Verso, 1978), pp. 35ff.
[19] See for example, Adorno, *Negative Dialectics*, pp. 11ff. and 83ff., and Horkheimer & Adorno, *Dialectic of Enlightenment* (London: Verso, 1997), p. 17 and 28.
[20] See for example, Horkheimer & Adorno, *Dialectic of Enlightenment*, pp. 6ff., 16ff. and 29ff.
[21] See Braunstein, *Adornos Kritik der politischen Ökonomie*, p. 188.

critique of capitalism), societal *antagonism* and societal *principle of barter* (or exchange).

There are of course other themes strongly connected to Marx's philosophy—such as, for example, the dimensions of history and dialectics—but it seems more accurate to localize these themes to Adorno's work on Hegel. At the same time it seems reasonable to view his Marxism and materialism as historical-materialism.[22] Even if the theme of history will not be crucial here, it still indirectly plays an important role in several regards, for example in the historical reconstruction and the critique of the development of the domination over nature and subjectivity as well as in Adorno's critique of Hegel's preoccupation with the eternal in contrast to the temporary. In his text "Progress" (1969), Adorno sketches an inverted idea of history in contrast to the traditional idea of historical progress that for Adorno contains within it a destructive logic. Indeed, for Adorno, historical progress will not occur until the identity principle, which degrades and destroys all that is heterogeneous, is broken. Therefore real progress would mean the exit from the curse of progress; progress will not be progress until progress ends.[23] Here, dialectics will play an even more important role than history, and will, in the shape of his concept of non-identity, be presented as the main resource and precondition for his critique.

I will now address the concept of capitalism as well as the critique of capitalism in Adorno. Adorno often uses the concept of "late capitalism" instead of capitalism, which means that he (like many others at the time) historicizes the analysis of capitalism, such that capitalism is now regarded as entering its late phase, and perhaps close to its ruination. Still, Adorno is cautious about providing prognoses about this ruin. In his text on Adorno's critique of late capitalism, Fabian Freyenhagen notes how, in the eyes of Adorno, it is an essential characteristic of late capitalism that it has integrated the proletariat (and thereby defeated its revolutionary potential), making individuals conform with the economic principles of society and suffocating all critical possibilities from inside.[24] In his text "Late Capitalism

---

[22] Willem van Reijen, *Philosophie als Kritik: Einführung in die kritische Theorie* (Königstein: Hain, 1984), pp. 90 ff.
[23] Adorno, *Critical Models*, p. 150.
[24] Fabian Freyenhagen, "Adorno's Critique of Late Capitalism: Negative, Explanatory and Practical", in Karin De Boer & Ruth Sonderegger (eds.), *Conceptions of Critique in Modern and Contemporary Philosophy* (New York: Palgrave, 2012), p. 176; see also Fredric Jameson, *Late Marxism: Adorno, or, the Persistence of the Dialectic* (London: Verso, 2007).

or Industrial Society?" (1968), Adorno discusses if the concept of capitalism (and thereby Marx) is obsolete and if we should address society as an industrial society. In response, Adorno underlines that there are societal phenomena that only can be analyzed in a very superficial and arbitrary way if one lets go of the concept of capitalism, because societal power to a very large extent is channeled through economic principles. Society, when it comes to the stage of its modes of production, cannot be understood as an industrial society.[25] Adorno therefore argues that we need to hold onto the concept of capitalism for critical purposes; otherwise it will appear as if we have overcome capitalist domination. But according to Adorno this is not the case: human beings are still—perhaps even more than Marx stated in the mid-1800s—appendices to the economical machinery.[26]

The notion that capitalist society essentially (and not accidentally) has an *antagonistic* character and tears itself apart at the same time as it presents itself as cohesive precisely through the principle of its disruption is an insight that Adorno takes from Marx. Hendrik Wallat highlights the importance of this Marxian understanding of society in his book *Das Bewusstsein der Krise: Marx, Nietzsche und die Emanzipation des Nichtidentischen in der politischen Theorie*. The experience of an existing rupture between philosophy and the world and that both philosophy and the world are disrupted within themselves is according to Wallat an essential and motivating point of departure for Marx's thinking.[27] In Adorno's short text on "Gesellschaft" (1965), the antagonistic nature and the inner contradictions of society are in focus. Society must, according to Adorno, primarily be understood in terms of a process, and one understands society better through the analyses of its principles of development than by looking at polished, isolated and (posited) invariant attributions of society.[28] Adorno also writes that the self-formatting process of society is not being fulfilled beyond or despite the inner conflicts and antagonisms of society but precisely because of and through them, which at the same time risk to tear society apart.[29] Capitalist society is being formed and upheld through this inner tension, but also faces the risk of self-destruction. In the text "On the Logic of the Social

---

[25] Adorno, "Late Capitalism or Industrial Society?", p. 4 (http://members.efn.org/~dred mond/AdornoSozAddr.PDF).

[26] Adorno, "Late Capitalism or Industrial Society?".

[27] Wallat, *Das Bewusstsein der Krise: Marx, Nietzsche und die Emanzipation des Nicht-identischen in der politischen Theorie*, pp. 23 and 34.

[28] Adorno, *Soziologische Schriften I* (GS 8), p. 9.

[29] Adorno, *Soziologische Schriften I* (GS 8), pp. 14-15.

Sciences" (1962), Adorno writes that society is, on the one hand, to be understood as contradictory and irrational, but on the other hand as rational.[30] The point is that society, despite its destructive character, is not entirely chaotic. Instead, capitalism must be viewed in light of the enlightenment, science and reason. The tendency of capitalist society is precisely reason becoming unreason; through societal antagonism, counter-images against capitalism are being kept alive by capitalism itself. In functioning through this contradiction, capitalism prevents society from becoming entirely homogeneous. In *Negative Dialectics*, Adorno essentially emphasizes the contradiction between the common and the individual as yet another crucial aspect of the antagonism of society. Adorno criticizes the attempts in both politics and science to reduce the contradictions pregnant in the social realm to one common denominator. Any attempt to homogenize everything individual, integrating it into the systems' way of functioning, will fail.[31] For civil society exists through the tension between the common and the individual. Thorsten Bonacker describes this tension in a precise manner, when, in his text on Adorno's concept of the individual, he writes that the difference between pre-modern and modern societies lies in the fact that the individual only becomes a challenge to society in the case of the latter. Modern society exists by producing the individual, which on the one hand propels its development, but on the other is that which remains non-identical with society and that on which it is impossible to get a proper grip. The individual is thus a threat to society.[32] The system therefore keeps that very thing alive which for it is both a threat as well as the source of its existence. Precisely in this way the concept of non-identity, essential for Adorno's philosophical system, is preserved within it, as both a challenge and as a productive resource. Moreover, it is this principle that Adorno will use against Hegel.

The social antagonism is according to Adorno reproduced through the principle of barter,[33] a principle essential for capitalist society. The question of the rise of this principle plays a significant role in *Dialectic of Enlightenment*. Exchange as a societal principle is, according to Horkheimer and

---

[30] Adorno, "On the Logic of the Social Sciences" (http://www.autodidactproject.org/other/positivismusstreit/adorno-logic.html).

[31] Adorno, *Negative Dialectics*, pp. 10ff.

[32] Thorsten Bonacker, "Ohne Angst verschieden sein können: Individualität in der integralen Gesellschaft", in Stefan Müller-Doohm (ed.), *Die Gesellschaftstheorie Adornos: Themen und Grundbegriffe* (Darmstadt: Prius, 1998), pp. 141-142.

[33] Adorno, *Soziologische Schriften I* (GS 8), p. 15.

Adorno, produced because of the development of the law of equivalence: "Bourgeois society is ruled by equivalence. It makes the dissimilar comparable by reducing it to abstract quantities".[34] In order to be able to exchange things, to buy and sell them, everything has to be made comparable, even if such equivalence is impossible. But with help from a difference-erasing and monetary standard (money) the process of equalization is possible, draining nature of its quality with the natural world and becoming increasingly dependent on human exploitation and ownership.[35] Moreover, the specific and diverse needs of individuals are themselves equalized. The principle of barter is thus established as the general rule by which things and humans are mediated in civil society. At the same time, things and humans are kept apart through this principle; it is thus a process that further accentuates alienation. Human beings and all their relations are mediated by this capitalist logic and its murderous potential.[36] This reduction of differences with help from universal concepts and frameworks is a phenomenon that Adorno criticizes as identity thinking. Adorno especially highlights this as the main problem of societal and scientific systems: they erase differences. Still it is important to recognize, as Christoph Ziermann points out,[37] that Adorno holds on to the positive possibility inherent in the ideal of a free and just barter. Adorno holds onto its inherent promise, while he is categorically clear that this promise is not being fulfilled in capitalist society.

### b) Theory and praxis, the utopian, and the ban on images

The motivation for societal change is a decisive driving force for the Frankfurt School in general. This impulse is influenced by Marx and his injunction to transform fundamentally and revolutionarily capitalist society. Adorno's version of this transformation, although closely related to the Marxist tradition, is far more cautious with respect to a prognosis surrounding the possibility of such change. The relation of theory and praxis is a central question for Adorno, and it is one closely connected to the realization of philosophy. While, on the one hand, it is false to claim that Adorno thinks that the notion of praxis is impossible in the alienating and antagonistic world of capitalism, it is nonetheless true that he does not take

---

[34] Horkheimer & Adorno, *Dialectic of Enlightenment*, p. 7.
[35] See Braunstein, *Adornos Kritik der politischen Ökonomie*, p. 350.
[36] Adorno, *Negative Dialectics*, pp. 22ff. and 292ff., see also *Philosophische Elemente einer Theorie der Gesellschaft* (Frankfurt am Main: Suhrkamp, 2008), pp. 74ff.
[37] Ziermann, "Dialektik und Metaphysik bei Marx und Adorno", pp. 43ff.

this possibility for granted. According to Joan Alway, for example, Adorno is hesitant about the possibility of the rise of a proletarian subject as the agent of revolution.[38] In his text "Resignation" (1969), Adorno writes that the paths to a genuinely society-changing and oppression-negating praxis are almost entirely blocked within late capitalism.[39] The main reason for this is, for Adorno, society's ability to channel and disarm resistance.[40] But in so highlighting these obstacles for praxis, Adorno is not necessarily pulled into the direction of declaring praxis as impossible, as many commentators have claimed.[41] Adorno's critical theory aims rather at the discovery of available possibilities for free and non-reified praxis, but since these in many respects seem foreclosed, theory becomes (alongside art) a main reserve in which the hope for freedom is kept alive.[42]

This does not change the fact that, as Russell Berman writes in his essay "Adorno's Politics", it is a main theme of Adorno's thinking to ask the question how resistance can be thought within the tension between subjectivity and objective social forces.[43] It is for Adorno important not to be seduced by pseudo-activism.[44] As Adorno states in "Marginalia to Theory and Praxis" (1969), theory is already in itself praxis, maybe it is the only critical praxis possible in this dissimulated society. Regarding his own philosophical praxis he writes: "Wherever I have directly intervened in a narrow sense and with a visible practical influence, it happened only through theory".[45] Revolutionary praxis is obstructed, but theoretical praxis is being kept alive by not forcing itself into a pseudo-activity. The first words of *Negative Dialectics* outlines Adorno's view on the situation for philosophy: the philosophy which once seemed obsolete is kept alive because its moment

---

[38] Joan Alway, *Critical Theory and Political Possibilities: Conceptions of Emancipatory Politics in the Works of Horkheimer, Adorno, Marcuse, and Habermas* (Westport: Greenwood Press, 1995), pp. 64ff.
[39] Adorno, *Critical Models*, pp. 290ff.
[40] Adorno, *Critical Models*, pp. 291ff.
[41] See for example Lanning, *In the Hotel Abyss*, p. 2, Espen Hammer, *Adorno and the Political* (London: Routledge, 2006), p. 106, Inge Münz-Koenen, *Konstruktionen des Nirgendwo: Die Diskursivität des Utopischen bei Bloch, Adorno, Habermas*, (Berlin: Akademie Verlag, 1997), p. 123 and Ulrich Müller, Theodor W. *Adornos "Negative Dialektik"* (Darmstadt: Wissenschaftliche Buchgesellschaft, 2006), p. 126.
[42] See Adorno, *Problems of Moral Philosophy* (Stanford: Stanford University Press, 2000), p. 4.
[43] Russell Berman, "Adorno's Politics", in Gibson & Rubin (eds.), *Adorno: A Critical Reader*, p. 114.
[44] Adorno, *Critical Models*, pp. 290ff.
[45] Adorno, *Critical Models*, p. 277.

of realization has been missed.[46] Because the realization has not been actualized, critical thinking now finds itself in a situation in which it reflects on the question why the anticipated revolution has not arrived.

Nevertheless, Adorno almost only broaches the theme of such a utopian state of society in negative terms. He seldom gives expression of a more positive vision of the utopic, and on the few occasions he does he is very cautious, using the subjunctive mood: what would a better society be like?[47] A crucial concept in this negative circumscription of utopia is the concept of non-identity, which he receives from Hegel. In *Negative Dialectics*, Adorno's develops this concept in a way that differs from Hegel, turning it into a critical concept. This concept plays one of its most significant roles within the Hegelian critique of capitalism I am claiming Adorno develops. The non-identical is that which cannot be integrated into, or reduced to, mere moments within a closed system, neither as an individual within a given political system nor as particular things and humans within philosophical or scientific systems. Because it cannot be subsumed under common concepts or be explained systematically the non-identical also presents the impossibility for systems to be closed entities. The non-identical stands for a critique of the identical and the logic of identity, which, according to Adorno, is the principle of homogeneity that erases differences.[48] This critique of systemic domination over the non-identical allows for the utopic task of rescuing the non-identity from the claws of identity. More strongly put, the recovery of the non-identical would here not only be the negative counterpart to the identical, rather it would open up for the possibility of developing its own positive end as a unique singularity.[49]

A main reason for why Adorno claims that it is necessary to address the utopian in negative terms is that he sees danger in trying to grasp the new in the terms that already predominate within society. Such an approach runs the risk of asphyxiating the new immediately.[50] Instead Adorno tries to release a positive force through the employment of negative formulations.[51]

---

[46] Adorno, *Negative Dialectics*, pp. 3 ff., see also Schaap, *Die Verwirklichung der Philosophie.*

[47] See Anders Bartonek, *Philosophie im Konjunktiv: Nichtidentität als Ort der Möglichkeit des Utopischen in der negativen Dialektik Theodor W. Adornos* (Würzburg: Königshausen & Neumann, 2011), p. 227.

[48] Adorno, *Negative Dialectics*, pp. 3ff.

[49] Adorno, *Negative Dialectics*, pp. 6ff.

[50] Adorno, *Negative Dialectics*, pp. 204ff.

[51] Adorno, *Hegel: Three Studies*, p. 80.

He has two sources of inspiration for adopting such cautiousness. One is the Jewish ban on images, which, together with Horkheimer in *Dialectic of Enlightenment,* he invokes in the following way: "Jewish religion allows no word that would alleviate the despair of all that is mortal. It associates hope only with the prohibition against calling on what is false as God, against invoking the finite as the infinite, lies as truth".[52] The danger is to present that which is not utopian *as* utopian and thereby hindering the utopic from coming into life. The other source of inspiration is the philosophy of Marx, and Adorno is referring to his refusal to deliver positive and specific images of the classless society.[53] Adorno suggests that Marx secularizes the theological ban on images, so as simply *not* to prevent the transformation of society. For Adorno, this ban avoids any counterproductive sliding into a defense of pseudo-activity.

### c) Materialism

The concept of materialism plays a significant role in Adorno's negative dialectics, and Marx is again a primary source for Adorno here. Materialism has two major dimensions for Adorno. On the one hand, it points to how society, far from being a harmonious whole, is constructed through disruptions and antagonisms. On the other hand, a materialist standpoint shows in what ways the objective and material are impossible to reduce to the ideal and identical. Accordingly, materialism serves as a way of critiquing both political systems and identity-systems.

On the relationship between societal antagonisms and Adorno's materialism, Mauro Bozzetti, for example, writes in his book, *Hegel und Adorno,* that Adorno uses materialism as an indicator for society that is both discontinuous and dialectical in itself.[54] On this interpretation, Adorno is closer to Marx and his critique of Hegel's idealistic philosophy. Adorno develops his critique of philosophy in connection to Marx's materialism.[55] This materialism consists in Adorno's attempt to give the objective and non-identical—that is, the material that thought encounters—protection in relation to instrumentalizing and subsumptive thinking. Hegel's idealistic philosophy gives priority to thinking over the material: thinking is what forms and gives determination to the real. For Adorno, this means that thinking must

[52] Horkheimer & Adorno, *Dialectic of Enlightenment,* p. 23.
[53] Adorno, *Critical Models,* p. 277.
[54] Bozzetti, *Hegel und Adorno,* pp. 210f.
[55] Adorno, *Philosophische Terminologie,* Bd. 2, p. 255 and *Negative Dialectics,* pp. 204ff.

be self-critical. Adorno adopts the role of the defender of things, choosing to speak in terms of a preponderance of the object (*Vorrang des Objekts*). This request for thought to respect the object means resisting the subsumption of the object under thought's concepts. Thinking, therefore, should not force things into its nature-dominating patterns.[56] Precisely, only a thinking that prioritizes the object can be materialist, a mode of thinking, moreover, that sees in things themselves a resistance toward idealistic abstraction.[57] It is here that, arguably, Adorno's materialism transcends even that of Marx.

In *Negative Dialectics*, Adorno argues that these dimensions of materialism are connected. Underlining the disruptive nature of society and the materialistic critique of idealist philosophy are two sides of the same coin. According to Adorno, any materialism worthy its name must not only critique idealism, but it must also, and essentially, present a critique of existing societal reality that demands political transformation. This parallel critique of society and philosophy plays an important part for Adorno's critique of capitalism with help from Hegel, for his Hegelian Marxism. Adorno uses the same "weapon" against both: the concept of the non-identical.

## Adorno's Hegelian Marxism

Adorno's relation to Hegel is ambivalent. On the one hand he criticizes fundamentally Hegel's construction of a closed system-identity—the most elaborate version of such a system within the tradition, starting from Parmenides' identification of being with itself.[58] On the other hand, Adorno receives his most important critical tool and concept from Hegel's identity system.[59] The importance of the concept of non-identity for Adorno should not be underestimated. In Hegel, non-identity is a concept that refers only to a productive negation for and within the system.

Adorno's reformulation of the concept of dialectics, from the Hegelian positive version to his own negative redescription of it, is programmatically addressed in his book *Hegel: Three Studies*. However, things are developed in a more elaborate fashion three years later in *Negative Dialectics*. In the Hegel-studies he writes that the purpose of the book is the preparation of a

---

[56] Adorno, *Negative Dialectics*, pp. 139ff., see also Thyen, *Negative Dialektik und Erfahrung*, pp. 207ff. and Simon Jarvis, "Adorno, Marx, Materialism", in Huhn (ed.), *The Cambridge Companion to Adorno*.
[57] Adorno, *Negative Dialectics*, pp. 192ff.
[58] See Adorno, *Hegel: Three Studies*, pp. 40ff.
[59] See Bozzetti, *Hegel und Adorno*, pp. 9ff and 55ff.

transformation of the concept of dialectics,[60] and in the preface to *Negative Dialectics* he formulates his ambition as wanting to release dialectics from its traditionally affirmative meaning. Adorno refers to Plato's philosophy in which the principle of dialectics contains the negation that is supposed to lead to the creation of something positive.[61] On account of Adorno's critique of an affirmative dialectics, it seems problematic to say, as Yvonne Sherratt does, that a positive dialectics is still retained by Adorno, even if it is true that Adorno's thinking is not purely negative.[62] Nonetheless, dialectics is a main theme in Adorno's philosophy, and for two reasons. First, dialectics is an object for philosophical critique; Adorno criticizes the reduction of the singular to common concepts, an operation carried out by positive dialectics as well as by the productive version of negation that constitutes the cornerstone of all systems. Second, dialectics is in itself a critical tool for Adorno. For this critical purpose Adorno's remodeled version of Hegel's concept of non-identity becomes essential for Adorno's critique of capitalism. Importantly, Adorno also criticizes Marx's philosophy for having problematic Hegelian characteristics: Marx accepts, for example, Hegel's idealism in the sense that he sees Hegel's thinking as an embodiment of the consciousness of the prehistory of liberation. Marx accepts this big dialectical picture and even time receives a subordinate place in the dialectical system of history.[63] In this manner, even Marx becomes problematic from the vantage point of Adorno's non-identity thinking.[64]

The main argument in what follows will be that Adorno, with help from the conceptual tool received from Hegel (the concept of non-identity), and which he gives a Marxist and system-critical direction, has the ambition to criticize closed systems in a philosophical (mainly Hegel) and political sense (capitalism). He criticizes both Hegel and the capitalist system with help from a Hegelian concept. The concept of "non-identity" will be the most important dimension here in order to formulate Adorno's Hegelian Marxism, that is, how Adorno mobilizes his thinking "with Hegel against capitalism". Of

---

[60] Adorno, *Hegel: Three Studies*, p. xxxvi.
[61] Adorno, *Negative Dialectics*, p. xix.
[62] See Yvonne Sherratt, *Adorno's Positive Dialectic* (Cambridge: Cambridge University Press, 2002).
[63] Adorno, "Reflections on Class Theory" (https://platypus1917.org/wp-content/uploads/readings/adorno_classtheory1942.pdf), pp. 94ff.
[64] See also Tischler's Negative-Dialectical Critique of Marx in Connection to Adorno; Tischler, "Adorno: The Conceptual Prison of the Subject, Political Fetishism and Class Struggle", in Holloway, Matamoros & Tischler (eds.), *Negativity and Revolution: Adorno and Political Activism*, pp. 103ff.

course, already Hegel was a critic of raw capitalism within civil society,[65] but nevertheless his political system ends in a typical form of closed identity (the state). Adorno criticizes both the identity of the common, which Hegel arrives at, and capitalism. He differs from Hegel in that he does not understand capitalism as an anti-universal principle; rather, capitalism embodies a system that gives priority to the common before the singular.

In the following, I will start by (a) presenting Adorno's critique of Hegel, but then also (b) show how and why Adorno holds onto Hegel, in order to, finally (c), develop the argument of Adorno's Marxist critique of capitalism through Hegel.

### a) Hegel as a problem

I have already pointed to Adorno's critique of Hegel's idealistic thinking and system, but here Adorno's critiques of the common, idealism and identity thinking will be presented in a more elaborated way. It is first against the background of this critique that Adorno's use of the concept of the non-identical, as well as his critique of capitalism, can be understood.

How are we to understand Adorno's claim that Hegel's system prioritizes the common over the singular and why is this a part of Hegel's idealism? Adorno's negative dialectics, which he also calls an "antisystem", consists in the attempt to uncover and criticize the appearance of a reality-constituting subjectivity.[66] For Adorno the task of thinking should itself be to question the idealist tradition by challenging the supposed ability of subjectivity to form reality. But this critique of thinking can also, according to Adorno, be directed toward philosophical traditions that are otherwise not idealist, such as positivism, as well as phenomenology and Heideggerian ontology.[67] This critique of the dominant way in which thinking relates to reality impresses on thought that things neither can nor should be subsumed under their concepts.[68] The role of dialectics comes to develop and present the difference between the singular and the common, a difference the common has kept concealed within its claimed identity.[69] Despite this critique, Adorno emphatically holds on to the very thinking he is criticizing, since it

---

[65] G. W. F. Hegel, *Elements of the Philosophy of Right*, trans. Allen Wood (Cambridge: Cambridge University Press, 1991), §§ 182-208.
[66] Adorno, *Negative Dialectics*, p. xx.
[67] See Adorno, *Negative Dialectics* and *Hegel: Three Studies*.
[68] Adorno, *Negative Dialectics*, pp. 3ff.
[69] Adorno, *Negative Dialectics*, pp. 6ff.

is only possible to criticize thinking with thinking itself (there is only one thinking, one reason). This is also why thinking, despite its necessary self-critique, sticks to the hope that in some way or some form it is able to reach a knowledge of reality that at the same time does not distort reality. Programmatically, Adorno writes that the utopia of knowledge lies in an opening up toward a non-conceptual conceptuality to which reality would not need to conform.[70]

In order to stay within Adorno's critique of Hegel the following questions can now be posed: according to Adorno, how does Hegel construct his identity system and what part does the non-identical play? Finally, what consequences follow from the way in which the Hegelian system relates to the non-identical? Adorno starts by writing that the tendency toward identification is an inherent dimension within thinking itself: to think means to identify.[71] This is one reason why he localizes the challenge within thinking: thinking turning itself against itself (and the identity-principle by which thinking is bound). Thinking is identification. But, at the same time thinking is dialectical, and therefore it has the ability to confront itself and become the negation of identification within thinking.[72] The problematic dimension of identity thinking lies in the fact that it tends to reduce all singularities to common concepts as well as turning them into mere moments of the system. Anke Thyen suggests, in her book on Adorno's negative dialectics and the concept of experience, that it is possible to locate a distinction between identifying something "with" something and to identify something "as" something. The oppressing form of identification would in this case be the first, through which a thing is reduced to its likeness with other things and therefore robbed of its uniqueness. The latter form must, in contrast, take into account the thing's specific content.[73]

But the primacy of the concept and its power over reality is still predominant. This principle of identification derives according to Adorno from the history of the domination over nature and the reign of subjectivity, a history that is reconstructed in *Dialectic of Enlightenment*. The relation between the enlightenment, science and the capitalist economy to nature—both outer and inner nature—is characterized by a categorizing, classifying and calculating as well as an instrumental reason, and is initiated as well as

---

[70] Adorno, *Negative Dialectics*, p. 10, see also 15.
[71] Adorno, *Negative Dialectics*, pp. 4ff.
[72] Adorno, *Negative Dialectics*, pp. 135ff.
[73] Thyen, *Negative Dialektik und Erfahrung*, pp. 115ff.

developed and refined through the exploitation of nature. This dominating and instrumental relation to nature and reality is in *Negative Dialectics* addressed by Adorno as the problem of identity thinking, that is, the critique of the "subsuming cover concept",[74] which degrades the non-identical. For Adorno, this identity and its domination over non-identity is both real and mere appearance at the same time. Where on the one hand the identity thinking as well as the economical praxis within civil society and scientific activity really have had a negative effect on reality, things and humans, on the other hand the non-identical as such embodies the general impossibility of a closed system, in which the conformity of all things is established. In this sense identity is just an appearance.[75]

For Adorno, the non-identical cannot really be subsumed under identity, for it resists integration. The non-identical therefore contains those aspects in a thing that are insoluble within the classification schemes that attempt to subsume the thing.[76] This means that the non-identical embodies the contradiction within identity systems or rather it shows that identity cannot hold itself together as a closed system. The problem of non-identity, however, can only come forth in relation to identity, as a divergence. Instead of forcing the non-identical into the pattern of identity, thinking should, according to Adorno, develop a consequent awareness of the problem of non-identity.[77] This requires that thinking affirms its identity character, precisely in order to be able to identify the problem of identification.

### b) Hegel and the critical potential of dialectics

Without dialectical and therefore identity thinking it is not possible to address the problem of identification and then a recovery of the non-identical would not possible. The task that Adorno issues to thinking is that it changes the direction of its concepts. It should no longer prefer and prioritize the identical, the eternal and common, but negative dialectics must rather focus on the non-identical and its constitutive meaning in and for thinking. It is important to be aware of the fact that thinking is essentially formed by the non-conceptual; only by force can thought claim to be independent from reality.[78] This mediation of subjectivity and objectivity,

---

[74] Adorno, *Negative Dialectics*, p. 408.
[75] See Adorno, *Critical Models*, pp. 245ff.
[76] Adorno, *Negative Dialectics*, pp. 148ff.
[77] Adorno, *Negative Dialectics*, pp. 4ff.
[78] Adorno, *Negative Dialectics*, pp. 13ff.

which is not the same as an identity, prevents thinking from dominating a nature apparently outside itself.[79]

The tragic moment for Hegel, which for Adorno is positive, is that Hegel is forced to keep the non-identical alive as a constitutive moment in his system that may irrupt as a threatening negativity. Without the negativity of the non-identical Hegel's system would stagnate and die, incapable of confronting new challenges and integrating them in his expanding realm. Out of necessity Hegel must hold onto non-identity, and yet Adorno will force the non-identical from out of the hands of Hegel, converting it into a weapon against identity. Non-identity is transformed into a critical tool against the system. Hegel is thus turned against Hegel. Instead of being a part of the system or even helping to generate it, non-identity cracks the system open.

First and foremost Adorno means that thinking neither should nor can negate the existing state of society by offering constructive suggestions of how the utopian should be, but practices what Adorno refers to as the determinate negation. A negation should in this sense question the positively given in order to open up for the possibilities of something new, without sketching out the nature of this novelty. The negation is determinate because it seeks to negate something very specific and concrete, that is, the existing society.[80] In *Hegel: Three Studies*, Adorno formulates the function of determinate negation as the nerve of dialectics as a method. Determinate negation seeks to release a force in a certain thing with the purpose of directing this force against the thing (in a critical sense) but also for the sake of the thing as empowerment. The thing is assisted here because it is now able to take the first steps toward self-determination, it is hindered however because no longer can it go on like before with a reified existence.[81] Determinate negation thereby mobilizes the non-identity in the thing against the thing, in order to break with the identical, but indirectly it also has the task to open a potential new future.[82]

But Adorno writes also positively and directly about Hegel's contributions, not only indirectly, with respect to his dialectics. In many ways Hegel's thinking already contains the courage to acknowledge the negativity

[79] See Adorno, *Critical Models*, pp. 249ff.
[80] See Elizabeth A. Pritchard, "Bilderverbot meets Body in Theodor W. Adornos Inverse Theology", in Gerard Delanty (ed.), *Theodor W. Adorno*, vol. 1 (London: SAGE, 2004), p. 191.
[81] Adorno, *Hegel: Three Studies*, pp. 80ff.
[82] See Bartonek, *Philosophie im Konjunktiv*.

in society and to follow it through to its most destructive and risky consequences. In the Hegel-studies, Adorno writes:

> These days it is hardly possible for a theoretical idea of any scope to do justice to the experience of consciousness but the embodied experience of human beings, without having incorporated something of Hegel's philosophy. But this cannot be explained in terms of the trivial apercu according to which Hegel, the absolute idealist, was a great realist and a man with a sharp historical eye. Hegel's substantive insights, which extended to the irreconcilability of the contradictions in bourgeois society, cannot be separated from speculation—the vulgar notion of which has nothing to do with the Hegelian notion—as though it were some kind of troublesome ornamentation. On the contrary, those insights are produced by speculation, and they lose their substance as soon as they are conceived as merely empirical. The idea that the a priori is also the a posteriori, an idea that was programmatic in Fichte and was then fully elaborated by Hegel, is not an audacious piece of bombast; it is the mainspring of Hegel's thought: it inspires both his criticism of a grim empirical reality and his critique of a static apriorism. Where Hegel compels his material to speak, the idea of an original identity of subject and object "in spirit", an identity that becomes divided and then reunites, is at work. Otherwise the inexhaustibly rich content of his system would remain either a mere accumulation of facts, and thus pre-philosophical, or merely dogmatic and without rigor.[83]

Adorno underlines Hegel's courage to devote himself to the dynamic dialectics of reality, and he shows how Hegel is very far from both establishing a static view of the empirical and advocating a static aprioristic theory. One must not misunderstand Hegel like this, but rather see his ambition to mediate reason and reality through the labor of spirit, which only can be done if reason hazards itself in reality. But this does not change Adorno's critique of Hegel and his integration of reality into his own philosophical system. Through a more radical negativity, dialectics must instead mobilize reality against reason in order to negate the negative and the dissimulated image of society that has subsumption as its principle.[84]

## c) Hegel as a capitalism-critical weapon

In order to return to Adorno's Marxism, the connection (from the perspective of identity thinking) between philosophy/science and politics/economy

---

[83] Adorno, *Hegel: Three Studies*, pp. 2-3.
[84] See Bonefeld, "Emancipatory Praxis and Conceptuality in Adorno", pp. 141ff.

that he establishes must now be clarified. Identity thinking takes shape both philosophically and politically, and it is this connection that makes his Hegelian Marxist critique of capitalism possible. Adorno's argument regarding this connection is constructed around their common history surrounding the domination of nature. The principles that characterize reality and that make it antagonistic are the very same principles that through the spirit of science cut through nature and humanity with calculative rationality and classificatory schemas. In both cases, domination over nature is at play and both science and capital expand their power over humans through the identity-principle. Through this principle, reason embraces everything external to itself and makes all identical with itself.[85] Society is torn apart in atomized individuals, things alienated from one another, but at the same time the diversity of things remains controlled by a common denominator. This connection between societal-capitalistic-equivalence and philosophical instrumental reason as two forms of nature domination is something that Horkheimer and Adorno already established in *Dialectic of Enlightenment*. Against the background of a historical breaking-point between subject and object, through which the subject (seemingly independent from reality) became able to dominate the objects, this domination becomes a scientific as well as societal (economic) reality.[86] The later Adorno writes, in the text "On Subject and Object" (1969), that critique toward society is a critique of knowledge and vice versa.[87]

But the decisive formulation in this matter, on which I am grounding my argument of Adorno's Hegelian Marxism, can be found in *Negative Dialectics*:

> The barter principle, the reduction of human labor to the abstract universal concept of average working hours, is fundamentally akin to the principle of identification. Barter is the social model of the principle, and without the principle there would be no barter; it is through barter that non-identical individuals and performances become commensurable and identical. The spread of the principle imposes on the whole world an obligation to become identical, to become total.[88]

Here Adorno shows how, on the one hand, the principle of barter fundamentally is related to the principle of identity, but also, on the other hand,

---

[85] Adorno, *Lectures on Negative Dialectics* (Cambridge: Polity Press, 2008), p. 9.
[86] Bartonek, *Philosophie im Konjunktiv*, pp. 83ff.
[87] Adorno, *Critical Models*, p. 250.
[88] Adorno, *Negative Dialectics*, p. 146.

that the principle of identity has its societal form in barter, and finally, that barter would not exist without the principle of identity. Adorno interprets the societal principle of barter and thereby also the fundamental principle of capitalist society in terms of identity. The principle of barter is a form of the identity-principle, which also takes shape in philosophy, science and enlightenment. In the quotation above, the principle's effect on the non-identical is also underlined: through this principle, singular and non-identical things are made comparable with each other and reduced to a common denominator as well as to the identical.

This means that Adorno with help from the concept of the non-identical criticizes the identity-principle both in philosophy, science *and* in capitalism. Hegel therefore becomes the main resource for Adorno's critique of capitalism. The non-identical reveals the oppression of philosophy and capitalism. But since he has adapted the concept of non-identity and holds onto his critique of Hegel as a thinker of totality,[89] his position should be considered as "Hegelian" Marxism, that is, with quotation marks. Even if Adorno criticizes capitalism through the question of identity and Hegel, Adorno turns the argument around, for example in his Hegel-studies, and writes that the falseness of society is a sign of the falseness of Hegel's philosophy. The conditions of civil society, which Hegel integrates and subsumes in his system, is a sign of the untruth in Hegel and that his system oppresses the non-identical in its totality.[90] This aversion of Adorno towards the concept of totality differs him from Lukács, who was more affirmative towards Hegel's conception of it.[91] Returning to Adorno's "Hegelian" Marxism once more, we can say that he uses the identity-concept to understand capitalism and the concept of non-identity to criticize it.[92] But what would the utopian be in relation to this critique? Expressed negatively, as a determinate negation, freedom would be the freedom from capitalism and its alienation; and for the non-identical, it would mean no longer being *for* the system. The system is questionable not least because it is defended in the

---

[89] Martin Jay, *Marxism and Totality* (Berkeley: University of California Press, 1984), pp. 245 and 261.

[90] Adorno, *Hegel: Three Studies*, p. 24.

[91] See Adorno, *Philosophische Früschriften* (GS 1) (Frankfurt am Main: Suhrkamp, 2003), and also Georg Lukács, *History and Class Consciousness* (Cambridge: MIT Press, 1971), pp. 12ff., and Braunstein, *Adornos Kritik der politischen Ökonomie*, p. 34.

[92] See also Vouros, "Hegel, 'Totality', and 'Abstract Universality' in the Philosophy of Theodor Adorno", for a discussion of Adorno's Hegel-inspired "anti-method" as a critique of capitalism, but which does not focus on the concept of identity.

name of the common, but, moreover, it is always to the benefit of a particular and powerful agent. Or as Adorno puts it: "The Hegelian subject-object is subject".[93]

This connection between Adorno's critique of capitalism and his identity critique is addressed by a number of commentators, but mostly only in passing, without specifically discussing the relation between them.[94] Braunstein is one of a few discussing this relation in greater detail and also points to how best to understand Adorno's critique of capitalism in the light of the question of identity.[95] He does this, though, without a reference either to the question of Adorno's Hegelian Marxism or to the relation between Hegel and Adorno. This may account for why Braunstein is somewhat unclear about the connection between capitalism- and identity-critique. At one point he suggests that the identity question is derived from the question of capitalism and exchange,[96] but in other passages he claims that the identity-perspective is the tool for interpreting the principle of capitalism.[97] Despite these interpretative ambiguities, Braunstein raises an interesting detail when he refers to a protocol from a seminar on economy and society 1957–1958 in which Adorno took part. Here a discussion is documented on the question whether the principle of barter comes out of an existing principle of thought directed towards the domination over nature, or if the opposite is the case: are the forms of thinking and their relation to nature determined by the principle of barter? But according to this source, Adorno argues that this way of putting the question is undialectical.[98] By only choosing one of these options, the question of their mutual influence is ignored. Braunstein himself also seems to suggest they are developed in a parallel way.[99] The question raised is whether a one-sided answer ignores how the principles have interacted dialectically and historically. But this is not all, one also runs the risk of ignoring their inseparability. This seems to be a significant argument against my presentation of Adorno's Hegelian Marxism as foun-

---

[93] Adorno, *Hegel: Three Studies*, p. 13.
[94] See for example: Gibson, "Rethinking the Old Saw: Dialectical Negativity, Utopia, and Negative Dialectic in Adorno's Hegelian Marxism" and Henry W. Pickford, "The Dialectic of Theory and Praxis: On Late Adorno", in Gibson & Rubin (eds.), *Adorno: A Critical Reader*.
[95] See also Sangwon Han, *Konstitutive Negativität: Zur Rekonstruktion des Politischen in der Negative Dialektik Adornos* (Bielefeld: Transcript, 2016), pp. 97ff.
[96] Braunstein, *Adornos Kritik der politischen Ökonomie*, pp. 389 and 395.
[97] Braunstein, *Adornos Kritik der politischen Ökonomie*, pp. 195, 388 and 390.
[98] Braunstein, *Adornos Kritik der politischen Ökonomie*, p. 274.
[99] Braunstein, *Adornos Kritik der politischen Ökonomie*, p. 396.

ded on the application of identity-critique on capitalism. But it does not change the fact that Adorno uses the concept of identity to criticize identification on the societal level.[100] Even if capitalism and identification are historically intertwined, Adorno primarily understands capitalism through the concept of identity and not identity through capitalism. Identity is not primarily being criticized as capitalism, but capitalism is mainly being criticized as identity.

In summary, Adorno can be understood as a Marxist critic of capitalism equipped with Hegelian tools. He addresses the problem of capitalism with help from his critique of identity systems, in which the non-identical is oppressed and where Hegel turns it into a constructive but subordinate moment within his system. In contrast, Adorno remodels the non-identical so that it becomes a system-critical concept, by virtue of which capitalism and Hegel are criticized in the same way. Both contain the problem of subsuming reality under criteria of identification. At the same time, Adorno understands the capitalist system as the most fundamentally idealistic form of identitarian thinking, historically derived from the thinking of ancient Greece. Here it becomes reasonable to interpret capitalism through the problem of identity, although it is important not to ignore the historical and dialectical meditations at play between capitalism and identification. Since Adorno criticizes Hegel's all-embracing system in the same way as capitalism, his Marxism can only be cautiously described as "Hegelian". One goes too far if Adorno is called a Hegelian. He devoted much of his work to fight against what Hegel stands for. Nevertheless, he defends much of Hegel's thinking as well, and is the beneficiary of much of Hegel's critical energy when Adorno develops his own critique of capitalism.

[100] See also Vasilis Grollios, *Negativity and Democracy* (New York: Routledge, 2016), p. 135.

# The Revisionist Within: Unity and Unilateralism in Hegelian Marxism and Beyond

*David Payne*

## Marxism's integrity

What today is at stake in revisiting the scene of the relation between Marx and Hegel, or, more broadly, in recalling to our own present Marxist interpretations of Hegel as well as Hegelian understandings of Marx? At the very least we might have to entertain the possibility that answers to this question are today not immediately forthcoming. The question surrounding where Marx stands with respect to Hegel is obviously a question that can be posed. But, if the question abides, there is the nagging doubt that it does so for principally logical rather than existential reasons. The relation between Marx and Hegel marks out a point of systemic undecidability inherent in Marxism itself: since the polysemy of both Marx's and Engels' own writings bear no stamp of clarity on the issue, then what follows is that, interpretatively, a decision *must* be taken—and taken interminably. But a decision for what? To what end? Why decide to decide?

These counter-questions are to be considered as one measure of our present malaise. For what we are arguably still in the process of coming to terms with is how the necessity of taking a decision on this issue has lost its sense of avowed urgency. Not only this: the collective experience of our own present is a fragmentation of the very *stakes* that had permanently been in play when the relation of Marx and Hegel was a question of utmost significance for previous generations of Marxists. What of these stakes specifically? They represent what Lenin famously canonized as the "three sources and three components of Marxism": Marxism is born from the confluence of French socialism, English political economy and German idealism.[1] These sources do not serve merely as historical antecedents, as the triangulation of lived traditions accounting for the contextual conditions out of which Marxism historically emerged; they index in a metonymic fashion the three distinct modes of practice in and by which Marxism is engaged: politics, science and philosophy. They are, as Lenin speaks of them, the component parts of Marxist thought, the co-existence and synchronicity of which secure for Marxism its operativity as both *perennis et universalis*.[2] If it is comprised of these three distinct and differentially calibrated practices, the stakes do not simply correlate with the practices as such, staking out the contiguous loci of Marxism's concern; the image of a Marxist engaged *in*, or even *by*, "politics", "science" and "philosophy" is liable to mislead, since Marxism immanently transformed the practice of these practices.[3] What therefore comes to be at stake is among other things the meaning of the practices that are recast in a new image. This shows itself in the variable ways in which Marxists interpreted Hegel, not just with respect to the meaning of the "philosophical", but with equal insistence in terms of the meaning also of the "scientific" and the "political".

Three stakes, then, can be provisionally enumerated, which, in one way or another, are thrown into relief by tracing out the elasticity of the distance separating Hegel from Marx:

1) The *practico-political*. Marxism not only carries within itself a concrete political demand for the real transformation of the social relations

---

[1] V. I. Lenin, "The Three Sources and Three Components of Marxism", *Collected Works of Lenin*, vol. 19 (Moscow: Progress Publishers, 1973).

[2] It is in this short propaedeutic that Lenin famously writes that "Marxism is all powerful because it is truth." He goes on to attribute this omnipotence, and the truth that is the cause of its force, to Marxism's comprehensiveness and, more significantly, its *integrity*: "It is comprehensive and *harmonious*, and provides men with an *integral* world outlook irreconcilable with any form of superstition, reaction, or defense of bourgeois oppression. It is the legitimate successor to the best that man produced in the nineteenth century, as represented by German philosophy, English political economy and French socialism." Lenin, "The Three Sources and Three Components of Marxism", p. 22.

[3] A point made with especial force by Louis Althusser. Please see: *Philosophy and the Spontaneous Philosophy of the Scientists and Other Essays*, ed. Gregory Elliot (London: Verso, 1990) and "On the Materialist Dialectic", trans. Ben Brewster, in *For Marx* (London: Verso, 1996). At the same time, we must not neglect the fact that Marxism has been described—often by its critics—as the negation of these practices i.e. as an "anti-science" (see, for example, Karl Popper), as an "anti-politics" (see Hannah Arendt) and an "anti-philosophy" (Karl Jaspers). Since, however, Marxism would augur a new understanding of what is possible and thinkable *as* a science, politics, and a philosophy—demanding no less than a transvaluation of the criteria by which each is indexable—then it is no surprise that Marxism became a principal site of contestation over the very meaning of each of these practices or modes of thinking.

and forms of economic production of capitalism, it opens up both a new political terrain and a new mode of political existence. Class antagonism reframes the very meaning of political practice. And at stake is the precise character of "class struggle" and the terms by which this struggle is waged. But, on this fundamental point, the history of Marxism contains within it a series of ambivalences about its own politico-strategic consequences. Mutually exclusive possibilities sit side-by-side: "spontaneity of the masses or party organization?", "reform or revolution?", "insurgency or hegemony?", etc. These questions, which function more as ultimatums, bring to a head the crucial question surrounding the principal subject of transformative political action, and Marxism's position with respect to this emancipatory subject. On the one hand, Marxism indexes a subject that is anterior to it (i.e. the laboring classes of industrial capitalism). On the other, Marxism is itself the site for the active production of an emancipatory subject—the "Proletariat", which can be said to be the result of, and be sustained through, Marxism and its attendant political apparatuses. Is the political agent for emancipatory transformation referable as a *datum*, as something given, a real existent with an objective basis in the lived relations of social production? Or is this collective subject itself an ideality that must be brought into existence by means of a *political* operation? Marxism's understanding of class identity roughly divides between, on the one hand, an empirical realism and, on the other, a genetico-constructivism. The very encounter between Marx and Hegel touches on these very questions. We can see how, for example, Georg Lukács' *History and Class Consciousness* or, even, Antonio Gramsci's idea of hegemony used Hegel to undermine the means and methods of thinking class in determinate and objective terms, and likewise how certain counter-responses, provided by the likes of Colletti and Althusser, identified within these Hegelian solutions the traces of voluntarism, historicism and subjectivism.[4]

2) The *scientificity* of Marxism, that is, the extent of the *theoretical* revolution effected by Marx—what Louis Althusser pronounced (borrowing a term from Gaston Bachelard) as the "epistemological break" locatable

---

[4] Please see: Louis Althusser, "Marxism is not a Historicism", *Reading Capital*, trans. Ben Brewster (London: NLB, 1970) pp. 119-144 and Lucio Colletti, "From Bergson to Lukács", in *Marxism and Hegel*, trans. Lawrence Garner (London: NLB, 1973), pp. 157-199, as well as Colletti, "From Hegel to Marcuse", in *From Rousseau to Lenin: Studies in Ideology and Society*, trans. Judith White & John Merrington (London: NLB, 1972) pp. 111-143.

within the work of Marx,[5] the result of which was an irreversible rupture
with its philosophical and politico-economic pre-history. Marx induced a
science, "historical materialism", which opened up a new continent for
knowledge. Just as the names of Pythagoras and Thales are assigned to the
founding of Mathematics and Galileo to Physics, Marx (referred to by Galvano della Volpe as the inventor of a "Moral Galileanism"[6]) discovered the
science of history, thereby effecting a double displacement. First a displacement of history from philosophical speculation to its scientific
analysis, and second a displacement of the "eternal ideas" of classical
political economy onto the terrain of history.[7] At issue was not simply *if*
Marxism designated a science, and not solely *how* it broke ineradicably with
the ideological precursors of both classical political economy (Smith,
Ricardo) and the philosophy of the left Hegelians (Proudhon, Feuerbach,
Bauer); the very meaning of science was at stake. As Simone Weil writes:
"you cannot claim for 'scientific socialism' if you have not a clear idea of
what science is, if consequently you have posited in clear terms the problem
of knowledge, of the relationship between thought and its object."[8]

3) The *philosophical* import of Marxism. Despite *prima facie* the question of Marxism's scientificity seemingly resting on the annulment of philosophy, alongside the clear textual discontinuities that one can locate in the
writings of Marx and Engels (e.g. *Theses on Feuerbach*, 1845, *The German
Ideology*, 1846, *The Poverty of Philosophy*, 1847), all of which would stage a
break with their erstwhile "philosophical consciences", a philosophical
practice is nonetheless incubated, even if it is not positively circumscribed
by Marx and Engels in the same way that applies to the fields of "science"
and "politics". The "dialectic" would be one such philosophical operator
present in Marxian thought, and for which, in the official organon of Soviet
Marxism, "*dialectical* materialism" (understood as the philosophical complement to the scientific discourse of 'historical materialism'), indexes. Notwithstanding the official classification of Soviet Marxism, western Marxists
(in varying degrees of opposition to Soviet "orthodoxy") continually retur-

[5] Louis Althusser, *For Marx*, trans. Ben Brewster (London: Verso, 1996), pp. 32-38.
[6] Galvano della Volpe, "For a Materialist Methodology of Economics and of the Moral
Disciplines in General", in *Rousseau and Marx and Other Writings*, trans. John Fraser
(London: Lawrence and Wishart, 1978), p. 201.
[7] Louis Althusser, *Lenin and Philosophy and Other Essays*, trans. Ben Brewster (London:
Monthly Review Press, 2001), p. 23.
[8] Simone Weil, *Oppression and Liberty*, trans. Arthur Wills & John Petrie (London: Ark,
1988), p. 29.

ned to the Marxian texts, locating therein a certain philosophical mutation, and seeking to draw out the implications for the expounding of a specifically Marxist philosophical practice. Such philosophical experiments may or may not imply the dialectic (whether methodologically or ontologically construed), but in any case, a confrontation with Hegel is unavoidable.

Politics, science and philosophy: the three constitutive practices of Marxism, each constituting a *necessary* but, in isolation, an *insufficient* condition in accounting for Marxism. It is at once a matter of recognizing, as Louis Althusser always insisted, the "differential specificity" of these moments,[9] as well as placing due emphasis on the specific difference of "Marxism" itself, as the proper name of a "discourse" that, so to say, is forged in and through the unification of the three irreducible instances of "politics", "philosophy" and "science".[10] It is on the basis of the co-existence of its constituent parts, on account of its wholeness and *integrity*, that Marxism summons its potency—or as Lenin makes clear, its *omni*-potence. On this very same basis, a *fourth* issue or stake reveals itself. It is a stake that does not relate to a further as-yet unnamed practice, but instead concerns the interrelation between these practices; in this regard, it can be said to overarch the others. It addresses the problem of the *revisionist*. The revisionist puts into question the equality between these constitutive features of the Marxist discourse, through the unilateralization of one practice or mode of thought at the expense of the others. Against the threat offered by the revisionist, what is at stake is to preserve or re-secure the very integrity of Marxism. Marxism, as a totalizing discourse, depends on the perfect coordination of its constituent parts. But, and this is from where our present sense of reticence springs: in the long drawn out night of Marxism's retreat, it is precisely its omnivalent pretensions that appear to have receded furthest from sight.

## Postmodern disintegration

If today we remain under the condition of the postmodern it is on account of the general state of incredulity shown toward meta-narrativity and *mutadis mutandi* to the systematizing proclivities of Marxism, as they have been presented above. Marxism, as necessarily a meta-discourse—as a "Discourse" that provides refuge for the "discourses" of the political mili-

---

[9] Cf. Althusser, "On the Materialist Dialectic".
[10] Althusser, *Lenin and Philosophy*, pp. 11-43.

tant, the philosopher and the scientist—has been a principal victim of such incredulousness. This indifference derives from the vitiating and paradoxical effects to which a "Discourse" succumbs when, in seeking a perfect balance between its constitutive elements, it must account for this wholeness by presenting it discursively, doing so, though, without reinscribing this unity within any one of the particular discourses with which it is in a relation of equiprimordiality. This leads to two suboptimal outcomes. Either Marxism must secure its unity by means of a fourth discourse, which supervenes onto the site of the unification of its three founding elements, but which, in not being immanent to the whole it founds, remains itself unthought. Or the very unity of its system must be accounted for by appeal to one of its constituent parts—either the philosophical, scientific or the political—as the privileged means by which the unity of ends is established. In doing so, though, the principle of equivalence is indubitably compromised for the unilateralization of one of its interiorized elements (whence the result of "revisionism"). Either way, the necessity of the composite integrity of Marxism, its unity and wholeness, is categorically compromised in times when a general fragmentation of the stakes and the heterogeneous ends that regulate them is collectively felt.

The logic of this disintegration of the "tasks" and "ends" of genres of discourse was, as we know, the subject of Jean-François Lyotard's report on what he diagnosed as the crisis of legitimation indicative of the "postmodern condition", according to which a series of conflicts arise

> between a language game made of denotations answerable only to the criterion of truth [science] and a language game governing ethical, social and political practice that necessarily involves decisions and obligations, in other words, utterances expected to be just rather than true and which in the final analysis lie outside the realm of scientific knowledge [politics] (...) and speculation [philosophy] that functions as a meta-subject in the process of formulating both the legitimacy of the discourses of the empirical sciences and that of the direct institutions of popular cultures.[11]

This heightened awareness of the "logic of disintegration" invades the Marxist problematic from within; by virtue of this recognition it is possible

---

[11] Jean-François Lyotard, *The Postmodern Condition: A Report on Knowledge*, trans. Geoff Bennington & Brian Massumi (Manchester: Manchester University Press, 1984), pp. 33-35.

to read the history of Marxism as a series of reflexive attempts to bring into accord the relatively autonomous discursive practices that are operative within it, changing emphasis and accent on the order of determination between its three levels, as an oarsman steadies his boat by veering in the opposing direction to compensate for any oversteering.[12]

This lengthy introduction has been taken to lay the groundwork for what is to follow for the remainder of this inquiry. It is from the outset to sound a cautionary note, in that the terrain upon which we today embark in investigating the relation between Marx and Hegel—and, in its mediated form, an investigation into how the history of Marxists received the question of Hegel and his relation to Marx—is evidently such that the once perspicacious stakes have been largely obscured and fragmented. Which is not to say, that, when taken singularly, there are no real questions to be heeded from within the provinces of politics, philosophy and theory. Rather, from the position of our own conjuncture, it is a matter of raising two redoubtable problems. Firstly, whether Marxism (in its Hegelianized form or otherwise) has any longer the capacity to bring into *general* relief and to present as a *unified* whole the stakes and tasks of philosophy, politics and science? And secondly, perhaps more fundamentally still, whether, under the condition of the irreversible fragmentation and heterogeneity of these practices, the very attempt of any such synthetic act invariably brushes up against its own impossibility?

## For Hegel: Philosophy unilateralized

In the history of Marxism, to broach the relation between Marx and Hegel is not solely to engage in a scholastic exercise; the value and effects of posing the question of their relationship has never been limited to the bounds of Marxist "philosophy", in any restricted disciplinary sense of the term. This

---

[12] In this connection, Lyotard offers some remarks in truncated form, noting how: "It would be easy to show that Marxism has wavered between the two models of narrative legitimation I have just described. The Party takes the place of the University, the proletariat that of the people or of humanity, dialectical materialism, idealism, etc. Stalinism may be the result, with its specific relationship with the sciences: in Stalinism, the sciences only figure as citations from the metanarrative of the march towards socialism, which is the equivalent of the life of the spirit. But on the other hand Marxism can, in conformity to the second version, develop into a form of critical knowledge by declaring that socialism is nothing other than the constitution of the autonomous subject and that the only justification for the sciences is that they give the empirical subject (the proletariat) the means to emancipate itself from alienation and repression: this was, briefly, the position of the Frankfurt School." Lyotard, *The Postmodern Condition*, pp. 36-37.

much has already been established. But the fact that the consequences of this interpretative encounter between Marx and the strictly philosophical thinking of Hegel reverberated outwards into other contiguous areas of concern, held within it the risk that the philosophical, as a specific mode of thought, would be carried too far beyond itself, encroaching illicitly on both the question of Marxist science and Marxist politics. The risk was that the *differentiae specificae* of these other constitutive parts of Marxism would be resultantly compromised.

Two notable thinkers, Louis Althusser and Lucio Colletti, operating within two quite distinct intellectual contexts and political situations, were very much alert to this problem. Even though the problematic is articulated in quite different ways, the works of Althusser and Colletti are unparalleled in showing a sensitivity towards: (i) the co-origination of a triptych of practices of thought by which Marxism is, we could say, "initially baptized"[13] as well as (ii) the difficulties of remaining consequent in this originating gesture, when the lived history of Marxism has, at every turn, been haunted by the risk of revisionism, which reveals itself through an encroachment of one of its constituent practices upon and over its other parts. This insight is in evidence when in a lecture on Hegel, dedicated to Jean Hyppolite, Althusser describes that:

> The Marx-Hegel relationship is a currently decisive theoretical and political question. [As] a theoretical question: it governs the future of the number-one strategic *science* of modern times: the science of history, as well as the future of the *philosophy* linked to that science: dialectical materialism. A political question also derives from these premises. It is inscribed in the class struggle at some level, in the past as in the present. (translation modified)[14]

A reckoning with the extent of the relationship between Marx and Hegel has wide implications. But as Althusser goes on to explain, in investigating the Marx-Hegel relation, the indexing of these implications will itself be affected by the manner in which the "philosophical" and the "non-philosophical" are brought into contact with one another: either the relation between these two thinkers constitutes an object for a general questioning,

---

[13] A term borrowed from the work of Saul Kripke. Cf. *Naming and Necessity* (London: Blackwell Publishing, 1981), pp. 96-97, 135-140.
[14] Louis Althusser, "Marx's Relation to Hegel", in *Politics and History: Montesquieu, Rousseau, Marx: Politics and History,* trans. Ben Brewster (London: Verso, 1982), p. 164.

traversing the entire field of Marxist practice (political, scientific and philosophical), or it implies a philosophical questioning that is simply generalized to cover non-philosophical practices. In the case of the former, philosophy becomes itself a datum for the practices of non-philosophy; whatever is at stake in, through and between Marx and Hegel is filtered through the distinct prisms of politics and science: non-philosophical questions are raised at philosophy for extra-philosophical ends. In the case of the latter, philosophy *informs* (in both senses of transmitting and shaping) the precise ways and wherefores of science and politics; whatever is at stake in other sites of Marxist practice gains its fullest expression in and through its philosophical articulation: philosophical questions are directed towards non-philosophical practices for the purposes of the solicitation of philosophical ends. What the latter possibility results in is the *unilateralization* or *superordination* of philosophy. For Althusser (as well as for Colletti), it remains a question of ascertaining the precise interrelation between the "philosophical" and the "non-philosophical", without falling victim to a treatment of Hegel and Marx that has as its principal purpose the universal accreditation of Marxism through its philosophical circumscription.

The temptation of a certain unilateralism of the philosophical in and through the treatment of Hegel and Marx is obviously great, since the question at stake already gains its immediate field of intelligibility internal to philosophy, as part of its own history. And yet this would be a simplifying assumption. What is considerably more crucial is that the possible unilateralization of the philosophical arises out of conditions that are not exclusively philosophical but are themselves *extra*-philosophical.

We can point to an important phase in the history of Marxism in which the value of Marxist philosophy reveals itself in all its lucidity. From around the 1920s up to the 1960s, a specific but dispersed filiation of Marxist thinkers—what we can designate loosely and not altogether unproblematically as "Hegelian Marxists" (Karl Korsch, Georg Lukács, Antonio Gramsci and Herbert Marcuse, foremost among them)[15]—responded to the direction of both Marxist science and Marxist politics, and to the double

---

[15] Like all such designators, "Hegelian Marxism" suffers from imprecision in capturing this somewhat disparate filiation of Marxists. Not only is there the obvious problem surrounding the extent to which the individual thinkers would themselves assent to such a label, there is more incisively the issue whether their works are in any way *sufficiently* Hegelian for the term to be warranted. Cf. Gillian Rose, *Hegel contra Sociology* (London: Athlone Press, 1981). Gillian Rose sees in much of Western Marxism the traces of Fichte and not Hegel.

crises it identified therein. This philosophical recuperation arose out of, and in opposition to, the "degenerative" Marxism of the Second International, with the purpose of replotting through Hegel the philosophical coordinates of Marxism, in order to reorient both its sense and direction. Reactivating the relation between Hegel and Marx served thus an extra-philosophical function: a direct refutation to both the nomological scientism of the Second International and its attendant political reformist and opportunist tendencies (tendencies incubated in, for example, the work of Kautsky, Plekhanov and Bernstein). To reassess the relation between Hegel and Marx served as a bulwark against the destructive one-sided implications of a putative scientific and concomitantly reformist Marxism that had increasingly become estranged from its own originary sources. This necessary counterpositioning, and the far-reaching implications of a renewed appreciation of Hegel's contribution to Marxism, was to have two principal effects: 1) the *rectification* of a seeming forgetting of the philosophical origins out of which the Marxian texts emerged and which they incubated within themselves and 2) the positing of philosophy as the *general* and *effective* means in the reassertion of Marxism's revolutionary force and its theoretical novelty.

This double gesture is, for one, captured in Karl Korsch's *Marxism and Philosophy*, published in 1923. Korsch reclaims Marxism for philosophy and philosophy for Marxism.[16] This means first the proper elucidation of Marxism's specific and essential intervention in the history of philosophy. But secondly, and more essentially, Korsch's act of reclamation touches on the role and function of philosophy in the wider field of Marxist practice. As Korsch himself describes, and in a way that will be seen as exemplary of Hegelian Marxism more widely understood: the force of philosophy serves as the *real* precipitate in the revolutionary upsurge of the masses on the march; the active, vitalizing and revolutionary elements of Marxism coalesce when precisely philosophy is itself ascendant within Marxist thought.[17] Philosophy is the ideological seal on revolutionary political practice (a part of a wider "historicist" interpretation of Marxism, uniting Korsch, Gramsci and Sartre).[18] Just as the philosophy of the German Idealists shored up the

---

[16] The same argument is advanced by Antonio Gramsci in his *Prison Notebooks,* trans. Quentin Hoare (London: Lawrence and Wishart, 1998), pp. 332-336.
[17] Korsch, *Marxism and Philosophy*, tr. Fred Halliday (London: New Left Books, 1971) p. 47.
[18] Here we would need to consider Sartre's claims in his *Search for Method* (New York: Vintage Press, 1968): "every philosophy is practical, even the one which at first appears

worldview within which the revolutionary political tendencies of the bourgeoisie fomented, Marxist philosophy is the necessary complement to the
historical emergence of the proletariat upon the political stage;[19] the physio-
logy of emancipation is comprised of the head of the philosopher and the
heart of the proletarian, as the young Marx was to write.[20] And yet in times
when Marxism is on the defensive—in the aftermath of severe political
defeat and disappointments, of aborted revolutions and suppressed re-
volts—philosophy is abandoned and the objectifying power of science takes
prominence.[21]

Philosophy does not only represent the flow of the subjective side of
history, i.e. when history is on the move and ideas take on a material
force—in contradistinction to the ebbing tide and political stagnation that
marks out the rise of "passive" science; philosophy is that mode of thinking,
which presents the necessity of both moments in the fullness of their
dialectical movement. It is the discourse that, once "the umbilical cord of its
*natural* combination has been broken"[22] by the vitiating effects of a vulgar
scientism and political reformism, returns Marxism to its founding unity. In
this way, philosophy comes to occupy a double position. Against the pas-
sivity of science, it is on the active side of history. But it is not only one side
of a two-sided historical process. It is the only discourse capable of comprehending this two-sidedness, that is, of presenting the dialectical movement of history itself. The privileged position of philosophy, and of Marxist
philosophy specifically, is on account of its modus, what specifies its
method, namely the dialectic—more precisely, the *materialist* dialectic.[23]

---

to be the most contemplative. Its method is a social and political weapon" (p. 5). The
entire description of philosophy that Sartre provides in this short text resonates greatly
with Korsch. On the question of 'historicism', consider Antonio Gramsci in the following passage from the *Prison Notebooks*, p. 442: "The philosophy of praxis is absolute
'historicism', the absolute secularization and earthliness of thought, an absolute humanism of history. It is along this line that one must trace the thread of the new conception of the world."

[19] Korsch, *Marxism and Philosophy*, p. 41.
[20] Karl Marx, "Contribution to the Critique of Hegel's Philosophy of Right: Introduction", *Marx and Engels: Collected Works*, vol. 3. trans. Richard Dixon *et al* (Moscow:
Progress Publishers, 1975), p. 186.
[21] This dialectic of philosophical hope and scientific circumspection is also noted by
Maurice Merleau-Ponty in chapter 3 of *Adventures of the Dialectic,* trans. Joseph Bien
(London: Heinemann, 1974), p. 64.
[22] Korsch, *Marxism and Philosophy*, p. 53.
[23] Georg Lukács, *History and Class Consciousness*, trans. Rodney Livingstone (London:
Merlin Press, 1971). Lukács famously announces that Marxism discovered the "dialectics
of history itself", its distinct philosophical contribution consists in comprehending that

Korsch's insight here is a point more widely shared by other variants of Hegelian Marxism.

The principal means to restore a sense of philosophical impetus to Marxism was to shore up the ineliminable traces of Hegel within the writings of Marx. What these Hegelian interpretations of Marxism rediscovered in Hegel was, in general terms, the source of Marx's own revolutionary *method*: "to be clear about the function of theory", writes Lukács, "is also to understand its own basis, i.e. its dialectical method."[24] Indeed, as Lukács claims in "What is Orthodox Marxism?" (more explicitly than Korsch), the methods of the empirical sciences stand in direct conflict with the revolutionary process that Marxist philosophy, in its very method, emboldens; the vulgar Marxists of the Second International, divesting themselves of the critical weapons to further proletarian struggle, and inveigled by the methods of the positive empirical sciences, served but to reproduce the conditions of existence of capitalist production:

> the dialectical method was overthrown and with it the methodological supremacy of the totality over the individual aspects; the parts were prevented from finding their definition within the whole and, instead, the whole was dismissed as unscientific or else it degenerated into the mere "idea" or "sum" of its parts. With the totality out of the way, the fetishistic relations of the isolated parts appeared as a timeless law valid for every human society.[25]

Like "every fetishistic science" the vulgar Marxists strayed into the illusory realm of an empirically verifiable "objectivity", having at their disposal a set of categories that merely sustained the fiction of capitalist reality, keeping it in a state of unquestioned pre-eminence.[26] The "fetishistic" form of science reveals itself in its objectifying and rationalizing propensity,[27] resulting in

---

"dialectics is not imported from history from outside, nor is it interpreted in light of history (as often occurs in Hegel), but is *derived* from history made conscious as its logical manifestation at this particular point in its development" (p. 177).

[24] Lukács, *History and Class Consciousness*, p. 3.

[25] Lukács, *History and Class Consciousness*, p. 14.

[26] Lukács, *History and Class Consciousness*, p. 10.

[27] The same mode of argumentation is adopted by Max Horkheimer, in his programmatic statements about "critical theory" and the future direction of the Frankfurt School, in "Traditional and Critical Theory". He writes: "The assiduous collecting of facts in all the disciplines dealing with social life, the gathering of great masses of details in connection with problems, the empirical inquiries, through careful questionnaires and other means, which are a major part of scholarly activity (…) all this adds up to a pattern which is, outwardly, much like the rest of life in a society dominated by industrial

science being blind-sighted twice over: once, on the side of the real, by the allure of a "phantom objectivity" revealing itself in its factical immediacy and second, on the side of cognition, in the form of a reified mind composed of a set of assumed and naturalized categories, "regarded as the true representatives of social existence."[28] As Lukács claims, more generally:

> the fetishistic illusions enveloping *all* phenomena in capitalist society succeed in concealing reality, but more is concealed than the historical, i.e. transitory, ephemeral nature of phenomena. This concealment is made possible by the fact that in capitalist society man's environment, and *especially* the categories of economics, appear to him immediately and necessarily in forms of objectivity which conceal the fact that they are the categories of the relations of men with each other. Instead they appear as things and the relations of things with each other.[29]

A line of reasoning seemingly of a piece with Marx's own insights into the fetish character of the commodity form, namely that "the definite social relation between men assumes, in their eyes, the fantastic form of a relation between things."[30] With one significant twist, however: the "fetishistic" form is no longer specifically tied to the commodity and to the capitalist system within which commodities are produced and consumed, exchanged and circulate. Attention now turns toward the empirical sciences that, according to Lukács, lay the very conditions under which a society of general reification is possible and endures; "by *scientifically* deepening the laws at work"[31] and by seeking to give a transcendental gloss to the categories that organize our experience as subjects of capitalism, science ensnares consciousness within a state of reified immediacy, thereby imprisoning thinking and acting in a perpetual reproducibility of what is, in its brute facticity, and thus effectively debarring the *actual* possibility of its transcendence. The technical and empirical sciences form the "web of rational calculation", from out of which is further spun the entrapment of modern man under the specific historical conditions of capital.[32]

---

production techniques." *Critical Theory: Selected Essays*, trans. Matthew J. O'Connell et al (New York: Continuum Press, 1995), p. 191.
[28] Lukács, *History and Class Consciousness*, p. 93.
[29] Lukács, *History and Class Consciousness*, p. 14.
[30] Marx, *Capital: A Critique of Political Economy*, vol. 1, trans. Ben Fowkes (London: Penguin, 1976), p. 163.
[31] Lukács, *History and Class Consciousness*, p. 113.
[32] The consequence here, as Lucio Colletti adeptly points out, and as we shall examine in greater detail later, is that the critique of science becomes total, in Lukács specifically, but

Lukács extends the famous Marxian analysis of commodity fetishism, in order to cover the sciences as the progenitor of reification. Certainly, the move is not entirely unwarranted. We can recall how in Marx's account of the commodity form, the sensuousness of the object as commodity, i.e. what confronts the gaze, conceals within itself what is imperceptible to the senses, namely the *supersensuousness* of its wider social and historical existence.[33] It is through laying out this description that Marx presents the structure of ideological misrecognition constitutive of commodity societies, a description that can equally be made to apply to a certain scientific procedure. Famously, Marx writes:

> in the act of seeing, of course, light is really transmitted from one thing, the external object, to another thing, the eye. It is a physical relation between physical things. As against this, the commodity form, and the value-relation of the products within which it appears, have absolutely no connection with the physical nature of the commodity and the material relations arising out of this.[34]

The ideological structure of the fetishized commodity mirrors the critique of the sensuous (empirical) materialism of Feuerbach that appears in the first of Marx's *Theses on Feuerbach*: Feuerbach's own sensualizing of matter ends up merely reproducing the classical image of contemplative detachment, surrendering thereby the vitality of active practical life to Hegelian philosophical idealism.[35] In both cases (in the analysis of the fetish character

---

in Hegelian variants of Marxism more generally: "reification is engendered by science. And since there is an absolute homogeneity and solidarity of nature between science and capitalism—to the point that science appears as an institution of the bourgeois world, destined to be swept away with it (…) Capitalist reification, in short, *is the reification engendered by science itself.*" *Marxism and Hegel* (London: NLB, 1973), p. 182. What precisely gets jettisoned, according to Colletti, is the exactitude of a critical analysis of capital (the very hallmark of Marxian thought), which requires a scientific practice in order to effectively understand and explain the complex structuration and operativity of capitalism. Anything that falls short of this simply repeats the "romantic critique of the intellect and science, and contributes little to a socio-historical critique of capitalism", p. 175.

[33] Marx, *Capital*, vol. 1, p. 164.

[34] Marx, *Capital*, vol. 1, p. 165.

[35] Marx, "Theses on Feuerbach", *Marx and Engels Collected Works*, vol. 5, trans. Richard Dixon *et al.* (Moscow: Progress Publishers, 1975). The first of Marx's theses on Feuerbach famously states: "The chief defect of all previous materialism (that of Feuerbach included) is that things [*Gegenstand*], reality, sensuousness are conceived only in the form of the object, or of contemplation, but not as sensuous human activity, practice, not subjectively. Hence in contradistinction to materialism, the active side was set forth abstractly by idealism—which, of course, does not know real, sensuous activity as such.

of the commodity form and in the first thesis on Feuerbach), the fallacy of empiricism is circumscribed. The concrete is not the material particularity of a physical thing that meets the gaze; exactly at this point of *immediacy*, when what appears to the eye in its physical form does not penetrate any further than its manifest appearance, and thus leaves unrecognized the variety of determinations that account for its *social* existence, the concrete is itself abstract. A thinking of the social whole is debarred in advance by a science that handles only determinate and particular things. In contrast, philosophical, that is, dialectical thinking makes possible the active articulation of "the concrete totality of the historical world, the concrete *and* total historical process."[36] The concrete *qua* concrete, Lukács quotes Marx, is "a *synthesis* of many particular determinants",[37] a "*unity* of diverse elements."[38] As a *unity* of the diverse, the concrete is the preserve of the whole, of totality. As a *synthesis*, this totality is not given as a datum, but the active result of thought: "the intellectual reproduction of reality"[39] brings a real diversity into accord with reason as the totalizer or totalizing instance. From within the province of Marx, Lukács secures a Hegelian insight otherwise disowned by the obdurate scientific materialism of the epigones of the Second International: the substance of the real is not matter; *a contrario*, "to posit oneself, to produce and reproduce oneself—that *is* reality."[40]

That Lukács (alongside the other Hegelian Marxists) repudiates the scientific Marxism of the Second International is not in question. What does remain in doubt is the presumption that an excessive scientism be rectifiable by and through a strictly philosophical counter-movement that risks burying entirely the problematic of science and the specificity of its practice; a philosophical destruction of science and scientific method that nonetheless makes possible a clearing for Marxism's philosophical grounding. Lukács, as we have already noted, claims that "to be clear about the function of theory is also to understand its own basis i.e. its dialectical method." This is a principal concern for the filiation of "Hegelian Marxist", more generally. What subtends Marxist theory is the dialectical method, and this methodological elucidation has strictly Hegelian provenance.

Feuerbach wants sensuous objects, really distinct from conceptual objects, but he does not conceive human activity itself as *objective* activity" (p. 6).

[36] Lukács, *History and Class Consciousness*, p. 145.
[37] Lukács, *History and Class Consciousness*, p. 9.
[38] Lukács, *History and Class Consciousness*, p. 9.
[39] Lukács, *History and Class Consciousness*, p. 9.
[40] Lukács, *History and Class Consciousness*, p. 15.

Hegelian philosophy: the last and ultimate expression of philosophy, for which, as Martin Heidegger put it, no "future, still higher standpoint over against it" is possible.[41]

It is in the very recuperation of the philosophical stakes of Marxism— through a reevaluation of the extent of Hegel's contribution to Marxism— that the problem of the *unilateralization* of the philosophical reveals itself. In returning to Marxism after a renewed exploration of Hegel, Hegelian Marxism preserves and deploys certain categorial distinctions that run counter to the purpose of effectively coordinating the three-fold relation between the orders of the political, scientific and the philosophical, from which Marxism gains its potency. Principal among them is the distinction between *Verstand* and *Vernunft*; a conceptual coupling already philo- sophically overdetermined, providing no neutral schema within which to carve out the differences between Marxist science, politics and philosophy, and by which to think the relative autonomy of each of its constituent practices. The stringently anti-Hegelian interpretations of Marx developed by Lucio Colletti and Louis Althusser were especially alive to this problem in their immediate Marxist forebears. While cognizant of the specificity of the practice of Marxist philosophy ("the paradoxically precarious existence of Marxist Philosophy",[42] as Althusser would speak of it), they understood that this need for the preservation of a distinct Marxist practice of philo- sophy should not encroach upon the stakes and function of class struggle and the scientific inquiries into the functioning and structuration of capi- talism.[43] For the rest of this chapter, however, attention will focus especially

---

[41] Martin Heidegger, "Negativity: A Confrontation with Hegel approached from Nega- tivity", in *Hegel*, trans. Joseph Arel & Niels Feuerhahn (Indiana: Indiana University Press, 2015), p. 3.

[42] Althusser, *For Marx*, p. 28.

[43] Louis Althusser poses the questions clearly in his important introduction to *For Marx*: "What is Marxist philosophy? Has it any theoretical right to existence? And if it does exist in principle, how can its specificity be defined?" (p. 31). Certainly, beyond the bounds of this particular investigation, it is nonetheless of significance to remind the reader that Althusser was especially uncertain with respect to what this specificity of Marxist philosophy consists in. His philosophical trajectory would see him providing quite different answers to the originary questions set forth in *For Marx*. Whence his later position, advanced for example in his lecture "Lenin and Philosophy", that "philosophy has no history, philosophy is that strange theoretical site where nothing really happens, nothing but this repetition of nothing. To say that nothing happens in philosophy is to say that philosophy *leads nowhere because it is going nowhere*: the paths it opens really are, as Dietzgen said, long before Heidegger, *'Holzwege'*, paths that lead nowhere." *Lenin and Philosophy*, p. 33.

on Lucio Colletti's critical appraisal of the philosophical unilateralism of Hegelian Marxism.

### In Hegel and against Marx: The absolution of reason, the sequestering of science

For Lukács and other Hegelian Marxists, a clarification of Marxist theory depends on attending to its philosophical basis—that is, on settling accounts with Hegel. Both the task and the object of this elucidation is the dialectical method: the gift of philosophy. Lucio Colletti's *Marxism and Hegel*, published in 1969, is a forensic and immanent scrutiny of this philosophical basis, in order to better elucidate both the philosophical and non-philosophical sacrifices that are the by-product of any such Hegelian clarification. Colletti demonstrates that attending to the dialectical method as the philosophical base of Marxism ends up producing the obverse effect. It produces a set of confusions and figurative evasions that render less clear the unity of Marxism as a science, philosophy and a politics. In Colletti's own words, the variety of restorative interpretations of Hegel provided by Marxists gave rise to a fundamental and necessary "error that now lies at the basis of almost a century of theoretical Marxism."[44] In what does this fundamental error consist? For Colletti, it is locatable in the restitution of both the Hegelian critique of *Verstand* and in its concomitant retrieval of *Vernunft*: the counterpositioning of sensuous intellect against the super-sensuousness of speculative thinking as reason, that is, the empirical factum of reality against the rational truth of thought as what is real. As Hegel himself writes in the *Science of Logic*: "the understanding *determines*, and holds the determination fixed; reason is negative and *dialectical*, because it resolves the determinations of the understanding into nothing; it is positive because it generates the universal and comprehends the particular therein."[45] We already see the distant echoes of this difference reverberate in the writings of both Korsch and Lukács; what transpires in the Marxist recuperative interpretations of Hegel is not only the confirmation of the inner diremption and prioritization of the faculty of "reason" over and above the "intellect" (or the "understanding"), but the further counterpositioning of "Philosophy" and the "sciences", setting two constituent parts of Marxism into direct conflict with one another. Preserved within Hegelian Marxism is

---

[44] Colletti, *Marxism and Hegel*, p. 27.
[45] G. W. F. Hegel, *Science of Logic*, trans. Arnold V. Miller (Atlantic Highlands: Humanities Press, 1993), p. 28.

the very content with which Hegel had ascribed to the opposition between *Verstand* and *Vernunft*, namely that the power of reason rests on philosophy fully unbridling itself from the determinate materialist sciences, realizing its own essence as an unmitigated idealism.[46]

For his part, Colletti begins by reconstructing the very principles of Hegel's philosophy out of which Marxist philosophy, tied to the dialectic, is said to emerge. Returning to Hegel's second remark at the end of the chapter on "determinate being" in the *Science of Logic*, Colletti underlines the definitional problem that any Marxist Philosophy, which takes sustenance from Hegel in expounding the necessary philosophical stakes inscribed in Marxist practice, is forced to encounter, namely Hegel's claim that, *in esse*, philosophy is consubstantial with idealism.[47]

The trouble, according to Hegel, is that the historical existence of philosophy has invariably been inconsistent with its own essence. Despite the principle of idealism, particular philosophies have retained an extra-logical substrate—heterogeneous to all conceptual mediation—that stands as the facticity of being and the halting-point for thought. Kantian philosophy would be foremost among them, which in the name of philosophy nonetheless subtracts something qualitatively vital from it, namely its speculative interest. Hegelian philosophy would be the purification of philosophical thought, cleansed of all such extraneities and limitations. Hegel's critique of Kant will for Colletti be of principal significance;[48] the acceptance of Hegel's critical account of Kant by those putative Hegelian Marxists would explain, according to Colletti, the superordination of philosophy as the principal instance in Marxist thought, as well as, by the very same token, accounting for a tendential regression behind the theoretical breakthrough of a Marxian materialist science.

For Hegel, Kant's refutation of the ontological argument for the existence of God dramatizes the glaring inconsistency of a philosophy not properly consequent with what it means to philosophize; Kant's claim that existence is not a *real* predicate, is a materialist postulate of scientific and thus *non*-philosophical derivation. The postulation is a function of the understanding. Once existence is predicated to a concept, the concept does

---

[46] Hegel, *Science of Logic*, p. 27: "Philosophy, if it would be a science, cannot, as I have remarked elsewhere, borrow its method from a subordinate science like mathematics."
[47] Hegel, *Science of Logic*, p. 154.
[48] Colletti, *Marxism and Hegel*, see esp. chapters 6, 7 and 8.

not become *etwas mehr*.[49] Kant exemplifies accordingly: while the concept of one hundred thalers is no more than one hundred thalers, only the depositing of one hundred *actual* thalers positively affects the creditor's bank balance. The most basic materialist postulate (shared by the empirical sciences) arises from this: being and thought, real existence and the "idea", are non-identical. A first-order implication for Hegel is that if this Kantian refutation of the ontological argument for the existence of God holds, it does so in a way that goes against the interests of reason and of philosophical thought. Kant is guilty of misapplying the conditions by which objects of experience are apprehended—that is, the rules governing the understanding (the faculty par excellence of science and of common sense)—in order to censure philosophical speculation about a Being that, precisely as supersensible, cannot be made to yield to the rules of the understanding.[50] Hegel accordingly turns the tables on Kant. If Kant's critical gesture consists in reeling in the excesses of speculative metaphysics by divining the line separating legitimate from illegitimate knowledge claims (such that the critical task results in the sequestering of reason by means of the finitude of the understanding) then Hegel takes issue with Kant's illicit over-extension of the understanding, which serves as the universal arbitrator of the legitimate ends of knowledge, and seeks instead to liberate reason from the shackles of the finite, thus unbridling thought from the faculty of the understanding. While for Kant the ontological argument proceeds erroneously through the misapplication of the categories that regulate the understanding, for Hegel, the Kantian critique of the ontological argument operates defectively by misapplying the rules of the intellect to legislate over a thinking that necessarily exceeds the scope of its dominion. Hegel thus writes: "the *genuine* criticism of the categories and of reason is just this: to make *intellect* aware of this difference and to prevent it from applying to God the determinations and relationships of the finite."[51]

A second and related implication of this minimal postulation of materialism is, according to Hegel, to have consecrated the finite and *mutadis mutandi* to have vanquished the infinite. The infinite is banished to the farthest reaches of what is conceivable, to what is other than being or simply

---

[49] Immanuel Kant, *Critique of Pure Reason,* trans. Werner S. Pluhar (Cambridge: Hackett Press, 1996) A598/B626-A600/B628. For Hegel's refutation of Kant's position, please see Hegel, *Science of Logic,* pp. 86-88
[50] Hegel, *Science of Logic,* p. 89.
[51] Hegel, *Science of Logic,* see pp. 90 and 45, where a similar point is made.

non-being. "Finitude is the most stubborn category of the understanding";[52] riveted to the sensible, the understanding is bound to what is determinate, particular, conditioned, in short to what is given. Whatever is finite is a determinate positivity, but as conditioned and determined, it is a positivity that cannot be mistaken for self-sufficiency. The finite is a limited being, and as limited it is infected by what is on the hither side of its limit, namely that it is not. The point of externality vis-à-vis a determinate being is an "otherness" that nonetheless is an interiorzsed and reflected moment of the in-itself of *that* particular being: "something has a limitation", states Hegel, "insofar as it has negation in its determination, and the determination is the accomplished sublation of the limitation."[53] What the understanding cannot properly grasp is this accomplishment through sublation, through rational mediation, even if it *partially* apprehends that finitude is at once what is in its immediacy a positivity *and* is invaded by a negativity, which impels it to move beyond its determinate limit, condemning it to "having-ceased-to-be": the understanding is at one with common sense in surmising that the empirical law governing all things is that "the hour of its birth is the hour of its death";[54] what comes into existence will fade from being, the presence of something is haunted by its inevitable absenting into nothingness. Where the understanding errs is by converting nothingness into an "imperishable absolute", so that the very ceasing-to-be is absolutized: "the determination or destiny of finite things takes them no further than their *end*."[55] A melancholic elegy is composed from the wistful serenade of the understanding, converting non-being as "the determination of things and at the same time making it imperishable and absolute." As Colletti will summarize Hegel's argument against the *finitism* of the understanding, "finitude, never ceasing in its ceasing, is thus eternal."[56] This is the spurious infinity Hegel repudiates, on account of the two related errors it commits: first by "infinitizing the finite" (the movement of which has been described above) and second by finitizing "the infinite" (the result of the understanding's dualistic and "one-sided" apprehension of the finite and the infinite).[57] The spurious

---

[52] Hegel, *Science of Logic*, p. 129.

[53] Hegel, *Science of Logic*, p. 133.

[54] Hegel, *Science of Logic*, p. 129.

[55] Hegel, *Science of Logic*, p. 130.

[56] Colletti, *Marxism and Hegel*, p. 10.

[57] Hegel, *Science of Logic*, p. 91: "The commonest injustice done to a speculative content is to make it one-sided, that is, to give prominence only to one of the propositions into which it can be resolved."

infinity of the understanding resolves infinity into the open series of a succession of finite things, which rise and fall, emerge and fade, *ad infinitum*. The infinite is solely the outcome of the movement of perpetuity of the ceasing-to-be of things at the same time as it remains itself external and indifferent towards them.

Were the infinite external to the finite, then the former would be just the presentation of one side of a conceptual couplet, rendering infinity just a finite particular. To be equal to the infinite requires that it not be one of a pair, a part of a whole, but the whole itself, the very movement within which the determinateness of being is carried forth, like the suspended sedimentary particles within the sea, dissolving and crystallizing, separating and rejoining: "the finite is *in* and *of* the infinite"[58] and thus does not stand opposed as the determinate finite being does to the aloofness of an Idea beyond, held at an unreachable distance. As the "determination of the finite in the infinite", it is none other than the expression of the movement of ideality.[59] The finite thereby relinquishes its self-sufficiency as a real and concrete datum, the finite thus becomes itself ideal: "the ideal *is* concrete, veritable being, and on the other hand the moments of this concrete being are no less ideal—are sublated in it; but in fact what is, is only the concrete whole from which the moments are inseparable."[60] As the very medium by which the finite as determinate being is seized, the infinite makes its crossing over into the actual, it is immanent to *this* world: spirit is "made flesh", the Idea "transubstantiated".

As Colletti notes (following the early Marx), this immanentization of the infinite plays a double game: it means *first* the realization and fulfilment of the essence of philosophy as the consummation of speculative idealism but *second* it represents the consolidation of the Christian Logos through the repatrification of God;[61] the absolute is pulled down from its position of indifference towards the world, shoring up the place of God not as the "there" of a "nowhere", but as a "here", already within the ambit of the real. With respect to the first point, reason is finally superordinate over the understanding, it presides over the sublation of the finite into the movement of the whole. This Hegelian operation is affirmed by Lukács, Korsch

---

[58] Hegel, *Science of Logic*, p. 151.
[59] Hegel, *Science of Logic*, p. 143.
[60] Hegel, *Science of Logic*, p. 155.
[61] Colletti, *Marxism and Hegel*, pp. 10-20; Karl Marx, "The Poverty of Philosophy", *Marx and Engels Collected* Works, vol. 6, trans. Richard Dixon *et al.* (Progress Publishers: Moscow, 1976), pp. 162-165.

and Marcuse, as the revolutionary thrust of Marxist *philosophy* in contrast to the conservationist analytic of the sciences. In both Hegelian thought and in Marxist theory, the realization of philosophy comes about through a methodological rectification: the principle of "(non-)contradiction"—sacrosanct for the understanding—is dispensed with and is substituted for the dialectical method, which bespeaks "the identity of identity and non-identity." It puts philosophy on the right methodological track, delivered from the syncretism that had otherwise dogged it. As Colletti sums up Hegel's—and *mutadis mutandi* Hegelian Marxism's—abjuring of the intellect: "the intellect reifies everything that it touches. It transforms that which is not a thing into the *finite*. It is not the principle of philosophy or idealism, but of *Unphilosophie*."[62] While for philosophy proper, "there are no things, there is only reason; there is no exclusive determinacy, 'a right this here', that excludes its opposite, but a rational inclusion, 'a this together with that'—i.e. the unity of "sameness" and "otherness", of "being" and "non-being", of finite and the infinite, *in* the infinite." [63]

Colletti's rendering of the Hegelian reaffirmation of philosophical (dialectical) reason over the limits of the understanding is neither neutral nor innocent;[64] it filters the Hegelian logic through those attempts by Marxists at a restorative interpretation of Hegel. In Lukács, we had earlier noted in what way the faculty of the intellect is not only *transmuted* into the very progenitor of the reificatory logic, but moreover that reification becomes correlated with the sciences as such. The empirical or regional sciences which, in Hegel's *Logic*, are bound to the "immediate", are in Lukács beholden to a pernicious "phantom objectivity", that, in the words of Herbert Marcuse, "confin[es] men within the existing order of things and events."[65] Lurking behind this homage to Hegel is Weber's sociological thesis concerning the "iron cage" of scientific rationality; modern societies are marked by a series of systemic rationalizations "whose unity derives from its orientation towards that aspect of the phenomena that can be grasped by the *understanding*, that is created by the understanding and hence also subject to the control, the predictions and the calculations of the understanding."[66] The understanding condemns thought to a circularity that solely assents to

---

[62] Colletti, *Marxism and Hegel*, p. 12.
[63] Colletti, *Marxism and Hegel*, p. 12.
[64] Of course, on strictly Hegelian premises, dialectical reason constitutes a pleonasm.
[65] Herbert Marcuse, *Reason and Revolution: Hegel and the Rise of Social Theory* (London: Humanities Press, 1991), p. 20.
[66] Lukács, *History and Class Consciousness*, p. 113.

what is, to the present state of affairs. The appropriation of dialectics is a methodological necessity, since it is the only *rational* method that affords a breaking-out of the empiricist allure of the immediacy of the object and its substitution with a genetic and dynamic seizing of the movement of history as a whole. A possibility that finds, in Lukács, its compressed elucidation in the following passage from Hegel's *Philosophy of Right*:

> What is actual is necessary in itself. Necessity consists in this that the whole is sundered into the different concepts and that this divided whole yields a fixed and permanent determinacy. However, this is not a *fossilized* determinacy but *one which permanently recreates itself in its dissolution.*[67]

A "fossilized" determinacy: this is the determinate being—static, particular, reified—of the understanding, in contradistinction to the *process* of determination of the parts through the whole, which constantly resolves itself out of its own compositional dissolution, that the dialectical reasoning of Hegelian philosophy accomplishes. Marxism and Hegel would be brought into tandem on this point of philosophical method.

But, as Colletti reminds us, the Hegelian assuaging of the intellect in the name of reason plays a game that at the same time is other than methodological: Hegel's *Logic* is the transliteration of logic into the "Christian Logos". The immanentization of the infinite does not solely mean the final overcoming of the limitations of the understanding by reason; it serves as the consecration of the absolute, of God. Hegel's *Logic* is thus a philosophical method in the service of an onto-theo-logic.[68] Reason restored through the dialectic represents the abjuring of the understanding and, against the non-attribution of existence to the concept (an entailment of Kant's prioritization of the intellect over reason), restores the ontological proof concerning God's existence. The "logic" or "method" of the dialectic does not stand apart from the ontological proofs to which the method lends itself. Colletti writes, with respect to Hegel: "the world was negated *in order to* give way to the immanentization of God; the finite was 'idealized' *so that* the Christian *Logos* could incarnate itself and so pass over from the beyond to the here and now."[69] The method is a *function* of the ends on which Hegel puts the dialectic to work; it is teleologically inscribed. And for Colletti, this

---

[67] Hegel cited in Lukács, *History and Class Consciousness*, p. 16.
[68] Colletti, *Marxism and Hegel*, p. 106.
[69] Colletti, *Marxism and Hegel*, p. 80.

is the most debilitating outcome, it is a method, whose results could not be any different, even were they extricated from the philosophical system under which dialectical reason operates.[70]

## The mystifying shell and the rational kernel

The question animating the Marxist reception of Hegelian philosophy has always been whether the "revolutionary" dialectical *method* can be salvaged from the "reactionary" character of the *system* within which the former is imprisoned. This question, invariably raised, has with equal persistence convoked as a response the curiously convoluted and mixed metaphorical figures that Marx employs in the Postface to the Second Edition of the first volume of *Das Kapital:* "With him [Hegel], it [the dialectic] is standing on its head. It must be turned right side up again, in order to discover the rational kernel within the mystical shell."[71] An operation that contains within it not one, but two tasks: an inversion and an extraction. The *inversion*, which necessitates putting the dialectic on its feet and an *extraction* requiring that the rational content of the dialectical method be pulled out from the retrogressive forms imprisoning it: the real substantializations or hypostases of the absolute in the form of God and the Prussian State.

We are now in a position to make a more general summary of the stakes over which Hegelian Marxism presided. First, the "rational kernel" to be saved is the philosophical affirmation of "reason" over the "intellect". The dialectical method certifies what is proper to philosophical thinking, that is, the grasping of the "whole" and thereby the traversal of the conditioned limitations self-imposed by the "intellect"—the faculty of both common-sense and the sciences. In his analysis of the *Science of Logic*, Colletti cogently demonstrates that the dialectic reveals its rational essence by first overcoming the intellect on its way to fulfilling philosophy as *idealism*.[72] Even when delivered out of the "mystical riggings" of the absolute—i.e. the onto-logical demonstration of the existence of God, the ascension to absolute knowledge or the consecration of the bourgeois State—the dialectical method is fundamentally compromised by way of its inherent idealism. The

---

[70] Colletti, *Marxism and Hegel*, p. 48.

[71] Marx, *Capital*, vol. 1, p. 103.

[72] Colletti, *Marxism and Hegel,* pp. 47-51. Althusser also reproached Hegelian Marxism for seeking to say something substantive about Marxist theory from the convoluted metaphor adopted by Marx, and reprised many times subsequently. See "Contradiction and Overdetermination", in *For Marx*, pp. 89-94.

"dialectic" is delivered up in the name of "idealism" by way of idealism. Taken on its own, therefore, the extraction of the rational kernel of Hegelian philosophy is incapable of providing Marxism with its differential features, both as an ostensive materialism and as a critical *science* of political economy. Nonetheless, it is with the discrete operation of an "extraction"— with the opposition between the intellect of the "sciences" and the reason of "philosophy" preserved—that some notable restorative Marxist interpretations of Hegel have plied their intellectual labor. Indeed, Lukács diligently transcribes this metaphorical gesture found in Marx's Postface to *Capital*, so as to separate out "the progressive part of the method" from the "corpse of the written system [that] remained for the scavenging philologists and system-makers to feast upon",[73] claiming that in extracting the rational method Marxism is unimpeachable. Marcuse, with equal certainty, proposes that "what Marx criticizes as the dialectic is the foundation and actual 'content' of Hegel's philosophy—not its (supposed) 'method'."[74] For "while Marx criticizes, he simultaneously *extracts* the positive aspects, the great discoveries made by Hegel."[75]

Since the *extraction* appears insufficient on its own, it would seem that the task of an inversion is both indispensable and primary. As a precondition for laying claim to the "rational kernel" of Hegel's philosophy, the dialectic must first be put on its feet, in order that philosophy is convertible from an essential idealism to a materialism. This is how precisely Marx puts the case in the Postface to the first volume of *Das Kapital*: "It must be turned right side up again, *in order to* discover the rational kernel within the mystical shell". The problem is that the sign-posting of this causal direction does nothing to waylay the awkwardness of the metaphorical construction; an awkwardness that reveals a fundamental incompatibilism between the "extraction" of a dialectics and the achievement of materialism through "inversion". Here we encounter what Colletti describes as a "heterogenesis" of tasks: the "extraction" and the "inversion" operate neither on the same level nor do they refer to the same object.[76] As referent, the dialectic is in each operation at cross-purposes. Through inversion, the dialectic stands the right side up: "material conditions determine consciousness", it is "not consciousness that determines ideas." But what is achieved in the course of

[73] Lukács, *History and Class Consciousness*, p. 18.
[74] Marcuse, *Reason and Revolution*, p. 41.
[75] Marcuse, *Reason and Revolution*, p. 41.
[76] Colletti, *Marxism and Hegel*, p. 79.

the inversion (the founding of the "materialist dialectic") is unsupported by the outcome of the extraction (the traversal of the intellect by reason and the realization of philosophy's essence as an idealism). Colletti will present the dilemma in the following way: *either* a dialectical materialism is possible but it cannot sanction the extraction of the "rational" kernel of the Hegelian method, since it is precisely Hegel's claim that dialectics inclines toward idealism, which is in question. *Or* the commitment to the materialism of the dialectic is inessential and therefore the entire thrust of Hegel's methodological breakthrough can be retained but its commitment to materialism vanquished. In the case of the former, "dialectical materialism is simply an idealism unaware of its own nature,"[77] and in the latter, by being aware of its own nature, a Marxist dialectics is forced to drop the very identificatory traits (i.e. its "materialism", its claim to "scientificity") that would serve to specify the distinguishing characteristics of "Marxism" over its Hegelian antecedent. Colletti thus sees the law of the "broken middle" taking its revenge. This reveals itself historically, in the way that the Marxist recuperation of Hegel bifurcated between two tendencies. On the one hand, the "official" codification of "dialectical materialism", which leant on principally Engels, Plekhanov's and Lenin's restitution of a "dialectic of matter" and, on the other, what became known as "Western Marxism".[78]

Separated in what is otherwise the inseparable unity of Marxism is its philosophical and scientific determinations. "Science" and "philosophy", metonymically indexed by way of the "intellect" (or "understanding") and "reason", come to be in dispute. The integrity of Marxism, comprised of the three co-originary practices of politics, philosophy and science, is torn asunder. Exemplary in this is the argument that Marcuse develops in *Reason and Revolution*, and which Colletti represents in the following way:

> The "understanding" i.e. common sense and science, which adhere to things and real factual data, represent positivism and the safe and sound world of the bourgeoisie; they stand for conformism and preservation, and that "false" and "self-assured" consciousness which sticks closely to objects, knowing full well that if "this security disappears", it will be driven into "unrest" and will undergo fear and anguish. Contrariwise, Reason, which denies that things exist outside of thought and states that things are truly "real" when they are no longer things but thoughts—this Reason represents the destruction of the established order. The "intellect" is positive thought, thought that recognizes existing reality. Reason,

[77] Colletti, *Marxism and Hegel*, p. 60.
[78] Colletti, *Marxism and Hegel*, pp. 61-62.

on the other hand, which negates the world (…) for the sake of the Idea, is negative thought. The understanding (intellect) is Reaction—Reason is Revolution.[79]

The relative autonomy of the variable instances of Marxist practice ("philosophical practice", "scientific practice", "political practice"), is placed in doubt. Colletti indexes the crisis accordingly: philosophical reason divides *and* conquers. It divides the understanding—the province of science and common sense—from reason, in order to sequester science as a *sub*-ordinate instance; but it also, in the same process, covets political practice, by converting it into a mirror image of itself. "Reason *is* revolution": as the use of the copula indicates, an identity is metonymically advanced between a certain mode of philosophy (dialectical philosophy) and a particular type of politics (transformative, that is, emancipatory politics). The individuated "faculties" are thus assigned a political destination, resolving revolutionary politics into Reason and the understanding into, at best, reformism, but at worse a quietist acceptance of the way things are. Only the Marxist dialectic, by means of a philosophical elucidation, can surmount not only the pitfalls of science but also the political compromises of the understanding. As Lukács will write, once the terrain of dialectical materialism is relinquished, politics is forced to wage its struggles "on the 'natural' ground of existence, of the empirical in its stark-naked brutality".[80] But in doing so, it is caught within the yawning divide between the received objectivity of the situation (the "milieu of the facts") and the subjective force of an action necessary for the transformative overcoming of that situation. "Being" and "action", the "is" and "ought" stand opposed to each other. The faculty of the will (for the young Lukács) is lobotomized in the absence of any dialectical mediation.[81] Politics, for its revolutionary capacity to be realized, must place itself in the service of dialectical (philosophical) reason.

Inversions and extractions, then. For Colletti, out of this fog of metaphors, the situation becomes clear. The method and system of Hegel cannot be separated in the way that countless Marxists, reiterating Marx of the Postface, had otherwise supposed. Neither an inversion nor an extraction, nor (more accurately) an extraction on the basis of a prior inversion of the Hegelian priority of the being of the Idea over matter was in any way

---

[79] Colletti, *Marxism and Hegel*, p. 77.
[80] Lukács, *History and Class Consciousness*, p. 23.
[81] Lukács, *History and Class Consciousness*, p. 23.

congenial to thinking the specificity of Marxism—not philosophically, politically nor as a science.[82] The *differentiae specificae* of Marxism had been irrevocably compromised. The superordination of a philosophical elucidation of the methodological bases of Marxism that, according to Hegelian Marxists, would serve to place Marxist theory and practice on a firmer footing, led however only to accentuate an instability between the differentiating tasks of Marx. How, though, could the indexing of this problem of philosophical superordination and the concomitant attenuation of the role of science be reckoned with without, on the one hand, re-drawing the lines of emphases from the opposing direction, such that once more the problematic of science would gain a paradigmatic status in the thought and practice of Marxism, resulting thereby in the unilateralization of science over and against its other sites? This problem is arguably insoluble, and we will not find the answer in Colletti.

For Colletti, materialism and not the dialectic constitutes the defining feature of Marxism. This goes beyond specifying on which of the two terms emphasis is to be placed. "Dialectical materialism"—which in the canon of Marxist orthodoxy represented the *philosophical* branch of "Marxism"—is exposed by Colletti as a *contradictio in terminis*. Marxism must decide: either the dialectic or materialism, either continuity with its immediate prehistory or a profound break with Hegelianism. *In nuce*, either philosophy or science. Colletti writes:

> "the intellect", the principle of non-contradiction, is common sense, the point of view of materialism and of science. Everything that philosophy or idealism asserts—that the finite "is not" and the infinite "is"—the "intellect" presents in the reverse order. Materialism and science are, therefore, the *Unphilosophie*, that is the antithesis or negation of philosophy.[83]

This attestation leaves little doubt about the mutual exclusion involved, and where, with respect to this opposition, Colletti positions himself. Marxism is first and foremost a materialist *science*, not a *dialectical* philosophy. It falls on the side of what was the object of Hegel's repudiation, the "understanding", which proceeds by way of determinate being, by way of the immediacy of what is perceived as appearance, as both finite, particular and

---

[82] Colletti, *Marxism and Hegel*. A similar (but by no means identical) point is made by Althusser in "On the Materialist Dialectic".
[83] Colletti, *From Rousseau to Lenin*, p. 113.

conditioned. This leads Colletti to admit the following mutually exclusive alternative: "If *scepsis towards matter* (…) is a moment that is indispensable to philosophy *qua* idealism, the critico-materialist point of view cannot help but imply a *scepsis* towards reason."[84] The critico-materialist standpoint, the position of a putative Marxist Science, vouchsafes for the principle of non-identity between thinking and being; the very principle, which at the beginning of the *Science of the Logic*, Hegel identifies in Kant, in order to break with Kant, and which Hegelian Marxism also puts into question as the insuperable starting point for an elucidation of its own philosophy. For Colletti, Marxism must not deviate from the most elementary materialist principle: existence is unassimilable to the concept (it is "extra-logical", a "something more" (*etwas mehr*)). Dialectical philosophy, which resolutely breaks with this basic materialist premise, cannot be anything other than idealism. As correlative terms, the real and rational convert existence into a logical category; the real movement of things is thereby said to mirror the movement of the concept, the two orders of *causa essendi* and *causa cognoscendi* are thus elided. The speculative pretensions of reason compromise a forensic analysis of the real and determinate conditions of capitalist expropriation and exploitation and the hazardous irruption of class struggle. Colletti (and Galvano della Volpe before him) shows the extent to which Marx was quickly alert to these Hegelian defects (even if many subsequent Marxists chose to ignore the warning signs). In Marx's early critical readings of Hegel and in his polemic against the Hegelianism of Proudhon in the *Poverty of Philosophy,* Marx diagnoses the litany of errors that follow from the methodological reasoning of the dialectic. "Just as by dint of abstraction everything is transformed into a logical category", it follows for Marx that

> one has to make an abstraction of every characteristic *distinctive* of different movements to attain movement in its abstract condition–a *purely formal* movement, the purely logical formula of movement. If one finds in logical categories the substance of all things, one imagines one has found in the logical formula of movement the absolute method, which not only explains all things, but also implies the movement of things.[85]

---

[84] Colletti, *Marxism and Hegel*, p. 92.
[85] Marx, "Poverty of Philosophy", p. 162.

The speculative pretensions of reason is exposed as scientifically fraudulent, a fraudulence that shows itself: (i) in the amphibologous reasoning it adopts, i.e. in confusing 'the logical formula' of change with real movement; (ii) in the subsequent manner that it resolves the contingencies of historical conditions into the logical deduction of their categorial unfolding; (iii) in the paucity of any determinate or actual knowledge that the "absolute method" of the dialectic is said to furnish. An interpretation of the history of social formations through the logical procession of the categories empties out history of its empirical density, evacuating thought of the very content required to incisively interrogate the actual historical conditions of societies, leaving thinking thereby to be ravaged by its own analytical impotence—what della Volpe diagnosed as its "cognitive sterility."[86]

The fault of those (Marxists or otherwise) who recognize in the philosophy of Hegel the revolutionary thrust of the dialectical method resolve the difficult labor of a direct confrontation with actual history, that is, with the concrete and specific conditions of overdetermined conjunctures, into a formal schema accounting for the movement of the whole as such, namely History and its *logical* unfolding.[87] It was as if the generic formulae for thinking change and movement that Hegel bequeathed—i.e. "the negation of negation", "the unity of opposites", the dialectical transformation from "quantity into quality", etc.—were sufficient to guarantee knowledge of the complex social, economic and political processes of capitalist societies; as though, equipped with such a formal demonstration, the critical categories of the Marxian critique of political economy could be extricated from the historical site of their theoretical production (principally from the volumes of *Capital*) and employed *a prioristically*—transformed into *generic* ideas, the analytical and explanatory power of which was supposed to apply, without exception, to all societies, past, present and future. Marx's own method—of which section three of the *Einleitung* (1857) to the *Contribution to the Critique of Political Economy* served as the most lucid expression—was, according to Colletti, at variance with this deductive approach. Marx produced *determinate* knowledge (for della Volpe and Colletti, following Kant, the only kind!) on the basis of a *specific* structuration of society, i.e. capitalist society, the actual existence of which constituted a *real object* for the understanding and not an ideality fabricated out of reason, forged

---

[86] Galvano della Volpe, "For a Materialist Methodology of Economics and of the Moral Disciplines in General", in *Rousseau and Marx*, p. 178.
[87] Colletti, *From Rousseau to Lenin*, p. 8.

through the "mere relation of idea to idea", the result of "an internal monologue within thought itself."[88] The task of the understanding is, from out of the phenomenality or the factuality of *this* society, to synthesize multitudinous *real* social causes and to reach an order of conceptuality that is neither *determined* exclusively by the bounds of particular empirical cases, from which knowledge has been induced, nor, through the genericity of an abstraction, is it rendered indeterminate. Avoiding the possibilities of both induction and deduction, a Marxist materialist science presents its knowledge through "determinate abstractions": a mode of concept whose explanatory and disclosive power is not restricted to the particular conditions from which it was induced but constitutes a historically conditioned model, law or rule that, despite its conditioned appearing, functions as an *explanans* for other contemporaneous concrete cases.[89]

For this purpose Marx needed no *philosophy* of history, which would contrive to fashion history in its own rational image but a science of the real object, of a determinate societal and historical conjuncture. We can see precisely in what way the priority between *Vernunft* and *Verstand*, between the ascendant heights of philosophical speculation and the activities of scientific calculation and common sense, is once again reversed by Colletti, and how the cascade of oppositions, said to take their bearings from this difference—"History" and "nature", "Being" and "determinate being", "the unconditional" and "the conditioned", "infinity" and "the finite", "the idea" and "matter", "negativity" and "positivity", etc.—find an arrangement that is something other than the dialectical surmounting that Hegelian Marxism seeks to present. As a reversal, though, Colletti does not jump out of the Hegelian shadow. Instead caught within the prismatic filter of the opposition between *Verstand* and *Vernunft*, seeking to wrest the scientificity of Marxism away from any crypto-metaphysics, preserving the "understanding" against the speculative pretensions of reason, he ends up converting the entire problematic into a simple alternative: either a Marxist materialist science or a Marxist dialectical philosophy.[90] The stakes are decisively clear,

---

[88] Colletti, *From Rousseau to Lenin*, p. 3.

[89] A determinate abstraction proceeds from the concrete to the abstract to the concrete again (notationally expressed by della Volpe as C-A-C$^1$). This is opposed to the circle augmented by generic abstractions, that takes the notational form of A-C-A. Please see: Galvano della Volpe, "For a Materialist Methodology of Economics and of the Moral Disciplines in General", pp. 194-197.

[90] The severity of this alternative becomes all the more pronounced in Colletti's later work, up to and including his irreversible break with Marxism. For an especially clear

but the terrain decidedly barren. And this is the problem, of course: in spite of himself, despite Colletti's own position as a philosopher, as a delicate reader of Kant and Marx, the entire philosophical vocation of Marxism gets tied to Hegelianism and vanquished as a result. All that remains is the promise of a Marxist Science, which itself, tied to the "understanding", comes close to simply taking its place next to the other empirical sciences.[91] But not only this. A political silence engulfs the alternative that Colletti lays bare. On precisely the terrain of Marxism, which compossibilizes "science", "philosophy" and "politics", the stand-off between Marxist science and Marxist philosophy turns Marxist politics into an unsuspecting residual instance.

It is symptomatic that in an essay entitled "Marxism: Science or Revolution?", Colletti is led back into a classically Leninist position: "building the party requires something 'from without.'"[92] This "without" meaning, of course, "science". Science becomes the conditioning moment for politics: "the working class cannot constitute itself as a class without taking possession of the scientific analysis of *Capital*."[93] This is no time to replay the entire history of Marxism from the point of view of what, from this investigation, would appear as the suppressed "third term", which, if only it had the proper space for articulation, would resolve the impasses and incurable

recapitulation of the unbridgeable divide between the means and ends of a Marxist science and a Marxist Philosophy, Cf. Colletti, "Marxism and the Dialectic", trans. John Matthews, *New Left Review* 1:93, September-October, 1975, pp. 3-29.

[91] Arguably, Althusser was more successful in his attempt to think the novelty of the Marxist practice of science, choosing as he did to rethink the very question of the scientificity of the sciences, which did not needlessly box the very practice of a Marxist science into an empiricist corner (the ultimate price paid by Colletti). Nor was the idea of a Marxist Philosophy forfeited (even if Althusser equivocated greatly on the question of what a Marxist Philosophy can do?). For Althusser's critical appraisal of Colletti and della Volpe (who ultimately stand charged of 'empiricism' and less explicably 'historicism'), cf. "Marxism is not a Historicism", *Reading Capital* (London: NLB, 1970). The empiricism of science becomes the unilateralized instance of Marxist practice. It becomes the model by which all other practices are validated. As Althusser clearly describes: 'Colletti (...) maintains that history, and even reality itself, have an '*experimental structure*', and therefore that in essence they are structured like an experiment. If real history on the one hand is declared to be 'industry and experiment' in this way—and if all scientific practice is defined as experimental practice, it follows that historical practice and theoretical practice have one and the same structure.' p. 135. Having said this, the value of Colletti over Althusser shows itself in the systematic interpretation that Colletti gave of Hegel, something that (for all manner of reasons) is not present in Althusser (notwithstanding Althusser's early "pre-Marxist" forays into Hegel's *Phenomenology of Spirit*).

[92] Colletti, *From Rousseau to Lenin*, p. 236.
[93] Colletti, *From Rousseau to Lenin*, p. 236.

blind-spots that have arisen from the received struggle between the Hegelian Marxists, who sought to revivify Marxist philosophy, and those who, in turn, had as their principal aim the scientific accreditation of Marxism. Were it now, as a matter of course, the immediate task of this chapter to raise the political instance of Marxism (that would find ample expression in the work of Lenin, Luxemburg, Sorel, Gramsci, moments in Althusser), we would however find that it is not itself immune to a recalibration of Marxism's interiorized relations that borders on an overcompensation of its own subordinate status. What results is the overextension of the bounds of political practice that encroaches on the relative autonomy and specificity of Marxism as a science and a philosophy. Gramsci's remark that "since *all* action is political, can one not say that the real philosophy of each man is contained in its entirety in his political action?", would be the respectable face of this politicism while the Lysenko affair would constitute its most destructive manifestation.[94]

*

To Marxism, societies today apply the pious moral dictum, *de mortuis nihil nisi bonum*. This is itself an indicative sign of its historical fragility, even if the sustained economic crises of the last decade have brought with them a renewed interest in elements of a Marxian analysis of capitalism—i.e. the cyclical crises of capitalism, of systemic unemployment and precarious labor, etc. The problem has been that the utility of the writings of Marx have become restricted to being just a further theoretical prism through which to sift through the veritable crises of capital. Concessionary analytical acceptance results in canonical domestication. Marx takes his place next to Smith, Ricardo, Bentham and Keynes, within some decontextualized ether. These are barely the crumbs of comfort to keep the infirmed hopeful, they are instead the offerings that serve more as a "halo of consolation". They thus serve notice, for one thing, on the disintegration of the unity of its ends as well as recognition of the acute difficulties surrounding the heterogeneity of the means (politics, philosophy, science) by which such ends were to be secured. It is, as Colletti feared already in the mid-1970s, namely that Marxism soldiers on emboldened by its principles alone but in denial of the facts:

---

[94] Gramsci, *Selections from the Prison Notebooks*, p. 326.

the only way Marxism can be revived is if no more books like *Marxism and Hegel* are published, and instead books Hilferding's *Finance Capital* and Luxemburg's *Accumulation of Capital*—or even Lenin's *Imperialism*, which was a popular brochure—are once again written.[95]

Ultimately, to repose the question of the relation of Marx and Hegel today runs the inevitable risk of being "the foible of a few university professors." But, this would be unnecessarily churlish. If the posing of this question serves a purpose in our own present then what it permits is a laying out of that immense history (at one and the same time philosophically, politically, scientifically charged) in front of us, even while at the same time today we deem it best to place the future of its recommencement behind us. In this sense, it might well be that by seeking to regain a time that has passed, by posing once more the extent of the connection or disconnection between Marx and Hegel, all we can possibly gain is a stronger sense of the times we have lost. This is said as much in respect to Marxism as much as it is to discredit our own times.

[95] Colletti, "A Political and Philosophical Interview", *New Left Review* 86, 1974, p. 28.

# A Lacanian Hegelianism:
# Slavoj Žižek's (Mis-)Reading of Hegel

*Anders Burman*

When reading Slavoj Žižek, it does not take long to realize that Hegel's philosophy is one of his most important theoretical points of departure. Unlike most other contemporary political theorists and thinkers, he does not even hesitate to call himself a Hegelian. In an interview from 2002, he says, for example, "even when I sometimes try to be critical of Hegel, I remain a Hegelian".[1] Like many other political radical Hegelians, Žižek is also in some way influenced by the theories of Marx as well as by Lenin and other later Marxist thinkers. Nevertheless, it would be incorrect to regard him as an orthodox or traditional Marxist. Ian Parker is therefore right when he writes: "Žižek does indeed see traditional Marxism as out of date, no longer applicable to new conditions of global capitalism", with the important addition, "and this does lead him back to Hegel".[2]

Žižek's readings of Hegel's texts are based on Jacques Lacan's theories of the subject and the unconscious, and less on Marx. Indeed, Žižek explicitly defends a psychoanalytically impregnated Hegelianism. With an implicit but obvious reference to Marx's eleventh thesis on Ludwig Feuerbach, he writes in *The Plague of Fantasies* that the motto of such a Lacanian reading of Hegel could be: "Philosophers have hitherto only interpreted Hegel; but the point is also to change him."[3]

This article examines Žižek's way of understanding and interpreting Hegel, but also how in different ways he changes the Hegelian philosophy in

---

[1] Slavoj Žižek & Glyn Daly, *Conversations with Žižek* (Cambridge & Malden: Polity, 2004), p. 63.

[2] Ian Parker, *Slavoj Žižek: A Critical Introduction* (London: Pluto Press, 2004), p. 109; see also p. 2.

[3] Slavoj Žižek, *The Plague of Fantasies* (London & New York: Verso, 2008), p. 122.

line with his own purposes and interests. So what does Žižek more precisely highlight in the works of Hegel, what does he tone down and why does he do all of this? These are the main questions to be pursued in the following essay. Furthermore, there will be reasons to look more closely at how in this context Žižek uses Lacan's psychoanalytic theories as well as evaluating the originality of his interpretation and use of Hegel.

That Žižek's interpretation of Hegel's philosophy is grounded on Lacanian psychoanalysis, as well as that his understanding of Lacan is based of Hegelian dialectics, was already clear from the doctoral dissertation he wrote in Paris under the supervision of Jacques-Alain Miller.[4] The dissertation, *Le plus sublime des hystériques*, was defended in 1982 and since then Hegel has been a standard reference in most of Žižek's texts. Hegel plays a more prominent position in some of them, such as *The Sublime Object of Ideology* (1989), *Tarrying with the Negative* (1993) and *The Ticklish Subject* (1999). But besides the French dissertation, one book stands out in Žižek's interpretation of Hegel, namely *Less Than Nothing: Hegel and The Shadow of Dialectical Materialism* from 2012. Unlike most of his other books, it deals almost exclusively with Hegel, although one recognizes much of its content and themes from other texts of Žižek. With a phrasing he has used about himself in another context, Žižek is indeed a master of cannibalization of his own earlier writings—so also with his texts on Hegel.[5] However, spanning more than 1 000 pages, *Less Than Nothing* appears not only to be Žižek's *magnum opus* (so far, it should be added), but it must also be said to be a substantial contribution to the already immense literature on Hegel.

Thus the empirical material is especially large for such an examination of Žižek's readings and uses of Hegel's philosophy.[6] Just as he does with Lacan,

---

[4] See Slavoj Žižek, *Le plus sublime des hystériques: Hegel avec Lacan* (Paris: Press Universitaires de France, 2011); in English, *The Most Sublime Hysteric: Hegel with Lacan*, trans. Thomas Scott-Railton (Cambridge, UK: Polity, 2014).

[5] Slavoj Žižek, *How to Read Lacan* (London: Granta, 2006), p. 121.

[6] There are also several previous writings about Žižek's readings of Hegel in general and *Less Than Nothing* in particular; see Sarah Kay, *Žižek: A Critical Introduction* (Cambridge & Malden: Polity, 2008), pp. 17-47; Todd McGowan, "Hegel as Marxist. Žižek's Revision of German Idealism", in Jamil Khader & Molly Anne Rothenberg (eds.), *Žižek Now: Current Perspectives in Žižek Studies* (Cambridge & Malden: Polity, 2013), pp. 31-53; Adrian Johnston, "'Freedom or System? Yes, Please!' How to Read Slavoj Žižek's *Less Than Nothing: Hegel and the Shadow of Dialectical Materialism*", in Agon Hamza (ed.), *Repeating Žižek* (Durham: Duke University Press, 2015), pp. 7-42; Agon Hamza & Frank Ruda (eds.), *Slavoj Žižek and Dialectical Materialism* (Basingstoke, Hampshire: Palgrave Macmillan, 2016). See also Dominik Finkelde, *Slavoj Žižek zwischen Lacan und Hegel: Politische Philosophie – Metapsychologie – Ethik*, 2 ed. (Wien & Berlin: Verlag Turia +

Žižek treats Hegel in relation to a variety of thinkers, phenomena and contexts; it can be anything from black holes and astrophysics to the class-consciousness of the proletariat, the shortcomings of identity politics or why Hegel is the ultimate Christian philosopher. As is often the case concerning Žižek, however, it is not always easy to determine which position he is taking when discussing Hegel. He sometimes seems to say one thing about Hegel's thinking, only on the next occasion—sometimes just a few pages later in the same text—say something quite different. Nevertheless, there is reason to claim that, on the whole, he is unusually consistent—for being Žižek—in his readings of Hegel, from the French doctoral dissertation to *Less Than Nothing*. Both thematically and perspectivally, there is in these many and in some ways heterogeneous analyses a fairly clear red thread, although his analyses has subsequently been deepened as well as widened.

## The delayed truth about Hegel

In line with the expanding tendency of his writings—that he constantly includes new areas of knowledge in his countless texts (not to mention all his talks and lectures) that have almost the character of a constantly ongoing monological discourse—Žižek in *Less than Nothing*, and more than in his previous work, makes some attempts to situate Hegel in the philosophical context of the late eighteenth and early nineteenth century. It is not a matter of a consistent intellectual historical contextualization that tries to link Hegel's philosophical project to the socio-economic and political situation in which he lived; but the fact remains that Žižek here, in a relatively systematic manner, relates Hegel to other thinkers in German idealism, from Immanuel Kant and Friedrich Hölderlin to Johann Gottlieb Fichte and Friedrich Wilhelm Joseph Schelling. In *Less Than Nothing* one can in other words perceive an implicit ambition to understand Hegel and the other German idealists on their own philosophical terms. It is also clear that Žižek has an affirmative understanding of German idealism, which he characterizes as an extremely rich period of intellectual creativity; in fifty years, more happens in the field of human thought—from the publication

Kant, 2013), Reinhard Heil, *Zur Aktualität von Slavoj Žižek: Einleitung in sein Werk* (Wiesbaden: VS Verlag, 2010), pp. 26-50; and Peter Dews, *The Limits of Disenchantment: Essays on Contemporary European Philosophy* (London & New York: Verso, 1995), pp. 236-258.

of Kant's *Critique of Pure Reason* 1781 to Hegel's death in 1831—than in the centuries following it or even in the millennium, taken as a whole.[7]

Interpreted through the theoretical prism of psychoanalysis, Žižek nevertheless insists that the originality and power of Hegel's thinking cannot be fully understood only on the basis of the context in which he lived. Instead, his philosophy must be interpreted on the basis of our own horizons. Today we necessarily understand Hegel differently from how others interpreted him, say, during his own lifetime or during the 1890s, 1930s or 1960s. According to Žižek, the very "truth" about Hegel, as well as Hegel's own "truth", seems to be or, more strongly put, *is* different today than before. In this regard, Hegel's philosophy may be compared with Sophocles' *Antigone*, which Žižek describes as follows:

> The "true" meaning of *Antigone* is not to be sought in the obscure origins of what "Sophocles really wanted to say", it is constituted by this very series of subsequent readings—that is, it is constituted *afterwards*, through a certain structurally necessary *delay*.[8]

Remarkably, Žižek refers in this context to Hans-Georg Gadamer and his thoughts on the significance of the history of effect in every interpretation. Although they may in many ways appear to be each other's theoretical antipodes, the wild speculative Žižek and the philologically careful Gadamer are completely in agreement about the futility of trying to get access to an author's original intentions. Žižek is of course no traditional hermeneutic thinker. To interpret Hegel based on our horizons means here to read him through a delayed, retroactive and—*nota bene*—Lacanian perspective. This is, according to Žižek, absolutely necessary. As he puts it in *The Sublime Object of Ideology*, "the only way to 'save Hegel' today is through Lacan".[9] One could say that Gadamer was open to many things, but most certainly he would not have entertained such a pronounced anachronistic and psychoanalytic reading of Hegel or other classical philosophers.

---

[7] Slavoj Žižek, *Less Than Nothing: Hegel and the Shadow of Dialectical Materialism* (London & New York: Verso, 2012), p. 8.

[8] Slavoj Žižek, *The Sublime Object of Ideology*, p. 243. See also Slavoj Žižek, *Antigone* (London: Bloomsbury Academic, 2016).

[9] Žižek, *The Sublime Object of Ideology*, p. xxxi.

## The fight against the standard image of Hegel

Against this background, it is not so strange that Žižek gives a quite different picture of Hegel than both Gadamer and most other modern interpreters of the German thinker. As Žižek characterizes the traditional view, Hegel was an idealistic and conservative system philosopher, who claimed that he had grasped and explained the current state, society and culture as well as everything that had happened in human history. In line with this understanding of the arts, religion and philosophy, as spiritual manifestations or expressions, Hegel maintained that ultimately all that has happened and all existing institutions can be brought back to the world spirit, a substance that is also a subject and that in its continual process of historical development grasps and consumes everything that stands in its path. With his all-encompassing system, the traditional Hegel claimed that he had given the definitive interpretation of spirit's development through the history of humanity and towards the absolute end of reason and freedom. According to this established interpretation of Hegel, which, according to Žižek, is based on gross simplifications and misunderstandings, Hegel was, in short, a holistic system thinker and an all-declaring "panlogical monster".[10]

Not immune from making simplifications of his own, Žižek claims that virtually all Hegel's critics in the last 150 or 200 years have assumed this fundamentally distorted picture of Hegel. Adopting his own psychoanalytic vocabulary, Žižek describes how Hegel's philosophy for his many critics touches on something real.[11] When making this claim, Žižek refers to one of Lacan's various determinations of the real, namely, as a void we can only know through its effects. From Søren Kierkegaard and the late Schelling, through Marx, Friedrich Nietzsche and Theodor W. Adorno, to Gilles Deleuze and contemporary poststructuralists, generations of thinkers have situated themselves in opposition to a reconciling thought system they have attributed to Hegel. But Žižek's point is that the "Hegel" used and reused in such a way is only a fiction, a construction; his name constitutes a void or an empty space, which we can only understand through its effects, just like the real.[12] In short, the Hegelian absolute subject, which swallows up everything that gets in its way, is the retroactive fantasy of his critics.[13]

---

[10] Žižek, *The Most Sublime Hysteric*, p. 1.
[11] Žižek, *The Most Sublime Hysteric*, p. 2.
[12] This understanding of the real as something that is present only through a series of effects is used by Žižek too in his interpretation of Hegel's dialectics of the relation between the master and the slave, though in a positive way. "[I]t is senseless to determine

The widespread standard view of Hegel also includes a specific under-standing of his relation to German idealism in general. The common interpretation of this highly influential philosophical tradition is that Kant's first two Critiques—*Critique of Pure Reason* and *Critique of Practical Reason*—established a gap between necessity and freedom, between *Sein* and *Sollen*, which then subsequently both Kant and the famous German Idealists who followed had the ambition to bridge. It was with his third Critique that Kant tried to solve the problem of the duality by means of judgment, but that bridging attempt was insufficient, according to the idealists, who in different ways attempted to take the step "beyond the Kan-tian line", as Hölderlin expressed it.[14] Friedrich Schiller, for example, high-lighted art and what he called the play drive as constituting such a connecting and reconciling force. In another way, Fichte put the human's—or rather the self's—free action at the center of things while Schelling, for his part, chose to ontologize Kant's critical epistemology and transcendental dialectics. Even Hegel, according to this standard interpretation, chose the ontologizing line, albeit in a different way from Schelling and the other idealists.

As Žižek reads Hegel—and this appears to be one of his more original contributions to the rich literature on the German philosopher—he was not, however, particularly interested in bridging the gap between Kant's first and second Critiques, at least not in a way that would reconcile the two. When Žižek explains Hegel's position on this particular question, he refers to the distinction between understanding and reason that was used already by Kant and then elaborated in different ways by the idealists, including Hegel, who came after him. According to Žižek, Hegel transformed this distinction for his own interests and purposes: the ambition of exceeding the duality is for him related to the conventional and limited level of the understanding. But, when viewed in the light of, the more advanced and complex dialectical reason, there is simply no need for such reconciliation. "In other words," Žižek writes in *Less Than Nothing*, "Hegel's move is not to

---

when this event could have taken place," he writes; "the point is just that it must be presupposed, that it constitutes a fantasy-scenario implied by the very fact that people work—it is the intersubjective condition, of the so-called 'instrumental relation to a world of objects'." Žižek, *The Sublime Object of Ideology*, p. 183.

[13] Žižek, *Less Than Nothing*, p. 261.

[14] Friedrich Hölderlin in a letter to Ludwig Neuffer, October 10, 1794, cited in Sven-Olov Wallenstein, "The Vicinity of Poetry and Thought", in Marcia Sá Cavalcante Schuback & Luiz Carlos Pereira (eds.), *Time and Form: Essays on Philosophy, Logic, Art, and Politics* (Stockholm: Axl Books, 2014), p. 289.

'overcome' the Kantian division, but rather to assert it 'as such', to remove the need for its 'overcoming' for the additional 'reconciliation' of the opposites".[15] From this, Žižek concludes—in contrast to the common inter-pretation of Hegel's relationship to Kant—that the author of *Phenomenology of the Spirit* did not at all attempt to ontologize his critical predecessor. The fact is actually the opposite: Hegel "de-ontologized" Kant, since in his three Critiques Kant had not been sufficiently consistent when he held on to the thing-in-itself and the distinction between phenomena and *noumena*.

Like dialectics itself, Hegelian reason is for Žižek associated with an over-shooting process, without any definite harmonious reconcilie. Reason and the dialectic open up, while understanding closes and delimits. This is the antagonistic way that Žižek reads the *Phenomenology of the Spirit*:

> far from being a story of its [the antagonism's] progressive overcoming, dialectics is for Hegel a systematic notation of the failure of all such attempts—"absolute knowledge" denotes a subjective position which finally accepts the "contradiction" as an internal condition of every identity.[16]

Absolute knowledge, which is the ultimate end of spirit's development according to the *Phenomenology of the Spirit,* and which Žižek in another context describes as Hegel's "name for a radical experience of self-limi-tation", is here equated with the crucial point in Lacanian psychoanalysis when the analysand realizes that the big other does not exist—*il n'y a pas de grand autre*.[17] In both cases, the crucial point is about a perspectival shift, through which what was previously seen as mistakes and failures now seem to acquire the character of something positive—in a sense, a truth. It is in line with this that Žižek emphasizes that the way to truth often passes through mistakes. Two positions that may appear as opposites might well be sublated in a third position, which includes these two at the same time as representing a new, higher form of truth. The idea of such an *Aufhebung*, which does not smooth over the original contradictions, conflicts and divisions, is an integral part of Hegelian dialectics.

[15] Žižek, *Less Than Nothing*, p. 267.
[16] Žižek, *The Sublime Object of Ideology*, p. xxix. See also Slavoj Žižek, *For They Know Not What They Do: Enjoyment as a Political Factor* (London & New York: Verso, 2008), pp. 99f.
[17] Slavoj Žižek, *Absolute Recoil: Towards a New Foundation of Dialectical Materialism* (London: Verso, 2014), p. 244, and Žižek, *The Most Sublime Hysteric*, p. 90.

## A philosophical Mozartian

Also on the subject of dialectics, which after all is at the heart of his readings by Hegel, Žižek makes his own original interpretation. With his own interest in ontology, Žižek certainly does not deny that Hegelian dialectics has an obvious metaphysical side, and he even writes that Hegel became Hegel when he abandoned the distinction between logic and metaphysics, after that he had realized, Žižek states, that "Logic *already is* Metaphysics". Here Žižek adds a further psychoanalytically inflected insight: "what appears as an introductory analysis of the tools required to grasp the Thing is already the Thing."[18] Nevertheless, it is clear that Žižek is mainly interested in the formal or structural dimensions of Hegel's dialectical thinking. For example, he describes the German philosopher as a "Mozartian", explaining that the "Mozartian practice of articulating the truth by the very distance of the form from its content finds its exact counterpart in Hegel's notion of the 'formal side [*das Formelle*]' articulating the truth of a given phenomenon."[19] Form has, Žižek writes elsewhere, "an autonomy and efficiency of its own."[20] This is said to be one of Hegel's most significant philosophical insights.

It is hardly possible to conceal that, from his Lacanian perspective, Žižek interprets Hegel selectively. As we have seen, his places particular emphasis on some aspects of Hegel thinking, while he chooses to ignore others. On the issue of the selective dimension of his interpretations, it is itself revealing that Žižek refers most often to the *Phenomenology of Spirit* and the Logic. This is not unusual. Indeed, it should be noted that this is something uniting many other leftwing theorists influenced by Hegel, among them Georg Lukács. In comparison with the author of *History and Class Consciousness*, however, it is in fact remarkable that Žižek refers also to Hegel's *Elements of the Philosophy of Right*, something that Lukács rarely did. Like many other Hegelian Marxists (with Herbert Marcuse as a notable exception), Lukács was in fact quite indifferent toward Hegel's arguments for a reformist state policy.[21] Since *Elements of the Philosophy of Right* belongs to Hegel's late conservative period, *Phenomenology of Spirit* and

---

[18] Žižek, *Less Than Nothing*, p. 49.
[19] Žižek, *The Sublime Object of Ideology*, p. 215f. In *The Parallax View*, p. 28, Žižek emphasizes that Hegel's Logic does not constitute "a system of universal ontology".
[20] Slavoj Žižek, *Violence: Six Sideways Reflections* (London: Profile, 2009), p. 125.
[21] On Lukács' uses of Hegel, see, Burman, "Back to Hegel! Georg Lukács, Dialectics, and Hegelian Marxism", and on Marcuse's Hegelian Marxism, see Anders Bartonek, "Herbert Marcuse: No Dialectics, No Critique", both in this volume.

some other of Hegel's earlier writings appear to be more fruitful from a radical Marxist perspective; this was in any case the view of Lukács and many other Hegelian Marxists during the twentieth century.

However, the ever-provocative Žižek finds radical elements even in the Hegelian philosophy of right. For example, a creative interpretation is made out of Hegel's description of the "mob" or the "rabble". It is hard not to perceive what Hegel writes on the "mob" as simply and squarely pejorative; the rabble is not something he appreciates, presenting it as a threat to the entire state. But Žižek makes a completely different point:

> When Hegel emphasizes how society—the existing social order—is the ultimate space in which the subject finds his substantial content and recognition, i.e., how subjective freedom can actualize itself only in the rationality of the universal ethical order, the implied (although not explicitly stated) obverse is that those who do NOT find this recognition have also the right to revolt: if a class of people is systematically deprived of their rights, of their very dignity as persons, they are *eo ipso* also released from their duties toward the social order, because this order is no longer their ethical substance (…).[22]

From Hegel's otherwise conservative discussion Žižek draws the radical, not to say revolutionary, conclusion that under certain conditions the poorest and most excluded parts of society are entitled to rebel. It is probably not necessary to add that this reading is hardly in harmony with the overall view that permeates Hegel's late political philosophy. But Žižek does not care so much about that. Rather, one is tempted to say that more important for his purposes is that Hegel's philosophy can be used in order to support and illustrate his own distinct philosophical claims.

In any case, on Žižek's reading, the excluded and the poor—the Hegelian rabble—represent an irrational element in an otherwise well-organized social order.[23] According to the same logic, but in an inverted way, something similar can actually be said about the king. With reference to Hegelian dialectics, Žižek maintains that the rational and symbolic order of the state

---

[22] Slavoj Žižek, "From Democracy to Divine Violence", in Giorgio Agamben et al., *Democracy in What State?*, trans. William McCuaig (New York: Columbia University Press, 2012), p. 116.

[23] In a similar context, Žižek also relates to violence and what he calls the "hidden truth" of Hegel's political philosophy: "the more a society forms a well-structured rational state, the more the abstract negativity of 'irrational' violence returns." Slavoj Žižek, "Answers Without Questions", in Žižek (ed.), *The Idea of Communism, vol. 2: The New York Conference* (London & New York: Verso, 2013), p. 182.

implies a particular, contingent and irrational moment; this is the position incarnated by the monarch. Žižek formulates the overall dialectical point of the argument as follows:

> the greatest speculative mystery of the dialectical movement is not how the richness and diversity of reality can be reduced to a dialectical conceptual mediation, but the fact that in order to take place this dialectical structuring must itself be embodied in some totally contingent element—that, for example, is the point of the Hegelian deduction of the role of the King: the State as the rational totality exists effectively only in so far as it is embodied in the inert presence of the King's body: the King, in his non-rational, biologically determined presence, "is" the State, it is in his body that the State achieves its effectiveness.[24]

The relation between the universal and the particular is, according to Žižek, the motor of dialectics. Since the universal in itself necessarily contains the particular, one can access something universally valid through something otherwise particular and partial. This does not apply to everything particular, but only to certain privileged elements and entities, with the proletariat as the clearest example. Relatedly, the same dialectical process between the universal and the particular characterizes also the individual subject. The subject, which for Žižek—following Lacan—is always a fragmented subject, is in fact situated between the universal and the particular. The subject is the emptiness of the universal substance, which is to say nothing at all or a pure negativity.[25]

Negativity is one of the most central concepts in Žižek's reading of Hegel. He rejects the usual image of the Hegelian dialectics as something that goes from a thesis to its antithesis before they are brought together to form a harmonious synthesis.[26] And the fact is that Hegel himself rarely describes dialectics in that way. Instead, both Hegel and Žižek prefer the more dynamic concepts of position, negation and negation of negation. The last term is described by Žižek as a "double, self-referential negation [that] does not entail any kind of return to positive identity, any kind of abolition, of cancellation of the disruptive force of negativity, of reducing it to a passing movement in the self-mediating identity process of identity". What

---

[24] Žižek, *The Sublime Object of Ideology*, p. 208.
[25] Žižek, *The Most Sublime Hysteric*, p. 49. See also Slavoj Žižek, *The Ticklish Subject: The Absent Centre of Political Ontology* (New York: Verso, 1999).
[26] Žižek, *The Most Sublime Hysteric*, p. 89f.

is crucial is that the negation of the negation preserves "all its disruptive power."[27]

It is also based on the concepts of negation and the negation of negation that Žižek understands and explains what he calls Hegel's radical anti-evolutionism. For Žižek, the Hegelian negation stands first and foremost *for* the possibility of thinking differently and *against* the current order. We can say here that the negative has the status of a kind of event. Incremental evolution is thus contrasted to the revolutionary act. Negativity becomes a concept critically calibrated against the contemporary capitalist social and political system, a category that points towards an affirmative opening for and a promise of something other—what Žižek presently prefers to call communism.

All in all, Žižek's interpretations of Hegel assuage philological fidelity towards the texts for an interpretative heterodoxy that frees up their radical potential, a radicality that he himself reads into them and that he is therefore responsible for actualizing in ever changing philosophical and political contexts. Thus, when in early books such as *The Sublime Object of Ideology*, Žižek regarded himself as a post-Marxist (mainly in line with Ernesto Laclau and Chantal Mouffe's *Hegemony and Socialist Strategy* from 1985), he claimed that Hegel was also a post-Marxist—indeed, the "first post-Marxist".[28] When Žižek later distanced himself from post-Marxism, he also stopped calling Hegel a post-Marxist. Today, applying the same interpretative logic, Žižek uses Hegelian philosophy as a theoretical tool in his struggle to restore the idea of communism. In this context, a passage by Alain Badiou—Žižek's communist brother in arms—from the first anthology on *The Idea of Communism*, deserves to be cited *in extenso*:

> Slavoj Žižek is probably the only thinker today who can simultaneously hew as closely as possible to Lacan's contributions and argue steadfastly and vigorously for the return of the Idea of communism. This is because his real master is Hegel, of whom he offers an interpretation that is completely novel, inasmuch as he has given up subordinating it to the theme of Totality. There are two ways of rescuing the Idea of communism in philosophy today: either by abandoning Hegel, not without regret, incidentally, and only after repeated considerations of his writings

---

[27] Žižek, *The Sublime Object of Ideology*, p. 199. On the negation of the negation, see also Slavoj Žižek, *The Invisible Reminder: On Schelling and Related Matters* (London & New York: Verso, 2007), p. 126.

[28] See, for example, Žižek, *The Sublime Object of Ideology*, p. xxix. Ernesto Laclau & Chantal Mouffe, *Hegemony and Socialist Strategy* (London: Verso, 1985).

(which is what I do), or by putting forward a different Hegel, an unknown Hegel, and that is what Žižek does, based on Lacan (who was a magnificent Hegelian—or so Žižek would claim—at first explicitly and later secretly, all along the way).[29]

## Homologies

In light of Badiou's comment, one may say that a fundamental assumption for Žižek's entire project is that Hegel's philosophy and Lacan's psychoanalytic theories can be translated into and be cross-fertilized by each other. Žižek writes that Lacan's psychoanalysis is basically a repetition of Hegel's philosophy,[30] and that Lacan was a Hegelian without knowing it himself. One relevant background detail in this context is that the French psychoanalyst was one of many thinkers—along with Georges Bataille, Simone de Beauvoir, Maurice Merleau-Ponty and Jean-Paul Sartre—who was inspired by Alexandre Kojève's Marxist reading of the *Phenomenology of Spirit*, which was presented in a seminar or rather a series of lectures at École pratique des hautes études in Paris in the 1930s. In his own writings and seminars, Lacan often quoted and made pleas to Hegel. For example, in his famous so-called seventh seminar on the ethics of psychoanalysis, he refers on several occasions to the dialectics of the master and slave in the *Phenomenology of Spirit*.[31] It was also Lacan who first described Hegel as the most sublime hysteric, a characteristic the Slovenian cultural theorist has often deployed, and a formulation he would even use for the title of his French doctoral dissertation.[32]

However, what interests Žižek when he says that Lacan was a Hegelian without himself knowing it, is not the question of whether explicit statements about the German nineteenth century philosopher can be located in Lacan. Rather Lacan's Hegelianism is implicit in his psychoanalytical theories about the subject and the unconscious. On an overall level, there are struc-

---

[29] Alain Badiou, "The Idea of Communism", in Costas Douzinas & Slavoj Žižek (eds.), *The Idea of Communism* (London & New York: Verso, 2010), p. 4.

[30] Žižek, *Less Than Nothing*, p. 6.

[31] Jacques Lacan, *The Seminar of Jacques Lacan: The Ethics of Psychoanalysis*, ed. Jacques-Alain Miller, trans. Dennis Porter (New York: W. W. Norton & Company, 1997).

[32] Žižek writes: "The truth at which we arrive is not 'whole,' the question always remains open, it simply becomes a question we ask of the Other. This is the perspective from which we should understand Lacan's statement that Hegel was 'the most sublime hysteric'; the hysteric asks questions because ha wants to 'burrow a hole in the other,' he experiences his own desire as if it were the Other's desire." Žižek, *The Most Sublime Hysteric*, pp. 108f.

tural similarities—or, with one of Žižek's favorite words, homologies—between Hegel and Lacan. In an interview, Žižek explains:

> My basic thesis is that the characteristic feature of German idealism—the de-substantialized understanding of the subject as a shortcoming in order—corresponds to the notion of "the object of little a", which for Lacan is a shortcoming.[33]

As Žižek repeatedly points out, there are also many other homologous relationships between Hegel and Lacan. Like Hegel, even Lacan (at least in Žižek's reading) tends to work with triads. The clearest example consists of the three registers—"the real", "the imaginary" and "the symbolic". Žižek also talks about the three stages of the symbolic in Lacan's thinking, which are also said to be easily translatable into the Hegelian idiom.[34] In addition, there are three different periods in Lacan's authorship (an early phenomenological phase, the structural or structuralist period during and around the fifties, and finally a late phase when he was primarily focused on exploring the real). Žižek often points out such formal homologies and similarities in the form of a standard rhetorical gesture, by asking the leading question: does not XX in Hegel correspond to YY in Lacan? This is rhetorically effective, because it is left to the reader to draw a conclusion that is not always convincing under closer examination.[35]

In fact, there is reason to claim that even if Žižek reads Lacan through Hegel in a similar way as he reads Hegel through Lacan, it is not—as Badiou puts it in the cited passage from *The Idea of Communism*—Hegel who is Žižek's "real Master", but Lacan. The latter has a certain structural determination over the Zizekian discursive universe, in the sense that Žižek's view of Lacan hardly stands and falls on account of his understanding of Hegel, while his interpretation of Hegel is completely permeated and penetrated by Lacanian psychoanalysis. At least as much as he interprets Lacan from a Hegelian point of view, one can say that he reads not only Hegel but also Lacan from a Lacanian perspective. It is symptomatic that Lacan besides Hegel is the most cited authority in *Less Than Nothing*, while it is not often the case that Hegel takes such a prominent position in Žižek's

---

[33] Žižek & Daly, *Conversations with Žižek*, p. 61.
[34] Žižek, *The Most Sublime Hysteric*, pp. 70f.
[35] This rhetorical trait of Žižek's is pointed out by Tony Myers in his book *Slavoj Žižek* (London & New York: Routledge, 2003), pp. 4f.

presentations and interpretations of Lacan; in *How to Read Lacan*, for example, the German philosopher is mentioned only once.

In other words and roughly described, Žižek is consistently reading Hegel from a Lacanian point of view just to find out that Hegel and Lacan, on the whole, say the same thing. Indeed, no matter how one prefers to estimate the fruitfulness of Žižek's non-traditional and controversial readings—or one may perhaps say his mis-readings—of Hegel, there is undoubtedly some kind of circular argumentation at play here. By extension, one could even ask whether a similar circularity is not characteristic for the whole of Lacanian psychoanalysis that Žižek adopts; the answers are to a large degree already embedded in the questions posed and that the conclusions are already implicit in the premises. In short, in some respects, Žižek's Hegel appears to be more Lacanian than traditionally Hegelian, at the same time as Žižek is claiming—as we have seen—that this is the only way through which we can "save" Hegel today.

All in all, one may conclude that Žižek has, in many regards, a one-sided view of Hegel's highly multifaceted thinking. To a certain extent, Žižek himself would certainly agree with that statement, based on his firm belief that "the *universal* truth of a concrete situation can be articulated only from a thoroughly *partisan* position." Indeed, he actually goes so far as to claim that "truth is, by definition, one-sided."[36] In any case, Žižek's one-sided and partial way not only to understand but also to change Hegel, shows that the dialectical philosophy of this German nineteenth century thinker can still be deeply inspiring in asking important political and philosophical questions as well as in developing the critical analyses of our late-capitalist societies.

[36] Slavoj Žižek, "Afterword: Lenin's Choice", in V. I. Lenin, *Revolution at the Gates: A Selection of Writings from February to October 1917*, ed. Slavoj Žižek (London & New York: Verso, 2004), p. 177.

# Authors

**Anders Bartonek** is lecturer at the Philosophy Department of Södertörn University, Stockholm. He specializes in German philosophy, mainly the Critical Theory of the Frankfurt School and German Idealism. He wrote his dissertation on the concept of non-identity and the negative dialectics of Theodor W. Adorno (2011). He is also involved in the Swedish translation of Hegel's *Elements of the Philosophy of Right*.

**Anders Burman** is professor of Intellectual history at Södertörn University. One of his main areas of research is the tradition of Hegelian Marxism. He has written, edited or co-edited almost thirty books, among them the monograph *Flykten från Hegel* ("The Flight from Hegel") and the anthologies *Att läsa Hegel* ("To Read Hegel") and *Tysk idealism* ("German Idealism").

**Sergei Mareev** is professor of Philosophy at Moscow International Higher Business School, "MIRBIS". He studies German classical philosophy and Marx, in particular the method of *Capital*. Being a pupil of the noted Soviet philosopher Evald Ilyenkov, he has developed his ideas in the field of the theory of scientific cognition and dialectical logic. In recent years he has in Russian published the monographs "E.V. Ilyenkov: To Live by Philosophy" (2015) and "L.S. Vygotsky: Philosophy, psychology and art" (2017).

**Elena Mareeva** is professor of Philosophy at Moscow State Institute of Culture. She specializes in the history of Russian and Soviet philosophy, paying a special attention to the evolution of Vladimir Lenin's philosophical ideas. A number of her works are devoted to various versions of "creative Marxism", especially to Evald Ilyenkov and Mikhail Lifshits, and to the "activity approach" in Soviet philosophy of culture. Her most important monograph is "The Problem of Soul in Classical and Non-Classical Philosophy" (in Russian 2017).

**David Payne** is currently a lecturer in Rhetoric at Södertörn University. He received his PhD in Political Theory from the University of Essex for his thesis, *A Critique of Post-Emancipatory Reason: Philosophical Visibility, Political Possibility and the question of Novelty* (2012). He has written articles on continental political thought, Marxism and Post-marxism, and is presently undertaking an investigation into the idea of the "proper" in contemporary politics as well as co-editing a volume on the people and populism.

**Sven-Olov Wallenstein** is Professor of Philosophy at Södertörn University. He specializes in German Idealism and modern European philosophy, with a particular emphasis on aesthetics and philosophy of art. He is the author of numerous books on philosophy, contemporary art, and architecture. Recent publications include *Madness, Religion, and the Limits of Reason* (ed. with Jonna Bornemark, 2015), and *Architecture, Critique, Ideology: Writings on Architecture and Theory* (2016). He is currently completing the first Swedish translations of Adorno's *Ästhetische Theorie* and *Negative Dialektik*, as well as monographs on Adorno and Lyotard.

# Index

# Södertörn Philosophical Studies

1.  Hans Ruin & Nicholas Smith (eds.), *Hermeneutik och tradition: Gadamer och den grekiska filosofin* (2003)

2.  Hans Ruin, *Kommentar till Heideggers Varat och tiden* (2005)

3.  Marcia Sá Cavalcante Schuback & Hans Ruin (eds.), *The Past's Presence: Essays on the Historicity of Philosophical Thought* (2006)

4.  Jonna Bornemark (ed.), *Det främmande i det egna: Filosofiska essäer om bildning och person* (2007)

5.  Marcia Sá Cavalcante Schuback (ed.), *Att tänka smärtan* (2009)

6.  Jonna Bornemark, *Kunskapens gräns, gränsens vetande: En fenomenologisk undersökning av transcendens och kroppslighet* (2009)

7.  Carl Cederberg & Hans Ruin (eds.), *En annan humaniora, en annan tid/Another humanities, another time* (2009)

8.  Jonna Bornemark & Hans Ruin (eds.), *Phenomenology and Religion: New Frontiers* (2010)

9.  Hans Ruin & Andrus Ers (eds.), *Rethinking Time: Essays on History, Memory, and Representation* (2011)

10. Jonna Bornemark & Marcia Sá Cavalcante Schuback (eds.), *Phenomenology of Eros* (2012)

11. Leif Dahlberg & Hans Ruin (eds.), *Teknik, fenomenologi och medialitet* (2011)

12. Jonna Bornemark & Hans Ruin (eds.), *Ambiguity of the Sacred* (2012)

13. Brian Manning Delaney & Sven-Olov Wallentein (eds.), *Translating Hegel* (2012)

14. Sven-Olov Wallenstein & Jakob Nilsson (eds.), *Foucault, Biopolitics, and Governmentality* (2013)

15. Jan Patočka, *Inledning till fenomenologisk filosofi* (2013)

16. Jonna Bornemark & Sven-Olov Wallenstein (eds.), *Madness, Religion, and the Limits of Reason* (2015)

17. Björn Sjöstrand, *Att tänka det tekniska: En studie i Derridas teknikfilosofi* (2015)

18. Jonna Bornemark & Nicholas Smith (eds.), *Phenomenology of Pregnancy* (2016)

19. Ramona Rat, *Un-common Sociality: Thinking Sociality with Levinas* (2016)

20. Hans Ruin & Jonna Bornemark (red.), *Ad Marciam* (2017)

21. Gustav Strandberg, *Politikens omskakning: Negativitet, samexistens och frihet i Jan Patočkas tänkande* (2017)

22. Anders Bartonek & Anders Burman (eds.), *Hegelian Marxism: The Uses of Hegel's Philosophy in Marxist Theory from Georg Lukács to Slavoj Žižek* (2018)

.